for A
who is even
more awesome

{ COMEDIAN
MASTERMIND }

THE BEST OF *FatCyclist.com*
2005–2007

than this book.
And that's darned
awesome indeed.

Fatty

ELDEN "FATTY" NELSON

{ COMEDIAN MASTERMIND }

FAKE NEWS
HOW-TOS
OPEN LETTERS
EPIC RIDES
EVIL RECIPES &
ADVERTISING INSIGHT
ALL BOUND
TOGETHER INTO
THIS BOOK
WHICH PROBABLY SHOULD
HAVE SIMPLY BEEN TITLED:

THE BEST OF *FatCyclist.com*
2005–2007

An Imprint of **Fatbooks** *Publishing*

ISBN-13: 978-0615563695
ISBN-10: 0615563694
First Paperback Edition

Book design by Kim Dow, dowhouse.com

Manufactured in the United States of America. Rock on.
www.fatcyclist.com

For The Hammer

Contents

Preface

ELDEN NELSON

WHEN I SEE THE PREFACE TO A BOOK, MY REACTION IS GENERALLY DISMAY. "DO I *HAVE* TO READ THAT IN ORDER FOR THE REST OF THE BOOK TO MAKE sense?" is pretty much what I ask myself.

I'm figuring you might be asking yourself something similar.

The answer is: No. You do not have to read this. Although — trust me on this — you *should* read all the Forewords. In order.

Still with me? OK. I'll make this quick.

This book is a compilation of what I consider to be my best work during the first two years of my blog: from mid-2005 to mid-2007. However, it's not exactly just a *Princess Bride*-ification (that is, only the good parts) of my blog. There are some differences worth noting:

1. **It's organized by topic instead of time.** So you can gorge on How-Tos or Epic Rides or Open Letters or whatever. This should make things easier for you to find. Oh, and also there's a table of contents! I have spared *no expense* in making this book both entertaining *and* accessible.

2. **Each post has a new introduction.** I thought you might be interested to know why I write the stuff I write, what kinds of events trigger my stories. If I was wrong, you can skip that part. But if, by chance, we see each other someday and start talking about this book, please pretend you took the time to

read these introductions or my feelings will be hurt.

3. **I've annotated this thing nigh unto death.** I wrote all these posts years ago. When I read (and edited) them now, I constantly had comments I wanted to add. So I did, in the form of footnotes. You can skip these, but, I for one think footnote humor is the *best*.

And really, that's about it.

That wasn't too painful now, was it?

Foreword

BOB BRINGHURST

ELDEN CALLED ME UP TO TELL ME HE HAD A WONDERFUL OPPORTUNITY FOR ME.

"What would you say if I told you that I'm willing to let you write a foreword for my Fat Cyclist book? And I'm asking nothing in return."

"Sounds too good to be true. Are you pulling my leg?"

"No, listen, this could be a win-win if you play your cards right."

"What do I need to do?"

"No Top Five lists."

"Fine."

"And no long descriptions of dance moves."

"Check."

"And no pretending you raced bicycles in Europe."

"I would never — "

"I'm serious. Just be yourself, and you'll do fine. Maybe drop a few big names. Oh wait. You've never met famous people like Levi Leipheimer and Lance Armstrong. Better leave that to me."

"I've met Lance Armstrong! We didn't actually meet, per se. He was sitting in the back of a pickup truck after he finished Leadville back in '08. He was cheering on riders who were getting ready to ride up The Boulevard. He looked straight at me and told me to 'Keep going.' He was drinking a beer."[1]

---

1   History does not record whether this beer was a Michelob Ultra.

"Wow, you're practically pen pals."

"I'm just saying that if we saw each other, he'd recognize me. He'd be like, 'Oh, there's that one guy who was trying really hard to finish the Leadville race in under 12 hours.' And I'd be all, 'Hey, Lance.' And he'd be like, 'Hey.'"

"Just let me do the name dropping. Can you write a foreword?"

"I can try."

"That's not good enough. I don't want you to fail and then act like a try-baby. Man up, and do it."

"I will!"

"That's better."

Foreword

KENNY JONES

I'VE KNOWN ELDEN NELSON, AKA FATTY, AKA THE FAT CYCLIST, FOR OVER TEN YEARS. WE BECAME ACQUAINTED THROUGH OUR SHARED PASSION for endurance mountain bike races, like the Leadville 100 and the Brian Head Epic. Through my friendship with Elden, I was introduced into a group of riders that we now refer to as "The Core Team."

Over the years, our friendship has grown as Elden and I have spent countless hours traveling to bike races and trailheads, not to mention all the hours spent riding together. In fact, I'm positive that Elden now considers me his dearest and best friend.

Despite our long friendship, few people know that Elden actually started FatCyclist.com because of me. I am now publicly taking sole credit for its beginning and I will, if this book becomes financially profitable, be serving Elden with a court injunction to ensure my cut of the pie.

It all started back in the Spring of 2004. Elden, like he does every year, had gained at least 50 pounds over the winter months. In April, he attended my annual RAWROD mountain bike ride: a 100-mile Ride Around the White Rim in One Day. The White Rim of Canyonlands National Park is a 100-mile dirt road that circles the Island in the Sky mesa. Each spring, we all dust off the cobwebs from our legs and join our friends in this joy ride to celebrate the beginning of bike season.

Well, this year seemed especially hard for Elden. Many times, I saw him pushing his bike up the gentlest of inclines. As the organizer of this event, I would hang back with the support vehicle and make sure that everyone and everything was secure after each planned stop. As I would start riding again, I would catch Elden at the back of the pack.

And each time I passed him, I couldn't help but notice his rather large tuchus.

Towards the end of the ride, the road begins a long climb up the Shafer trail. I caught Elden again around the twentieth switchback. He was off his bike, pushing up the hill, barely able to hold up his head.

That's when I said it. It wasn't planned. It just came out, the obvious thought verbalized, "Man, for an endurance cyclist you sure are fat." How could I have known that this pinnacle moment of insensitive male hazing would turn out to create something so huge?

A butterfly flaps its wings and a few years later, Elden becomes the Fat Cyclist. He creates a blog to publicly humiliate himself into losing weight and ends up raising a gajillion dollars for cancer survivorship and research,[2] all the while helping thousands of people get through their daily grinds with humor and creative writing.

People can feel Elden's generosity, compassion, and intelligence when they read his blog posts. It's no wonder that his readers feel like they know him, even though they have never met. I feel confident that this compilation of stories, fake news, and charitable contests will continue to entertain for decades.

In which case, Elden will owe me a buttload of royalties.

And if not, I have already secured the domain www.fitcyclist.com, where I will be posting humorous stories of extreme athletic activities. There will also be many contests and jerseys designed by my new favorite company, Twin 7.[3] Don't worry — all the proceeds will go to build awareness of osteoporosis due to excessive non-impact activities.

---

2   The FatCyclist.com "Team Fatty" fundraising efforts don't really come up in this book; the cancer awareness and contests came a little bit later in the blog's life. Trust me.

3   All FatCyclist gear is designed and distributed by a couple of very cool guys in Minneapolis: Twin Six.

Foreword

DUG ANDERSON

FIFTY BUCKS SEEMS A LITTLE LIGHT FOR WRITING A BOOK FOREWORD, EVEN IF THE BOOK IS SELF-PUBLISHED. BUT FIFTY BUCKS IS FIFTY BUCKS. That's, like, forty Diet Cokes.

Okay, here goes. When I first met Elden "Clyde" Nelson, he was wearing rollerblades, a goofy helmet, kneepads, and, if I remember correctly, goggles.

Some things never change.

Okay, some things have changed. For example, Elden moved away for something like four years and, through the magic of instant messaging and email, I didn't even know he was gone.

Then Elden moved back. I see him less now than when he was gone, but the magic is still there. For example, check out this IM conversation from when Elden lived in Seattle:

Me: I raced this weekend. I crashed, flatted, and hated it.

Elden: Hmm.

And here's an IM conversation from last week:

Me: Hey, now that I work right by where you live, let's do lunch Friday.

Elden: Hmm.

On the other hand, now that Elden lives three miles from my house, I can borrow cool bike stuff anytime I need it. The side door on his garage is usually locked, but if you lift the handle until you think it's about to break, then put your whole body weight into the door with your shoulder, the door will open just enough for a skinny guy to get in. So I bring my 13-year-old son, I open the door, and he goes in for the goods.

Elden, have your agent IM me. I'll do lunch with him.

Foreword

BRAD KEYES

I WAS THE FIRST OF THE CORE TEAM TO MEET ELDEN WHEN HIS SISTER MARRIED MY BEST FRIEND, LONG BEFORE HE TRADED IN HIS RED MIATA, sweatpants, cape, and Reeboks for a mountain bike. I barely remembered him when he showed up years later for a ride one day with Dug. Dug, what were you thinking?

I do however, remember being annoyed. Annoyed that we'd have to wait for him as he fidgeted with his bike at the trailhead. Annoyed that we'd have to wait for him at the top of a climb. This would be followed by more annoyance as he would fix his flat tire, clean his glasses, or remove trail debris from his derailleur.

It's a good thing he was funny and knew how to crash. Hard. And holler loudly when he crashes. Elden quickly endeared himself to our small group and no ride would be complete without a holler and a funny from him.

Then something happened. Elden moved away.

The group rides were never the same after that: no annoyance, no hollering, no funny. It took Kenny's RAWROD ride to get Elden to come back and ride with us. He didn't disappoint. Not only was he annoying and funny, he was chunky. Fat Cyclist-chunky. The stress of moving, the new job, family, and being too busy to ride had turned Elden into the Fat Cyclist.

Somewhere along the way, as Elden shed pounds, he got fast. Real fast. No longer at the back of the pack, he now contends for KOM. I don't know if it was the bizarre dieting, the caffeine, the ephedra/aspirin stack, or the public humiliation, but it worked. Thankfully, he still crashes and hollers.

You can't diet everything away.

It's not so easy anymore to call him the Fat Cyclist, but easy as always to call him a friend.

Foreword

RICKY MADDOX

WELL, WELL, WELL, WHAT CAN I SAY THAT HASN'T ALREADY BEEN SAID? I'VE BEEN PUBLICLY SHAMED AND HUMILIATED SO MANY TIMES ON FATTY'S blog that my first instinct is to lash back and defend myself. But I'm not that kind of buddy. So it is with that as a backdrop, I submit some thoughts.

As an original "Core Team" member, I am personally responsible for granting Elden membership to our little family. Elden's background as an intramural rollerblading superstar and part-time new-wave radio DJ, however, wasn't impressive enough for me to let him step up to the big leagues. Dug persuaded me to change my mind. Dug still plays rollerblading on weekends and "Ultimate Frisbee" at lunch, but I'll save that detail for Dug's book.

So just like that, Elden got in and we still really don't know why.

Over the years, Elden and I have spent a fair share of time traveling to destinations and trailheads. We've also spent countless hours doing what we love best: riding. I have observed many things about Elden. Some are interesting, some are borderline fascinating. He'll tell you all about those in this book. Just in case he doesn't, here are a few peculiarities that come up nearly every time we ride:

ELDENSYNCRASY 1

Despite Elden's lack of hair up top, he's actually a very hairy man. It turns out, he's a bit sensitive about the sheer quantity of hair on his body. With regard to the thick forest of follicles in his nose and ears, he's super sensitive. On a trip with the boys to Leadville, in 1999, Elden and I found ourselves close to each other in the backseat of the car. I don't remember whose car it was, but it was small. At a certain point, conversation broke out:

> **Me**: What the...? What is that in your nose?
>
> **Elden**: What?
>
> **Me**: And your ears. What is that?
>
> **Elden**: Stop it.
>
> **Me**: Don't you ever trim that stuff?
>
> **Elden**: Stop it, man.
>
> **Me**: I mean seriously. You can borrow my Panasonic. I actually brought it.
>
> **Elden** (noticeably angry): OK, stop it. I don't like talking about this sort of thing.
>
> **Me**: Did you catch any of that, Bobby...?

Elden prides himself on his gear and I must admit that I am totally envious of the stable of hardware he has in his garage. Going in there is like stepping into a bicycling museum. You would think that with the overabundance of cool stuff he has, he would worry less about maintaining all of it. Not true.

ELDENSYNCRASY 2

"Thou shalt not bump me, my bikes, or especially my wheels."

To entertain ourselves on long, boring fire road climbs (also to divert the suffering), Dug and I like to fling rocks at each other. We do this by looping our front wheels around rocks and snapping the handlebar and wheel, which effectively launches the rocks. We have a point system for the part of the bike or leg the launched rocks hit. Sometimes, we can actually volley the rock back and forth a few times.

Granted, this isn't the smartest little game to play but at the end of the day, we're on bikes in the dirt. C'mon! If you don't want to play, stay away, right?

Ahhh, not right.

On many occasions, when rocks get flung in Elden's direction, he sternly says, "Stop that. Stop it right now. I don't like that game. It's senseless and pointless." If the rock throwing persists, and it always does, rather than moving out of the line of fire, he sternly repeats his warning, just louder. Sometimes the expression on his face brings us to a stop until we can stop laughing.

I would love to go on, but you get the idea. Riding with Elden is always entertaining.

Foreword

BOB BRINGHURST

ELDEN HAS BEEN USING "THE CORE TEAM" TO REFER TO A CERTAIN GROUP OF RIDERS FOR YEARS NOW. I HAVE TO ADMIT THAT I DON'T ALWAYS KNOW which people to whom he's referring. I'm not even sure whether I'm still part of The Core Team. Now that I have this opportunity, I can remove all doubt and list all the members. And while I'm at it, I can help you learn more about them by describing their best dance routines as performed on stage. As Rene Descartes said, "I dance; therefore, I am."

Or maybe it was Patrick Duffy.

RICK MADDOX

Rick begins his performance in a narrow spotlight. He is tucked into a ball until Wild Cherry's "Play That Funky Music" begins. The fiery Italian uncurls himself slowly, menacingly, and begins to whirl across the stage. The tempo increases as Maddox moves into a lindy circle followed by a swing out. The spotlight can barely stay with him. When the song ends, he stops, licks his fingers, and slaps the buttocks of an imaginary partner. The spotlight narrows and fades as Maddox curls himself into a ball.

Brazen and hostile, yet charming. Rick is a director for a software firm.

BRAD KEYES

Brad dances as if he should be in a mosh pit, only he is alone on the stage with "Goodbye to Love" playing. His dance style is a cross between Travis Bickle and *The Breakfast Club*'s Andrew Clark. He jumps, leaps, and shakes in a constipated manner for most of the song. When the odd guitar solo begins, he stops dancing and looks perplexed and frustrated, as if he realizes he ate too much Fiber One for breakfast.

Violent and stubborn, Brad resides in Chicago.

ELDEN "FATTY" NELSON

Elden's dance begins with promise as the techno sounds of Devo's "Big Mess" charge the atmosphere. Fatty performs a robotic fall-off-the-log move that consists of a rock-step-stop followed by a kick-back-side-front. He forces a smile, and then repeats the fall-off-the-log move several times. The song ends, the lights fade, and the Fat Cyclist is still falling off the log in the darkness.

His performance shows a large degree of artistic intent and a small degree of artistic realization. Elden also works in the computer industry, usually in the form of giving advice.

DUG ANDERSON

Dug strolls onto the stage wearing a lumberjack shirt, leotards, and booties. The fixed look on his face wills the audience to take their seats and still their noise. As Dwight Yoakam's "A Thousand Miles From Nowhere" begins, Dug indulges in an odd combination of tango steps and modern-dance poses. His most impressive move — which only seems strangely accidental — is best described as a trade-slide double-turn out to an open halt.

Brash and forceful, yet unsubstantial, unlike other members of the core team, Dug does not work in the computer industry. OK, that's a lie. He just doesn't know how to use computers very well.

RICK SUNDERLAGE (NOT HIS REAL NAME)

Rick Sunderlage (not his real name) is dressed in a smart sailor's outfit on a well-lit stage. When Boston's "Don't Look Back" begins, the former horse whisperer thrusts his pelvis, slowly at first, and then more rapidly. Soon he thrusts his pelvis while walking in circles. He seems to lose interest. When the song ends, Rick appears to recognize the audience. He runs off the stage with face in hands.

Although Rick's quiet confidence sometimes erodes into unmistakable panic, he does use numerical analytics to track user data.

KENNY JONES

Kenny performs a soundtrack medley. Sporting skintight leather and taped feet, the Photoshop wizard spins in circles as he rubs his stomach and thighs to "Maniac." Water trickles over his body; he wheels and pounds his forearms against a chair. Kenny stops, looks wildly left and right, and then moves into a "stud strut" as "Stayin' Alive" rings out. Quick but effective tributes to *Fame* and *Dirty Dancing* leave the audience agape, but Kenny offers the true showstopper when he waves his hands quickly back and forth across his face, alternately revealing and hiding his anguish à la Elizabeth Berkley in *Showgirls*.

Refreshingly unrepressed and provocative, Kenny used to be a small business owner. He later became a smaller business owner. It is now believed that he is the owner of unemployment benefits.

BOB BRINGHURST

When "I Gotta Feeling" starts playing, I don't show any signs of being a dancer. I just kind of stand there against the wall, nonchalantly snapping my fingers and staring at the host of generic dancers on stage. The spotlight focuses on me as my foot begins to tap. My head starts bobbing, my knees start swerving, and I suddenly become a force of nature. Actually, that's not quite accurate. I become a sudden force of super nature. I dance my way onto the stage as the crowd of dancers part to the sides, clapping their hands in rhythm to the song as my dancing fills the stage. I dance with cold fury.

I am quite striking. Which reminds me of a story I like to tell whenever I have the talking pillow.

My friends act like it's no big deal that I used to race bicycles in Europe and sometimes even make fun of me because I never won a race there. Secretly, I know that they're jealous. They just want to bring me down to their level so I don't think I'm better than them. Ridiculous. I don't think I'm better than them. I may have lived a better life, and I may have done better things, and I may have hung out with better people, but that doesn't mean I'm better.

Where was I? Oh yes, cycling in Europe. Here are my top five victories: [*Editor's Note: Truncated for brevity and clarity.*]

1.
How It Began

I STARTED THE FAT CYCLIST BLOG IN MAY OF 2005. SINCE THEN, I'VE WRITTEN MORE THAN 1,500 ENTRIES AND I'M LUCKY ENOUGH TO HAVE had a lot of folks read a lot of what I've written.

But way back at the beginning of writing my blog, there was nobody to read it. Just me, writing to myself and hopefully a few friends as a way to chronicle my efforts to lose some weight. My plan was to hold my own feet to the fire by posting my weight each day.

But why had I gotten fat, anyway?

Well, I'm a stress eater. And the following things had all happened, in this order, in less than one year:

1. I took three pay cuts in my job as the editor-in-chief of a programmer's magazine, by which time my family was no longer making ends meet (Second half of '03).
2. I started interviewing for work, but found nothing local to our home in Utah (December '03).
3. My wife, Susan, was diagnosed with breast cancer (December '03).
4. Susan got a mastectomy. During this surgery, I got and accepted a great job offer at Microsoft, which paid well and had great medical coverage, but required us to move. I put the house up for sale and gave my old job two weeks' notice.

By the time Susan had awoke from surgery, our lives were as upside-down as is possible (January '04).

5. We — along with our four children, including twin toddlers — moved to Washington and I started a new job (February '04).

6. Susan started chemo (March '04).

7. We sold our house in Utah and bought a new house (April '04).

8. I was kind of busy. Not much time for training. I went from 158 pounds to 180 pounds.

9. And then I got Bell's Palsy and took steroids to get the use of the right side of my face back.

10. My weight went to 196 pounds, spitting distance from being a Clydesdale — what guys who weigh 200-plus pounds are called in bike races.

11. I resolved to lose that weight.

So I started a blog.

THE FIRST POST

In addition to my stated reasons for beginning a blog , I need to acknowledge my friend and, at the time, manager, Matt Carter. Microsoft, where we both worked, had been making a fuss about its new "Spaces" blogging service; Matt told me a number of times that I should start a blog. He even told me it should be about biking.

So I did. Hey, why not? I figured it would be a fun way to waste time instead of working and if Matt got angry at me for spending all my time blogging, I could say, "Well you were the one who told me to start it." So, Matt: thanks! And also: sorry!

It's crazy how much effect one person can have on another.

Hi. I'm Elden, and I'm a fat cyclist. That is, I am a fat person who rides a bicycle.

But I have not always been fat, nor have I always been a cyclist. I have, however, always been a rambling blowhard. It's a curse.

In the days[1] ahead, I will talk about some of the following:

- Why I am fat
- Why I love to ride my bike
- Why it's crucial that I lose 30 pounds in the next three months
- My craziest year ever (see "Why I am fat")[2]

First, though, I will tell you about what I did last weekend: Ride Around White Rim in One Day (affectionately known as RAWROD[3] '05), a 100-mile mountain bike ride in Canyonlands National Park, Utah, over the course of about ten hours.

---

1   When I started this blog, I figured that I, like most people, would tire of writing pretty soon and would abandon the project. I absolutely did *not* plan to keep writing for what's now closing in on seven years.

2   I look at this "craziest year ever" statement now and can't help but think how much crazier things would eventually get. That's a whole different book, though. Seriously, a whole book.

3   I am very pleased to boast that I am the person who came up with this acronym. For one thing, it's one of the rarest of all possible acronyms: it's easy to pronounce and remember, and the words in the acronym describe what the event is without having to resort to obscure words or strange ordering of those words. Most importantly, it's hilarious to say "rawrod."

Because while I am unquestionably fat, I have been doing endurance rides for around nine years now, which means I am, perhaps, not without hope.

> COMMENT FROM JOE S.
>
> It's late 2008 and I've lost 25 pounds this year and I'm still 245. You think *you're* fat?!? I better get moving.

> COMMENT FROM MICHAEL
>
> I'm 6' 0", 235 pounds, and love riding the bike. I've done six centuries and commute to work weekly, but I never manage to lose more than 10 pounds between events. I'm definitely the "fat cyclist" in my group.

RAWROD 2005

Apart from the obligatory preamble post, the first thing I wrote for my blog was a three-part description of an endurance ride. Which goes to show, I guess, that things don't change much. Over the course of six-plus years, I don't know how many of such stories I've written.

You'd think I'd get tired of them and by "them," I mean both the endurance rides and writing the stories. But I don't. Ever. Every time, the drama of doing something difficult is new. And every time I write the story afterward, I find myself thinking, "This is why I write."

If my job, for the rest of my life, were to go on big riding adventures and then tell the stories afterward, I would be utterly, perfectly happy.

I admit, I very nearly bailed out of riding the RAWROD '05. The embarrassment was almost too much to take. Consider that when I moved away from Utah 1.3 years ago, I weighed 158 pounds. Now I'm thirty pounds heavier.

When I moved away, I was one of the fast guys; now it would be questionable whether I'd even be capable of finishing the ride/race (technically, it was just a friendly ride. In reality, any time you have more than a few people in a riding group, at least some of them think it's a race).

And I was fairly confident at least a few of my old biking friends would try to jiggle my belly.

Still, I had bought the plane tickets, arranged for Rick Maddox to loan me a bike, had reserved a hotel room, and had professed enthusiasm for the ride. No backing out now.

Well, actually, I guess I could have bailed out. After all, Doug bailed out. Rick bailed out. Chucky bailed out. And none of them had better reasons than I.

Sure, there were still a lot of people riding — maybe as many as thirty. But I was still bummed that many of my closest friends had opted out of the trip. Maybe they had become fat, too.

FAT LOSER NERD, ALONE IN HOTEL ROOM

Kenny Jones, who put this massive group ride/race together, picked me up at the airport. He looks like he does nothing but ride his bike and shave his head. We made our way to Moab. It was rainy, windy, and cold. Moab's not usually like that. I began to wish I had stayed home.

I'm one of very few people who had planned to stay in a hotel room. I was ridiculed and scoffed at for not camping, but I smirked (choking back the tears), noting that it was, as I just mentioned, rainy, cold, and windy.

I went to my hotel room, got all my junk ready, and played Ridge Racer on my Sony PSP for a couple hours. If someone had taken my picture for the newspaper at that moment, the caption would have been "Fat loser nerd, alone in hotel room. Self-perception as endurance cyclist very questionable."

BEGINNING THE RIDE

During the night, the wind died down. Still plenty rainy and cold, though. The plan was to get going at 6:30AM. Around 7:00AM, we started going. Not bad for such a big group. Thinking how long it would take for this crew to regroup and get going at various stopping points, I loaded myself with enough food and water that I figured I could do the whole day with one stop, maximum.

I should note that while I was clearly having serious doubts internally about this ride, I wasn't saying anything bad about it. Kenny looked too excited; I didn't want to bring him down. One guy, though, who did look a little nervous about this ride was Ryan Benson. He's proud to be "America's Biggest Loser." In other words, he won a reality show series for losing more weight than anyone else. Still, losing weight is one thing. A ten-hour mountain bike ride is something else altogether.

"I'm giving you a 'good-time guarantee,'" I said to Ryan, having no idea whether he'd actually have a good time or not.

We started down Horse Thief at the beginning of the ride, which meant several miles of well-graded rolling dirt road, averaging slightly downhill. By the time we got to the bottom of Horse Thief, the rain had stopped.

I stopped thinking about how far I've sunk and started noticing that

I do, in fact, love to ride my bike. I mean, I really, really, really love it. So I'm slow. So what.

I picked a flower, put it in my shoulder strap — closest thing I had to a lapel — and decided I was going to have a good day.

TREACHERY

There are a couple of Strange Things about being a fat cyclist:

- You're reminded with every turn of the crank that you are, in fact, fat. How so? Because on the upstroke your quads squish up against your low-hanging stomach.[4]
- If you used to be a fast, competitive cyclist, the instinct to win doesn't go away when you become fat; it just festers.

I noticed Strange Thing #1 right away as I began riding around the White Rim. How could I not? But I didn't really notice Strange Thing #2 until I started climbing Hardscrabble Hill, a sandy, steep set of pitches. As person after person after person passed me, I realized that I would shortly be sorted to the back, where I would remain through the day.

And then a third Strange Thing happened: everyone started gathering at the top of Hardscrabble Hill, planning on picking up the food and water from our SAG vehicles that they needed to make it for the next section of the ride.

OK, that's not very strange.

The Strange Thing is the thought that occurred to me:[5] I had no need to stop. It was a cool day, so I hadn't used much water. I had enough food for the whole ride.

So I waved at everyone who had gathered, and I kept going. Abracadabra, I went from *back* of the pack to *leader* of the pack, knowing that since everyone was still waiting for the SAG wagons to catch up, I had picked up a 15-minute lead.

Is this niggardly, anti-social riding behavior? Why, yes. Yes it is. Am I

---

4   You can compensate for this problem with stem spacers, bigger stem angles, and riser handlebars, but only to a point. And I was well past that point.

5   Sure, you could assert that it's strange that a thought occurred to me, but that would just be mean. Don't kick a fat cyclist when he's down. It's not nice.

proud of myself for acting this way? No, no I am not.[6] Did I realize that I had used a particularly lame form of treachery to claim a spot on the trail that did not rightfully belong to me?

Yes, yes I did.

Did I feel shame and remorse to the extent that I would never do it again? I guess we'll see.[7]

NOT ALL ABOUT ME

For a little while, maybe half an hour, I mostly wondered how soon everyone would catch and pass me. Then I started noticing that the White Rim was the most beautiful it's ever been, and stopped thinking about other people, about me, about anything. I swear, I had one of Schopenhauer's[8] sublime moments, where I was simply immersed in the beauty of the profusion of wildflowers — white! red! yellow! purple! — and physics-defying sandstone structures.

To my left, cliffs towered beyond belief above me; to my right they dropped away so far down that my stomach would knot up.[9]

I was surprised that I was starting to get close to Murphy's Hogback: a long, difficult climb, at the top of which we were going to gather and eat lunch, and nobody had passed me yet. Ha! Maybe I'm in better shape than I thought! Maybe I'll be the first to the top of Murphy's, from which I can taunt the slower riders with my magnificent belly![10]

And then my good friend Brad Keyes passed me. On his singlespeed bike. While whistling an idle tune. Followed, within moments, by Mike Young — who is Pro Football Hall of Famer Steve Young's

---

6   Now that years have passed, I think I can admit that in reality, I *was* proud of this behavior. Or I wouldn't have written about it. In fact, it now occurs to me that if I were to write all the things I haven't written because I wasn't proud of the thought, I could write a whole different blog.

7   Yes, I would do it again.

8   I bring up Schopenhauer whenever I want to seem educated. I'd bring up other philosophers I remember from college, but Schopenhauer's the only one I feel confident nobody else in a typical room is going to have ever heard of, which means I'm unlikely to ever be questioned about his work. Which is good, because all I remember is his name, pretty much.

9   In the early days of my blog, it wasn't all that easy to include pictures. In fact, I'm not sure whether I even had a digital camera when I began the blog. And so I had to use *words* to describe things. What a hassle!

10   There is no way in hell I would actually ever do that.

more-athletic brother — who said, "Hey, you're not doing so bad, you big fat tub of goo!"

OK, Mike didn't say that.

But the fact that I had only been passed by two really fast guys made me feel much better about myself.

Oh wait, there were more coming up behind. I dug in deep, doing what I could to prevent anyone else from passing me before I got to Murphy's.

And then the climb began, putting an end to any thoughts I had of finishing strong. I went into my granny gear and just slowly spun up, not worrying about speed, not caring if anyone passed me. I just didn't want Mike, Brad, or the people behind me to see me get off and push.

Amazingly, I did it. I rode up the entirety of the Hog. Third guy up. Yay. Cori Jones was just seconds behind and did the whole thing one-handed[11] just for the heck of it, but still.

ON THE HOGBACK

The great thing about being at the top of Murphy's Hogback is you've got an incredible view of the trail you just climbed. It's very impressive. You get to watch everyone else ride in, cheer them on, and give them Very Helpful Advice as they get to the last ten extremely steep yards. Examples include:

- To Bill Freedman: "**C'mon! Ride a wheelie up that hill, you pansy!**" Of course, Bill (owner of a Ben and Jerry's shop, so naturally a wonderful person) complied. Then, as he summited, he put a little too much juice into it and wheelied over onto his butt. It was a perfect moment.[12]
- To Serena Warner: "**Need a push?**" To which she nodded assent. I quickly skittered down the hill to give her that push and up she went. I like to think that it's because I expended so much energy giving her that push that Serena would offhandedly blow by me toward the end of the ride.

---

11   No, not really.
12   I think it's one of those "picture's worth a thousand words" moments, in fact.

- To Ryan Benson:[13] "**Ry-an! Ry-an! Ry-an!**" Nobody expected Ryan to be able to clean that final pitch, but he did. Made it look easy. For that, Ryan would be awarded the "King of Shafer" trophy Kenny had made up, to be awarded to the male who suffered with the most class.

With everyone gathered, we all had lunch. And I fully intended, as soon as I was done, to hop on my bike and get riding before anyone else did.

After all, I had a non-race to win.

TIME FOR FUN

Kenny was crafty; he wanted to take a group photo before we all took off riding again. This defeated my plan of taking off ahead of everyone was foiled. So here's the photo. I'm the one with man-boobs and a white helmet, seated in the lower left corner, trying to look casual while sucking in my gut and using my arm to shield the camera from the incontrovertible evidence.

And, as expected, many people who were behind me didn't take long to pass. Knowing there wasn't much I could do about it, I enjoyed the ride. At least, I enjoyed the ride after the first ten minutes while my butt got used to the saddle again.

In the direction we were riding the White Rim Trail, the first half of the day is pretty hard work. There are several hard climbs, quite a bit of sand (which posed no problem whatsoever this trip, thanks to the way it got packed down with the previous night's rain), and very little downhill. That's why I always look forward to the second part of the day.

You start off with a few climbs and have to navigate a little sand (once again, not a problem on this trip; I have never ever ever seen the White Rim in such rideable condition). Then, gradually, the trail straightens out

---

13   After writing this post, for several weeks the biggest source of traffic to my blog was from people who had done a search on Ryan Benson. Of course, back then "biggest source of traffic" meant around ten page views per day. Even then, though, I watched my traffic stats obsessively and ten extra clicks was kind of an awesome thing to get. I started considering whether it might be possible for me to work Ryan Benson into additional posts. Alas, this never happened.

and becomes gently banked and downhill for miles at a time. The wind is usually at your back and you've got an opportunity to clock some wicked fast miles. Doesn't even matter that you're fat. Maybe it helps!

At this sheer-joy section of the trail, I was riding with Mark and Serena Warner,[14] along with Jilene Mecham.

Somehow I wound up riding behind Jilene (uh, maybe because she's faster than I am) and came to an astounding realization, which I am going to put on a separate line and in italics for emphasis:

Jilene Mecham picks a beautiful line.

Yep, Jilene was absorbing the right bumps, dodging the ones she should, and just in general making it really easy for me to not make any decisions at all. So I settled in and just tracked her line, noting that the sun was coming out, my legs didn't feel fried, and the temperature felt like it was in the high 60s. I thought to myself, "Well, I'd rather be a fat cyclist than just fat."

Eventually, the downhill ended, Mark flatted, and Jilene and I rode along together for a while. This is notable because:

- This would be the only time in the 100 miles I rode with someone.
- Jilene and I had a fairly serious conversation about how major life crises can change your priorities for the good.

And then Jilene got bored of riding slow and left me in the dust.

MORE TREACHERY...AND TERROR

We were now getting close to the end of riding the White Rim Trail. And as we did, I got more and more nervous. The ride finishes with several switchbacks as you climb up a very tall, steep cliff called Shafer's. And I just didn't have much power left. I could easily see myself needing to walk part of that, but I absolutely didn't want anyone to see me have to get off my bike and walk something I've ridden numerous times.

I am unbelievably vain.[15]

So once again, I resorted to treachery. I saw that everyone was gathering at Musselman's Arch. And, once again, I put my head down and

---

14   Note regarding the Mark/Serena dynamic: I learned this trip that it's OK for Serena to ride as far ahead of Mark as she pleases; the reverse is *absolutely forbidden*.

15   Strangely, as I've become increasingly popular and beloved — not to mention famous — I've become less and less vain.

kept going. Once again, I was ahead of most everyone, and once again, I knew it wouldn't last.

Shafer's Trail is always an impressive sight: you round a corner and see a massive cliff, evidently unclimbable. As you get closer, you can see sections of a road, hairpinning up the side of this cliff. And then, as you get to the base of the thing, you try to stop looking at the road, because it's just too damn demoralizing.

I shifted into my granny gear, put my head down, and vowed not to get off my bike. As people came down the trail, in trucks and on bikes, they gave me encouragement. I kept going, not wanting to let my fans down.

I looked back. People had left Musselman's Arch and were starting to climb. Some were going to catch me, I was sure of it. All I could do now was try to stay on my bike, keep my dignity.

It didn't happen.[16]

On one of the switchbacks, I just couldn't turn the crank one more time. So I got off my bike and did the walk of shame. Just one switchback's worth, then I was back on, but it was definitely a new low for me. It was during that walk that the idea for writing this very blog[17] occurred to me. "So I'm pathetic. Why not tell the world?" I thought.

Well, why not indeed?

Once you're[18] to the top of Shafer's you're on pavement for a few miles, and then you're done. During this pavement stretch, Serena and Jilene blew by me, evidently on a quest to emasculate me to whatever degree possible. Thanks, ladies!

And then I was at the campsite. I had made it. The Fat Cyclist had completed RAWROD '05.

---

16   I mean, I didn't keep my dignity. The part about people catching me definitely happened.

17   I wonder what would have happened if, instead of having a bad day on the bike, I had been out rollerblading. Would you be reading a book containing a collection of the best posts from fatblader.com? No, you probably wouldn't.

18   One of my signature rhetorical devices is to switch from first person to second person and back, seemingly without reason. Another is for me to switch from past to present tense and back, almost certainly without reason. See, if you acknowledge what you're doing, you get to call it a rhetorical device, rather than just sloppy writing.

CONSUME MASS QUANTITIES[19]

If you've never done an endurance event, you've never had a truly over-whelming appetite. The thing is, though, I *love* the massive hunger[20] that overtakes me about two hours after riding 100 miles on a mountain bike. A bunch of us went to Pasta Jays,[21] where I ordered way more food than I could ordinarily eat (big salad, gnocchi with a spicy red cream sauce) and finished it off no problem...then started looking hungrily at the fettuccine alfredo the person sitting next to me[22] had not finished.

The next day, on the way home, I would continue to eat constantly. By the time I got home and checked my weight, I had gained five pounds over the weekend.

So now, RAWROD 2005 is behind me. I'm glad I did it, even as a fat cyclist, but when the Leadville 100 happens this August, I'd just as soon be a tad thinner.

---

19   Gratuitous Coneheads reference, just in case you weren't sure.

20   Which is probably a pretty telling clue to the whole "fat cyclist" cycle I'm perpetually stuck in.

21   Restaurant in Moab, UT. Not a great restaurant unless you're starving after a big ride. Luckily for Pasta Jays, pretty much everyone in Moab is *always* starving after a big ride.

22   This person was Ryan Benson, by the way. I should have mentioned him by name; it would have probably been worth at least another fifteen or twenty clicks.

NEWS FLASH! OLN FIRES PHIL LIGGETT: FAILED TO MEET CONTRACTUAL OBLIGATION TO MENTION LANCE ARMSTRONG THREE TIMES PER MINUTE, SOURCES SAY

I was a couple months into writing my blog and a little bit concerned about the fact that, more or less, the same dozen-or-so people read it each day. Not that I was ungrateful, mind you. I just kinda hoped that my writing would catch like wildfire and in practically no time at all, I'd have a big audience.

The fact that I thought that I'd been patient by waiting for this not-yet-appearing massive audience for a whopping two months shows exactly how patient of a person I can (not) be.

Then MSN Spaces, which is where my blog was hosted at the time, highlighted me on their "What's Your Story" feature, where they used to spotlight pretty much any blog that wasn't written by a bored teenager.

A lot of page views came in. Thousands per day, where there used to be maybe a hundred.

And then I got lucky.

The 2005 Tour de France started. So naturally, I was writing about it, and poking a little fun at the Lance-mania that was in full swing. I wrote this piece in particular on the day MSN decided to promote my blog front and center on their homepage.

*Suddenly, I was getting 50,000 page views. Per **hour**. And a lot of those people forwarded this story on to their biking friends. And someone at CyclingNews saw it, then offered me a humor column.*

And in short, thanks to a nice set of coincidences, my blog went from having no traffic whatsoever to having a few thousand views per day, literally overnight.

And as a bonus, for the next three months, a Google search on "Phil Liggett" returned this blog post as the number one result. So, probably, Phil Liggett has read this piece.

I wonder what he thinks of it. But also, I kinda don't want to know.

PARIS, JULY 5 (FAT CYCLIST FAKE NEWS SERVICE) — Outdoor Life Network[23] today severed its contract with Phil Liggett, a perennial favorite cycling announcer both in England and in the United States. A spokesperson[24] for Outdoor Life Network (OLN) said, "We regret having to let Phil go, but he knew the terms of our agreement when he signed on. Namely, he is required to allude to Lance Armstrong three times per minute, with at least one of those mentions being by name. Most importantly, at no point in time shall forty seconds ever elapse without a mention of Lance Armstrong.

"Today, sadly, Mr. Liggett broke the terms of that agreement," continued the spokesperson. "When David Zabriskie had his unfortunate accident today, Phil failed, for 44 seconds,[25] to put it in the context of whether this would impact Lance Armstrong, or whether Lance Armstrong would have fallen, or asking what Lance Armstrong must be thinking about this accident right that moment."

When reached for comment, co-commentator Paul Sherwen said, "I had my 'Lance Stopwatch' going — it's what we use to help remind us when it's time to mention Lance again." Continued Sherwen, "When Zabriskie fell, Liggett started actually talking about how disastrous it was for the rider, instead of — as is proper — talking about how this would affect Lance and how he would no doubt have words of advice on the proper way to ride a bicycle for young Zabriskie.[26]

"When twenty seconds elapsed," said Sherwen, his voice quaking with emotion, "I signaled to the timer. Then thirty seconds elapsed — still no mention, so I made the sign of the Texas Longhorn, the code we use to signal that we need to *immediately* divert the conversation toward Armstrong. Still nothing."

---

23   That's Versus, now. Or NBC. Or something else probably, by the time you read this.

24   When I first started writing fake news pieces, I would avoid making up names, for some reason, instead going with generics. Later I would use friends' names when I needed an expert or spokesperson. Eventually, I decided I was protected by the first amendment and started going with actual spokesperson names. I have not yet been sued, but it might be scarily exciting if I were.

25   Originally, this said "40 seconds" but I just now changed it to "44 seconds," because it sounds more specific. And as everyone knows, specificity is the highest form of humor (fart noises are second highest).

26   At the time I originally wrote this, there was no paragraph break here. That's because I had not yet learned what I now consider to be the most important thing a person can learn to make their writing attractive and legible: write short paragraphs. Seriously.

Visibly shaken, Sherwen[27] finished, "On the forty-fifth second, Phil managed to bring the conversation back round to Armstrong, but by then it was too late. OLN Security was knocking at the door, ready to escort Phil from the premises."[28]

Interviewed in his hotel room in Paris, Liggett looked like a man who has lost his best friend. "I'm a huge fan of Armstrong," said Liggett. "I haven't pretended to be impartial for years. But between Bob Roll and that marionette Al Trautwig,[29] our Armstrong-centricism seemed pretty well covered and I suppose I briefly let my guard down. I wonder what Lance Armstrong thinks about that?"

Then, realizing the habit of mentioning Armstrong even when Armstrong is completely irrelevant to the conversation was still with him, Liggett briefly looked melancholy — which is the British equivalent of an American having a complete nervous breakdown.[30]

OLN has moved swiftly to replace Liggett, putting former color-commentator Al Trautwig in his spot. Said Trautwig regarding his promotion, "Lance Armstrong. Lance Lance Lance Armstrong. Armstrong Armstrong Lance Lance Lance Lance. Six-time Tour de France winner. Lance Armstrong Lance Armstrong, Lance Armstrong."[31]

"This is going to work out just fine," said the OLN spokesperson.

---

27   In the original version of this post, I misspelled Paul Sherwen's name each and every time (Sherwin), except one. Sorry, Paul. (Yeah, like Paul Sherwen's reading *this*.)

28   After I wrote the Phil and Paul quotes for this piece, I read them out loud to myself, trying to see if it sounded like them. At which point I discovered that I do a very poor British accent. Pip pip!

29   I have a theory: the people who get really upset at the way Craig Hummer commentates came to the sport after Al Trautwig stopped commentating the Tour de France. Never has such a great voice been matched with such horrible observations.

30   Stiff upper lip and whatnot, ho ho!

31   Yeah, that's about how it really was.

2.

Excellence in Advertising

I DON'T SEEK OUT ADS TO RIDICULE. I DON'T. AND IF I SEE AN AD THAT MAKES ME ROLL MY EYES, THEN I DO JUST THAT — ROLL MY EYES. AND then move on.

But once in a while, an ad speaks to me. And what it says is something like, "Please, Fatty. Make fun of me. I am so ridiculously bad that if you don't make fun of me, I am going to be angry at you."

"No," I reply. "I don't want to make fun of you. That's not nice. And I am a very nice person."

"My whole reason for existing is to be ridiculed!" the ad shouts. "I *want* you to make fun of me. I'm wearing a striped shirt and polka-dot pants. How could you *not* make fun of me?"

And the ad is right. I find that I am unable to not make fun of it.

This section, then, is a sampling of the times I've given in to the urge. I'm very sorry.

AN OPEN LETTER TO "CHAMPION: OFFICIAL SUPERMARKET OF THE TOUR DE FRANCE"

The first ad I ever felt compelled to write about was this one. And it's not like I saw the ad, considered it carefully, and then tried to find something peculiar to write about each person in the ad. I saw it, winced, looked more carefully at it, and then grabbed a post-it. On it, I wrote, "Lobotomy. Witch. Murderer. Terrified rider. Puffy sleeves."

After that, it took me longer to get a good scan of the ad than it did to write the post.

If there's ever been a piece that's written itself, this one was it.

Dear Champion Supermarket Chain,

Yesterday, I got my *Guide to the Tour*, a supplement to *VeloNews* magazine. I'm pretty sure this guide is simply a translated version of the Tour Guide published in France, ads and all.[1]

Champion, I am pleased that you are supporting the Tour and I am pleased that you are the Official Supermarket of the Tour de France. Alas, since I don't live in France, your ad never had a chance of getting me to buy anything, so you may want to reconsider how you spend your ad dollars next year. Still, if I ever go to France, now I know where to get my official Tour groceries and that's something. I guess.[2]

---

1   I have never actually verified whether this is actually the case, because fact-checking isn't something I'm especially concerned about, seeing as how 90% of everything I write is either impossible to verify or is an outright lie.

2   Last year I finally got a chance to visit France, and I totally forgot to visit a Champion Supermarket. Truthfully, I would have been kind of afraid to go inside anyway.

That said, Champion, I feel I must tell you that your full-page ad in this guide has creeped me out unlike any ad I have seen in recent memory.[3]

I submit the following reasons for why:

The cyclist has the largest, most terrified eyes I have ever seen.[4] He knows these people want him dead, and probably also realizes his bike is tilted so far up and to the left that there is *no way* he will not keel over onto his side. His terror is so great that he has forgotten to be embarrassed by the fact that he's tucked his jersey into his shorts.[5]

The adult male appears to have had a frontal lobotomy. He's looking into space and has a slack-jawed, lopsided grin. I'm confident the only reason we don't see drool is because it has been Photoshopped out.

He does not make me want to buy groceries.

The adult female is wearing the strangest baseball cap I have ever seen. No, calling it a baseball cap is inappropriate, for it is clearly a spotted turban with a bill.[6] Also, the expression on her face leads me to believe she is screaming for vengeance,[7] which I believe is the main reason the cyclist looks so scared.

She does not make me want to buy groceries, but she *does* make me want to buy life insurance.

The female child being held by the adult female is, I believe, a witch.[8] Her concentrated expression and the way she is making a hand gesture while looking directly into the eyes of the (again, terrified) cyclist leads

---

3   I was hedging because I hadn't really, at that point, spent a lot of time considering which ad has creeped me out most in my whole life. Now I have had time to consider and think I can say, with confidence, that the only ad that has creeped me out more than this one was…um…nope, can't think of any. This one is creepiest.

4   I have since seen larger.

5   Seriously, what is going on there?

6   I don't know why, but this is my favorite line in the whole piece. "Spotted turban with a bill" has a good rhythm to it, and it also happens to be a good description of what it looks like. And a spotted turban is kind of a funny idea, anyway.

7   I wonder what the cyclist did that made her so *mad*.

8   Second best line in the piece. Don't you think?

me to believe she is the instrument that will effect[9] the vengeance her mother wants so badly.

Also, the sleeve of her t-shirt puffs out as if it were inflatable. Perhaps this is a flotation function prepared against the likelihood of angry villagers trying to drown her?

The leftmost male child looks wistful, perhaps because he knows that his sister is placing a pox on the cyclist.

The rightmost male child is the only person in this photo who looks like he's actually cheering at a cycling event. However, due to his position, orientation, and where he's looking, he's clearly not cheering at *this* cycling event.[10] I notice, furthermore, that his left sleeve is big and puffy, in a manner similar to the way his sister's puffs.

I do not believe this boy is a witch, so am now reconsidering the "t-shirt-as-an-emergency-flotation-device" theory. I now, instead, believe this is how French children carry their cigarettes.

The smallest male...child?...dwarf?...mannequin?...undead zombie?[11]...is the real crux of the problem with this ad. His head is massive and he looks 40 years old. He's also completely expressionless. Like most of his siblings, he's evidently got either a life vest on under his t-shirt or lots and lots of cigarettes rolled up under the short sleeves.

This person makes me want to avoid your supermarket at all costs. In fact, he makes me afraid to go outside at all.

Champion, please believe me when I say that every single person in the United States would be better at producing ads for your

---

9   Yep, "effect." Not "affect." I know my verbs, bub.

10   There's another cycling event two blocks away.

11   "Undead zombie" is completely redundant, but I'm leaving the "undead" here because I'm too lazy to delete it. Plus, maybe if you kill a zombie but don't do a very good job and then a vampire bites it, it may come back to life as an *undead vampire zombie.* Hey, why not?

supermarket than what you've got here.[12] Give one of us a call. We'd
be happy to help.

Kind Regards,

COMMENT FROM DINGLEBOBBR
That manchild dwarf thing is scary. They ought to make a horror
movie with that character living in the basement of a library. The
electricity goes out, the library doors close, and the manchild
dwarf is hungry...

COMMENT FROM KJ
The Adult Female looks like Jennifer Jason Leigh at the end of
'Single White Female' when she freaks out on Bridget Fonda.
Maybe they're fueled by a similar hatred for Terrified Cyclist/
Bridget Fonda?

---

12   This is not hyperbole. Everyone here in the U.S. is *awesome* at producing ads.
Every. Single. One of us.

AN OPEN LETTER TO ASSOS

If VeloNews (now just called "Velo," because it no longer contains any news) had run the Luxury body ad in just one issue, I doubt I would have written this piece. I mean, it's pretty innocuous when you first look at it.

But they ran it issue after issue after issue. Right up front. There was no missing it. And so I started noticing odd little things about it. And more and more, it got under my skin.

Now, this part is a friend-of-a-friend story, but I still hope it's true. At Interbike, a year after I published this piece, someone asked the Assos guy at the booth what their marketing plans were for the following year. The booth guy went on for a while about budgets and campaigns and so forth, and then concluded, "Or we could just pray that the Fat Cyclist tears down another one of our ads."

Which kind of makes me wish they'd send me a pair of shorts or something. You know, as a "thank you."

Dear Assos,

I subscribe to *VeloNews* magazine, and have noticed that your ad (shown below for your convenience) has appeared in the premium inside-front cover spread for the past — oh, I dunno — maybe five thousand issues.

Assos, please believe that I have your best interests at heart when I beg you to pull this ad and replace it with something less ridiculous, such as a photo of a chimpanzee wearing a tutu.

Oh, you'd like justification for why I think this ad needs to be pulled? Well, if you insist.

MEET DEREK ZOOLANDER

Let's start with the model. I have no problem with companies using models in their ads. But the model you have selected for your ad and used throughout your website clearly does not ride a bike. At *all*.

He does not have the cycling jersey tanlines. He has a chiseled upper body. Most tellingly, however, is that he has silly little stick-like girly legs.

It's possible, Assos, that I'm actually complaining about a conscious decision you made in picking a non-cyclist to show off your cycling garb. After all, your website seems to indicate that you're really focusing on the non-cyclist part of the cyclist demographic. I quote:

"The less you ride, the more your body is fragile. The more you need garments that sustain and protect your body when riding your bicycle."

So, if I understand correctly, your point is that people who ride a lot *don't* need good bike clothes. People who *rarely* ride, however — or better yet, never ride at all — *should* buy your off-the-charts-expensive biking clothes.

That's a very original point of view and you should be commended for it.

Sadly, the originality of this point is offset by it being one of the stupidest things I've ever read.

LUXURY BODY?

Assos, I admit: the heading in your ad, "Luxury body," drew me in.

I think I can safely say, though, that it drew me in for reasons other than what you would like. Essentially, it perplexed me. Here are some of the questions — questions to which I have no answer — storming in my mind regarding your heading:

- What is a "Luxury body?"
- Why is "Luxury" capitalized, but "body" is not?
- Will your clothes make my body luxurious?
- Do I want a luxurious body? After all, I tend to look for luxury in my furniture. Having a "Luxury body" makes me think that I might be a good ottoman.

In search of these answers, I went to your website. Your explanation, if I can call it that, of "Luxury body" is:

"Assos is designed to give you the look, the style, the elegance & exclusivity. Assos enhances and makes you a luxury body!"

Assos, your explanation just leaves me with more questions. What look? What style? Who do I want to exclude? And that final sentence, ironically, gives new meaning to the word "meaningless." I mean, Assos enhances *what*?

So, I repeat, *what is a luxury body*? Please tell me, Assos. I must know.

LOREM IPSUM

Assos, I wouldn't have taken the time to write to you if your ad problems were limited to a silly model and a ridiculous headline.It was your ad copy that sent me over the edge.

One quick read-through convinced me that up until five minutes before this went to press, this was "lorem ipsum" text. You know, the fake Latin stuff used as place-holder whenever an ad designer doesn't know what the body copy ought to be.

> It's now!
>
> You've finally made time to get on your bike and do something for your body and soul
>
> These days it's a luxury to have time for yourself.
>
> This time is your own,
>
> it's about you and it's your choice!
>
> These moments are precious and should be treated as such.
>
> Don't spoil it by using ordinary equipment, which limits you and the entire experience.

Then, at the last moment, you realized your error, and hired the first non-English-speaker you could find to write "real" ad copy.

Let's take a look at that text, sentence by sentence.

It's now![13] *What's* now? I'm not asking just because this is vague. If you actually described what is now later, I'd be OK with it. Or maybe you're just pointing out a fundamental truth: no matter when you read this ad copy, you are reading it *now*. In which case, I apologize.

You've finally made time to get on your bike and do something for your body and soul. Assos, do you realize in which magazine this ad is running? It's *VeloNews*. Most people who read this magazine don't "finally make time" to go ride. We go riding *all* the time, often at the expense of our careers and family life.

These days it's a luxury to have time for yourself. Fair enough. I don't

---

13   This is the line that really got to me and forced me to write this piece. Fingernails on chalkboard, I tell you.

see where you're headed with this, though.

This time is your own, it's about you and it's your choice! Assos, this copy might work better in *Cosmopolitan* magazine. They're really into the psychology of making a personal statement or of having stuff be "about you." Most people with whom I ride, on the other hand, go riding because it's fun.

These moments are precious and should be treated as such. *Precious? Moments? Precious moments?* Here's a tip, Assos: the next time you want to do an ad, get a writer with experience outside the Geriatric Birthday Greeting Card business.

Don't spoil it by using ordinary equipment, which limits you and the entire experience. First off, Assos, I'm going to let you off the hook on your usage of "it" in this sentence, even though it's a pretty jarring switch from plural (moments) to singular (it). And the reason I'm going to let you off the hook is because you clearly outsourced your ad copy writing to whoever writes those wacky quasi-English phrases for T-shirts in Japan.

But are you really suggesting that ordinary equipment limits me and my entire experience? Isn't it at least *possible* that what's limiting me, as the non-cycling cyclist you've identified as your prime demographic, is the fact that I only ride my bike when I can find one of those *precious, luxurious moments* when I've finally made time to get on my bike?

Your ad copy problems aren't limited to your ad, Assos. Check out some text right on the home page of your website, once you wait for all the Flash fireworks to finally die down:

"The Assos Mission is total comfort regardless of price. Definitely not for everybody, but maybe for YOU."

Which is almost immediately followed by:

"Who needs Total Comfort? Everybody!"[14]

So, if I read you right, total comfort isn't for everybody, but it might be for me. On the other hand, everybody needs Total Comfort.

Maybe the difference is in the capitalization?

---

14   I really do love the way they contradict themselves within two lines. I imagine one ad guy saying, "We want to appear exclusive! Let's say Assos isn't for everyone!" And the other ad guy saying, "No, we want to sell as many $1200 bike kits as possible! Let's say Assos is for everyone!" And then, in unison, they say, "Let's say *both things!*" And then they hug.

ADDITIONAL QUESTIONS

Assos, I have a few other brief, ad-related questions I hope you can address:

Could you please change the name of  **your company?** I know you're Swiss and all, so you may not understand that you named your company something that reads and sounds just like an angry, obscene epithet. My young children are forbidden to pronounce your name.

What is a "Cycling Body?" Is that what a Luxury body aspires to become? Or is it the other way around?

They can ask *anything* else? In your website, you say, "When the development phase of a new Assos product begins, the one question our engineers, technicians, and tailors are not allowed to ask is: *'How much must this product cost in order for it to sell in volume?'.*" [emphasis, punctuation sic]

Is that actually *true?* Like, it's OK for them to ask, "What if we used a lot of sequins to make our jerseys really *pop?*" Or, "How about we make a chamois using nothing but magnesium rivets and barbed wire?"[15] Or — and it looks like someone answered 'yes' to this last question — "Should we make a bike outfit that makes the wearer look like he just stepped out of an 80s vintage Michael Jackson music video?"[16]

Thank you for your time, Assos. I look forward to your resolving this matter in a timely manner.

Kind Regards,

[signature]

PS: This doesn't have anything to do with your ad, but I thought you'd get a kick out of an experience I had with one of your products, Assos.[17]

---

15   That would be a very uncomfortable chamois indeed. Perhaps some Assos Chamois Creme would fix the problem.

16   OK, I admit that I would *totally* wear a *Thriller*-based jersey. And you would too. You know you would.

17   This story is totally true. I just thought I should let you know since most of my stories aren't.

I once purchased a container of Assos Chamois Creme, then applied it to my chamois just as I was about to begin a day-long mountain bike ride. Alas, I did not realize that one of the main ingredients in Assos Chamois Creme seems to be menthol, of approximately the same concentration as Ben Gay.

My nether regions were simultaneously aflame and freezing, which is nowhere near as nice a feeling as you might expect.

Wanting to make sure that I was not having a reaction nobody else would have, I hid my pain, exquisite though it was, and offered the container to everyone in the group, many of which thanked me for my generosity and applied your Chamois Creme to their chamois as well. Their subsequent yelps of pain let me know that I was not alone in my reaction.

I probably don't need to tell you that I did not finish the jar.[18]

---

18   I likely still have it somewhere on some shelf in the garage, though.

THE WIT AND WISDOM
OF DR. MICHAEL LÄMMLER

Sometimes people ask me whether the Dr. Lämmler letter is real. Is it really possible that someone could be so angry and indignant over a jokey analysis of an ad (The Assos ad teardown a couple pages back)?

The answer is: Yes. Meaning, I did not write it myself. It's too good. Too perfectly self-righteous. Too...well...snotty.

To date, consensus is that this is the funniest thing that has ever been posted on my blog.

Dr. Lämmler, true to his word, never commented again. But I owe him a huge debt of gratitude. I've hidden quotes from this letter in several of my jersey designs, and I've referred back to this letter from countless posts.

So, Dr. Lämmler, wherever you are: thanks. For reals.

Is it vain for me to sometimes go back and read some of my favorite Fat Cyclist posts?

It is? OK, just checking.

I ask because this past weekend I was engaged in just such a bout of vanity. Among other things, I re-read what is my favorite Fat Cyclist post of all time: An Open Letter to Assos. I continued on to read the comments that have trickled in on it during the past few months.

And that's when Dr. Michael Lämmler kicked me in the head.[19]

Judging from his comment — which he posted twice, as if to underscore his point — Dr. Michael Lämmler is not amused by my post about Assos. Nor, indeed, is he amused by my blog at *all*.

The wisdom of Dr. Michael Lämmler is simply too good to leave buried in the comments section of a months-old post. No, the whole *world* needs to read what the good doctor prescribes for me and my blog.

Here then, is what Dr. Lämmler had to say, along with my comments in *italics*. Because the Doctor is brilliant and I want to

---

19   I make it sound like a painful blow, but the truth is I got more and more excited as I read his comment for the first time. I instantly knew how I would reply to him and I immediately knew I would do so in my blog. All I had to do was write it up. This was genuinely one of those pieces that just write themselves.

retain all the flavor, nuance, and precision of his letter, I have not edited his remarks in any way.

hello fatguy,

I want to make it very clear that I do not follow your little pathetic, full time job website but happened (go figure) to end up on it.

*Actually, my little pathetic website is not **quite** full time. The guy who pays fat biking bloggers to write pathetic websites keeps my hours to a strict 25 per week. That way, he gets around having to pay medical benefits.*

Anyway, I'm curious: how did you end up on my site? And more importantly, who forced you to stay once you had discovered you didn't like it here?

I write to you because the content of your page simply upsets me and all the people I have shown it to.

So, how upset exactly? Like, do your eyes bug out? Do you begin foaming at the mouth? Do veins pulse visibly on your forehead? Do you write foaming-at-the-mouth comments? And to how many people have you shown this post? Could I ask you to please show it to more? Word-of-mouth is by far the most effective form of advertising, after all.

I am just a little european (although I have an american mother) ex-elite rider who has been riding the bike before I could actually walk.[20]

*Seriously? That's terrible. Why did it take you so long to learn to walk? And when you say you're a "little" European, do you mean that you're **really** little? Like Tom Thumb? If so, I'll bet your bike is just **adorable**.*

My english is not perfect but I hope your comedian mastermind this time around might actually get the point.[21]

I'll check with my comedian mastermind the next time he drops by. As for myself, nope, I haven't yet got the point. Are you planning on making one?

My bike was my playground and evolved into my tool of making a living.[22] This lasted three years until I realized I will never win a tour de france and that there actually is an easier way of making a living then racing my bike.

---

20   This actually raises a pretty interesting question: If he couldn't walk, how did he manage to get a leg over the bike? Sadly, Dr. Lämmler and I don't maintain a correspondence, so I'm pretty sure we'll never find out.

21   About the time I reach this point in the letter, I always start reading Dr. Lämmler's part in a Colonel Klink (from Hogan's Heroes) voice. I'm not alone in that, am I?

22   I can't help but wonder what kind of external forces would cause a playground to evolve into a tool.

Well, I'm sure that will come as quite a shock to all the pro racers I know, who have each stated clearly, "I race for a living because it's so easy." Also, I've got to admit that I spent some time Googling your name, Dr. Lämmler. It turns out that a search on "Dr. Michael Lämmler" yields exactly one result,[23] and it's not for your pro racing career. If I broaden the search out a little bit, I do find one recent race result. Triathlons, Doctor? For shame.

Now and for the last 16 years I ride the bike for quality of life reasons, because I love the bike, because the sport continues to fascinate me, because I enjoy suffering, because it keeps my mind and body in shape, because the technology and evolution fascinates me, because it lets me get away from my "business day"[24] and last but not least cardio reasons.

You know what, Doctor? I take everything I said earlier back. You and I actually have a lot in common. Let's make up and be friends, okay?

Why I take the time to write to you is because the way you are talking about people and companies is completely out of line. Your sarcasm is not funny but instead embarrassing to the US cycling community that a so called "cyclist" can actually act the way you act.

Hey. I thought we were friends now.

Why do you ride the bike????? Take a piece of paper and write it down!

Is it OK if I just continue writing the reasons in my blog, instead? You know, the way I do pretty much five times a week?

I bet you started a few years ago because somebody told you that cycling is the best way to loose your fat?

Actually, I started because I heard there was big money in pathetic full-time job blog writing. I expect the cash to start rolling in any day now.[25]

You have a complete lack of cycling cultural background,[26] never raced in your life (except maybe on some children, mother, pension event), knows nothing about the history of cycling, how it evolved,[27] the industry, who were the actors?[28]

---

23   This is, of course, no longer true. There is a Michael Lämmler who has a Facebook page, and a LinkedIn page for a Michael Lämmler, and a pretty disturbing photography site for a Michael Lämmler. But the top three results for Michael Lämmler are...all from FatCyclist.com.

24   I think he put "business day" in quotes because...well...OK, I have no idea why.

25   Six years later, I'm still waiting.

26   That is true. Still.

27   This is the third mention of evolution in this letter. Weird.

28   Well, I'm going to go on record that I hope Stanley Tucci was one of them. I'm a big fan.

You mean I've got to know all that?!? Hey, nobody told me there was going to be an entrance exam! And don't you go dissing my children/ mother/pension races. I beat that octogenarian and four-year-old girl[29] fair and square.

The maximum level of suffer you have experienced on the bike equals having to skip a nice juicy dinner, isn't it?

Mmmmm. Foooooood.

The disrespect you have shown in regards to Mr. Armstrong leaves me speechless.

You mean apart from the big ol' speech you're making here, right?

You are asking the guy "what have you done in your life?", "It's not easy to be fired?" etc. etc. ARE YOU FOR REAL or a comedian?

(Note to confused readers: Dr. Lämmler is now talking about the career advice I offered Lance Armstrong when he retired last year.)[30] Um, is that a trick question? 'Cuz I thought it was really obvious that offering career advice to the ultra-successful, ultra-rich, ultra-busy Lance Armstrong as if he were a hard-luck case who had just lost his job at the assembly line would have put me squarely in the "outrageously absurd comedy" category.

I am not an Armstrong fan and probably you don't find many Armstrong fans in europe, o.k. but regardless of his personality the physical achievements (clean or not clean does not matter anymore at that level) [*Oh, you're just saying that to sound world-weary, right Doctor?*] is simply worth admiration and is earned respect. Why? Well either you are a cyclist and you get it or you simply don't get it.

I get it. I think everyone gets it. I'm losing interest, Doctor. Pick up the pace a little, would you?

But if you don't get it, [*Hey, I just said I get it!*] then a little "fat nothing" should keep his mouth shut and instead of trying to be a comedian you should educate yourself in the matter.

So, a minute ago, when you asked me whether I'm for real or a comedian, you had already made up your mind that I'm a comedian? OK, that's fine. But if we both agree that I'm a comedian, then don't we also agree that saying that Armstrong needs career advice is comic? I don't get it. Maybe I need some education in the matter.

---

29   Separate races, it should be noted.

30   That letter is called, *An Open Letter to the Newly-Unemployed Lance Armstrong*, p. 262.

ASSOS? Luxury Body? Either you get it, or you don't.

I don't get it. At all.[31] *I'm very excited right now, though, because nobody else seems to get it either. By all means, please explain it!*

Do you realize that it is this little Swiss company who made it possible in the first place (although I am pretty sure this was not the company's objective), for fat people like yourself to be able to stay on a bike for more then 2 hours by "inventing" total comfort cycling apparel over half a century ago and has revolutionized an entire industry??

*Really? Assos invented cycling clothes? That's actually really interesting. They should put **that** in an ad.*[32]

The way you analyzed their ad simply shows that you are deeply perplexed.

True enough. But be fair: the way they created their ad is deeply perplexing. And I still don't know what a Luxury body is. I am beginning to suspect, however, that you're the guy who wrote the copy for that ad.

Deep in your mind you would love to have a luxury body (this is the reason why YOU are riding the bicycle), but when you look in the mirror all you see is the exact opposite (regardless of how many kilos you loose) of a luxury body.

*I refuse to commit to **wanting** a Luxury body until someone explains to me what a Luxury body **is**. Although, by inference, I'm now beginning to think you at least feel a Luxury body is the opposite of a fat cyclist's body. Which is a fair enough point, but I can't for the life of me make the connection between one's body and the type of cycling clothes one should own.*

Then you would like to buy some Assos luxury body gear but you can't afford it because you are sitting in front of your computer all day long trying to be a comedian.[33]

What can I say? Pathetic, full-time job websites don't pay what they should.

Then you had a little money left and were able to buy an ASSOS chamois creme, get a little glamour in your life; but not being cycling educated, you spalmed[34] it on your balls instead of your butt and this created even more, additional turbulence in your little "genius mind".

Turbulence, indeed. Wow! Though I must admit, the glamour of Assos

---

31   Still don't, even six years later. Most opaque slogan in the history of ever.
32   Seriously, "Assos: We invented CycleWear" would make a pretty good slogan.
33   Dude, get out of my *head!*
34   This is the best word in the world.

Chamois Creme was worth every moment of the searing pain I experienced on my spalmed balls.

I understand that writing might be a valve, a strategy to let go the frustration and complex (others ride the bike) you are facing in your life, but please, next time before you are using your webpage to do so — THINK! People do actually read your crap.

And it's a very upsetting experience for each and every one of them.[35]

Don't bather answering, I am not visiting your little paradise again.

Not even if I ask pretty-please?

sincerely yours,

Dr. Michael Lämmler

PS I apologize for my euro english but writing my message to you in german would be pointless, wouldn't?

Thank you for your unreserved and heartfelt apology for your Euro English. I accept your apology unconditionally. Let us not speak of it again.

Oh by the way, now I feel so much better, yes writing helps doesn't it?

If you say so, Doc. Though I've gotta say, when I need to work out some rage, I find a nice long bike ride works better.

> **COMMENT FROM HANS**
> That's too funny! But Lance still used Assos Chamois Creme in all his Tour de France victories. Good enough for him at least... Also, Assos was indeed the first to use Lycra (don't use the word spandex) in bicycling apparel.

> **COMMENT FROM TIMOTHY**
> Not only am I not sure what a Luxury body is, now I'm not sure how to know if I've spalmed myself. What are the signs and symptoms?

---

35   To those of you who have been with me the whole six years, I deeply apologize for the extraordinarily upsetting experience to which you have been subjected. And also, thank you for reading my crap.

COMMENT FROM JOEY

Fatty, You evil bastard! I opened up a fresh jar of Assos Creme and it was BLUE!! And no more tingle!! Just because one chubby, wussy blogger whined about the tingle, it's gone! At least the catalog is still soft porn.

COMMENT FROM UNKNOWN

OK I admit it, the Assos chamois creme actually works for me. Surely this must be a sign of the Luxury body! Perhaps the Luxury body has the innate ability to withstand the heat of errant spalmings?

3.
How To Do Very Important Things

"FAKE NEWS" PIECES ARE THE EASIEST KIND OF POST FOR ME TO WRITE, BUT "HOW TO" PIECES ARE THE MOST FUN. WHY? BECAUSE OF A LITTLE secret I'm going to let you in on right now:

I don't let the fact that I don't know anything at all about anything at all slow me down from acting like I'm an expert on everything. How to race faster? Sure. How to taper? Why not? How to evaluate your competition? Oh, I'm excellent at that.

That said, I'm a lot more likely to write about things in which I do have some experience. Like how to fall down. Or spit. Or be middle-aged.

Yeah, I'm a regular font of wisdom, I am.

HOW TO SIZE UP YOUR COMPETITION

When I am off the bike, I am the most non-competitive person you could ever meet. I'm easygoing to the point of being comatose. I actively try to lose arguments; I'm very good at this. I'd rather slow down than pass another car.

But when I'm on a bike, I undergo a subtle change. Who's in front **matters** *to me. My game face comes on — a terrifyingly serious game face, I can assure you. A friendly ride is actually a "friendly" ride. And if I finish ahead of you, you can bet that at some point in the future, I will find a reason to bring it up.*

Doesn't riding with me sound like a pleasure?

The thing is though, I'm pretty sure I'm as normal a rider as can be. It's just that I have more experience being needlessly competitive than most people. I'm so happy I can share this experience with you.

When does riding become racing? Two simple rules:

1. **When there are two riders:** It is possible for two cyclists to ride together without it turning into a race — but *only* if it has already been established that one of the two cyclists is the alpha rider.[1]

2. **When there are three or more riders:** If there are three or more cyclists, there will be racing, whether it be a race to the summit, a race to the next signpost, or a race of fatigue. The race may not be acknowledged,[2] but it is there.

Of course, before you embark upon any race,[3] you want to understand your competition. Today, I will begin to explain how you can assess your chances against your cycling foes.

---

1   Here, I'm talking about my fast friend Kenny. And Brad too. And Dug, but only on the descents. And Ricky too. And Bob. OK, I'm talking about pretty much everyone I ride with. Suddenly I'm depressed.

2   Indeed, it is bad form to acknowledge it. Because if you acknowledge that you were racing, you open yourself up to your friend/opponent saying, "Oh, if I'd known we were racing I would have tried. I thought we were just riding along."

3   Which you should be very careful to call a "ride."

THE CYCLIST

The first — and most obvious — thing you need to focus on is the fit of the clothes. The type and tightness of the jersey and shorts give you a good indication of the relative confidence of your opponent:

- **Loose fitting:** If the shorts and/or jersey are loose-fitting, the cyclist has something, i.e., fat, to hide. He knows he's not at the top of his game. Plan to destroy this cyclist on the climbs.
- **Form fitting:** You don't need me to tell you what this means. This is a person who has earned his physique. All you can hope for is that he earned it in the gym, not on the bike. The good news is that if he has a muscular, well-toned upper body with actual pecs and biceps and everything, he's more of an all-round athlete than a cyclist. There's a good chance you'll still be able to beat him, if you can hold on for the first twenty minutes (the average duration of a Gold's Gym workout).
- **Used to be form-fitting, but now looks uncomfortably tight:** Oh, that's me. Don't worry, I'm no threat to you.

Next comes sponsor branding. And this is complex. Bike clothes with sponsor branding can mean different things on different people.

- **Full team kit on a guy with hairy legs:** This person read a *Men's Health* article about the benefits of cycling a couple years ago and watched the Tour de France[4] last year, whereupon he decided to "get into" cycling. He has money to spend, but no biking skills whatsoever. Toy with him, then ride away.
- **Full team kit on a guy with shaved legs:** Could mean trouble. He's clearly a fanboy, and cares enough about cycling that he probably rides plenty. You're going to have to go to secondary clues: leg definition, evidence of a spare tire,[5] suntan pattern, bike clues.
- **Jersey advertising a non-bike-sponsoring consumer product:** This is a person who buys his jerseys at a bike store, as opposed to getting them as souvenirs for races he's done. This person

---

4   When I originally posted this, I wrote "Tour de Lance." Now whenever I hear people say "Tour de Lance" I can't help but roll my eyes. Apparently, though, I'm part of the problem. So of course I added a section to this book called *Tour de Lance* (see p. 257).

5   By which I do not mean a kit for repairing flats.

does not take biking seriously enough. A few intermediate sprints should demoralize him nicely. That said, I desperately want a Reese's Peanut Butter Cup jersey.[6] Have I mentioned that Saturday is my birthday? Size Large, please.[7]

- **Race/Event branding**: This is helpful only if you know the circumstances under which the jersey can be obtained. If it's a jersey you have to buy, it means your opponent wishes he were fast, but isn't. If the jersey can only be obtained by finishing, or worse, winning, a race, you may have a serious contender on your hands.

- **No branding whatsoever**: Inscrutable. This is clearly a guy who either wants to fade into the background because he sucks (70% chance), or likes to go stealth so that you feel that much worse when he cleans your clock (30% chance). Look for secondary clues.

Of course, the most important clue to how your competition, I mean, "friend," will ride are his legs. Evaluate his tan, his hairiness, and his quads and calves.

- **Tan = trouble.** But check *where* the tan starts and ends. If he's tan right up to the bike shorts line but not beyond, and his quads are *the* tannest part of his body, you've got a real cyclist on your hands. If his forehead has a strange tanning pattern on it that suddenly makes sense when he puts on his helmet and glasses, this spells trouble with a capital T.

- **Shaved legs = serious cyclist.** Why do shaved legs matter? Because they mean he's made a commitment to cycling. They also mean he's vain, because the purpose of shaved legs is to increase the visibility of your leg muscle definition.

- **Leg definition and size:** Finally, check the size and cut of his quads and calves. If he's just cut, you can probably take him on the flats. If he's just big, you can get him on the climbs. If he's both, just try to draft.

---

6   I eventually got this jersey, though I am proud to say that it is now too large for me. However, do you think it's a coincidence that the Fat Cyclist colors are the same colors as a Reese's wrapper? I think *not*.

7   I am only joking here. I am not hinting that I want another Reese's jersey. Please do not buy me one.

THE BIKE

Anyone who's ever gathered at a start line knows there's an awful lot of sly bike inspection going on. But gauging the quality of the cyclist based on what he's riding isn't limited to start lines. You can do it practically anytime. Looking at bikes on car racks and looking at the bikes people are riding as you pass/are passed are two common times. Today, let's take a look at how you can quickly size up the competition, just by looking at what they ride.

First, look for reflectors, or lack thereof. This is the absolutely most obvious way you can be sure someone's not serious about cycling. If he's left the reflectors on his bike, he's clearly not considering the extraordinarily deleterious (wow, I just used "deleterious" in a sentence!) effects on his speed that the weight and poor aerodynamics of the reflectors will have.[8]

The drivetrain is an excellent[9] indicator of the person's riding style:

- **Shimano** is all about efficiency and reliability. If the bike has high-end Shimano components, there's an 80% chance the rider also drives a Japanese car. There's also a high likelihood that the rider will be a good tactician and smart rider.[10]
- **Campagnolo** means the rider cares all about the history of cycling and the passion of cycling and will fly into a fit if you do not profess an undying love for Eddy Merckx. This person corners with passion. He climbs with passion. He descends with passion. He attacks with passion. And when you beat him, he will lose with passion. He is, in short, passionate.
- **SRAM**: This person isn't interested in beating you. He's interested in doing his own thing, man. If you suggest working together, he'll look at you like you're from Mars.[11]
- **Singlespeed** means that he no longer cares about winning, or

---

8   Disclaimer: I am not recommending you remove your bike reflectors. In fact, I recommend you put hundreds and hundreds of reflectors on your bike. Especially if you and I ever go on a "friendly ride" together.

9   When I originally posted this, I used the word "good" instead of excellent. I just changed it to "excellent" because this is the deluxe edition of the book. In the standard edition of the book, I will change the "good" to "OK."

10   The gag here is that I love Shimano components and drive nothing but Hondas, which may indicate why I'm saying such nice things about riders who love Shimano.

11   Back in 2005, SRAM was a real dark-horse component manufacturer, at least here in the U.S. Wow, things have changed.

at least wishes to project the image that he no longer cares.[12] He's jaded, like James Dean on a bike. *OR* it's possible that he is bringing enough game to the ride that he's confident he can beat you even without the benefit of technology.

And what about wheels? Well, everyone talks about wheels as if they're the biggest factor in how fast you go. Let me tell you a secret: your wheels aren't going to make you any faster or slower.[13] They're not going to change the quality of your ride.[14] So, if you see that your competition is riding with very expensive wheels, don't worry about him being faster than you. Instead, just make a mental note that this person is gullible and that you'll probably be successful at selling him Nu Skin products later.

As for the frame, well, a brand-new frame says more about your opponent's income than about his ability on a bike. It could mean he's new to biking. It could mean he just nailed a sponsor. It could mean he wore his previous bike out.

However, a well-worn bike says a *lot* about the rider. If it's well-used and well-maintained, count on a tough race. If the frame is a couple years old but still looks new, your competition is more likely riding a New Years' resolution — one that didn't work out — from a couple years ago. If he's riding a frame that's several years old and still in good shape, you know you're racing a lifer. If the rider looks strong, be ready for some serious competition.

And finally, most importantly, let's examine pedals. As in, it's better to have them than not.

Okay, I was just kidding about pedals being important.

COMMENT FROM BCMULL

What does it say if you are wearing a Team Fatty jersey?

---

12   This was before I started riding singlespeeds. Now I'd say something like, "This guy likes hedging his bets. If he beats you, he did it on a singlespeed. If you beat him, hey, he was just riding a singlespeed; what did you expect?

13   Honestly, I cannot tell any difference in how fast I go between a heavy wheelset and a light one. Can you? I mean, for real?

14   Unless they're out of true. Then they can change the quality of your ride *dramatically.*

COMMENT FROM TSURU

You missed one type of race: one rider vs. one rider. This is *very* different from two riders. Let me explain. Here's the scene: a lone rider is on a ride, then sees, up in the distance, another lone rider. Unbeknownst to the rider ahead, the race is on. It's a "bunch sprint" of one to some arbitrary point! But the winning moment is actually when the first rider, when about to pass, completely out of breath, in pain, but still chugging along, summons up just a little extra helping of oxygen to announce, "on your left" with a small grin holding it all together as he passes, waiting until the next bend or turn to try to hold back vomiting and passing out. Cavendish ain't got nuffin' on that finish.

COMMENT FROM VELOTEX

I usually laugh at the guys with shaven legs, but I never knew that it was done to show-off their leg muscle definition. Now I'm going to laugh even harder!

HOW TO DESPAIR

A lot of the posts I write have no truth in them whatsoever. And then there are the ones that have a little bit too much truth. Yes, I really do talk to myself when I'm trying to go faster.

What I don't mention in this post is the voice I hear in my head when I'm despairing. It's a "disappointed grandfather" voice: a stern-but-fair man who had high hopes for me, but now realizes that I'll never amount to anything.

*Seriously, with that voice in your head, who **wouldn't** despair?*

I've done a lot of endurance rides, more than a dozen 100-mile mountain bike races and probably more than a couple dozen events and just-for-fun rides.[15] I've learned that my mood arc, from beginning to end, is perfectly predictable:

- **Nervous excitement before starting**: Do I have everything I need? Is my equipment OK? Am I fast enough to keep up/not embarrass myself/reach my goal time?
- **Giddiness at the beginning**: Excited at the prospect of adventure, enjoying being around friends/like-minded cyclists, adrenaline from crossing a starting line.
- **Helpful/friendly "Mr. Roarke" (from *Fantasy Island*) phase**: Talking with anyone who'll engage with you about what lies ahead, discussing how to gauge/meter your effort, and generally exuding pleasure at having so much sage advice to give.[16]
- **In the moment:** Settling into the biking groove, no longer feeling a need to talk, thinking about whether I'm eating and drinking enough. This is the best mood of the race. Sometimes whole miles will elapse where I'm only peripherally aware of my surroundings: it's just me, my legs, and the sense of motion. It's a good place.
- **Despair:** I've slowed drastically and have begun talking to myself. I hate my bike, I hate the trail, I hate the other racers, I hate my former self: the obviously idiotic self who thought

---

15   Here I'm trying to build credibility, in spite of the fact that I have none.

16   I wonder how many times my Mr. Roarke phase has triggered someone else's despair phase.

doing another endurance race was a good idea. It's astounding how quickly I transition from the "In the moment" phase to the "Despair" phase. Sometimes I'll move back and forth between these two phases several times during the ride.

- **Anticipation**: My mind is on one thing only: crossing the line. I usually adopt a mantra for this part: "Five more miles. I can make it. Five more miles. I can make it. 4.98 miles. I can make it."
- **Resignation**: Once again, I finished. That's good, I guess. Once again, I didn't meet my goal. Too bad. Oh well, I'll get it next time.

TRASH TALKING TO MYSELF

I don't think I've ever done an endurance ride without going through all those stages, in that order. Of all these moods, though, I think "Despair" is the most interesting. It's absolutely the most *informative*, because a part of me I usually suppress comes to the foreground, and seems to feel that this is a good time to give me a frank assessment of my abilities, character, and priorities. Here are a few quotes from the conversations I have had with myself:

- For once, just *once*, can you try *not* being weak? Would it hurt *that much worse* to be strong and fast?[17]
- You have no business here. You have no strength, no speed, no endurance.
- You have no business on a bike whatsoever, for that matter. You have no technical skill, you can't climb, you can't sprint, you can't do *anything*.
- What did you think you'd accomplish by doing another long ride? Did you think you'd learn something? Did you think you'd be faster than before? Did you think you'd impress your coworkers?
- Your priorities are messed up. You waste all your time riding instead of being with your family. Or writing a book. Finish this ride, then sell the bike. Grow up.
- Another guy just passed you. And he's not going fast.
- You had a *whole year* to train and lose weight for this. So were

---

17   I'm pretty sure I've said this to myself in every single race I have ever ridden. Long or short.

the Oreos worth being fat and slow? Did they taste so good that you don't mind being out here pushing your bike up a hill when you could have finished right now?

- Do you think anyone would care if you quit? Nobody would. Get off your bike and tell people you were too sick to go on.

There are lots more. These are just the ones that come first to mind.

And yes, I always speak to myself in the second person during this stage. And yes, sometimes I do say these things aloud. And no, there's never an angel sitting on my right shoulder, answering the demon sitting on my left.

I never reply to the questions I ask myself. At least not out loud. Continuing to turn the cranks seems like the only answer there is.[18]

COMMENT FROM AARON

"I'm never doing this ride again." I have said that sentence at least a hundred times. I said it at the end of Leadville and I hope to say it again this year.

COMMENT FROM ANT

Fatty, you've really hit the nail on the head with this one — again. I usually include another stage: feeling guilty about all the money and time I have spent riding and working on bikes as well as the time away from my family — AND I WANT TO GIVE UP ON THIS STUPID RACE? Oh, and also thinking about the first possible point I can DNF without bringing complete and utter shame upon myself.

COMMENT FROM ROBERT

The Laramie Enduro was the only time I've ever gone into as dark a place as you describe. That was miserable. Oh, and Kokopelli's. And maybe Leadville. I'm usually more upbeat: "OK, so I just got passed on a hill by a guy wearing Levi's and a pinwheel hat. I'll catch him right after I throw up."

---

18 Wow, this post ended on a surprisingly serious note.

HOW TO BE A MIDDLE-AGED CYCLIST

I wrote this post in 2005, which means I wasn't even 40 yet. Now at 45, I'm trying very hard to remember how it's possible I considered myself middle-aged back then. Sadly, I cannot, because I no longer can remember anything at all. And besides, I need to go shout at the kids on my lawn.

Watching the Tour de France, you might reasonably come to the conclusion that all cyclists are dangerously thin, in their early twenties to early thirties, and can ride their bikes for up to three weeks without rest.

The reality is a little different. Most of us are middle-aged. Most of us need to lose weight. Luckily, by virtue of being middle-aged, we have the money that lets us *afford* this ridiculously expensive sport.[19]

So, if you want to become a bike enthusiast, you may as well learn how to be middle-aged too, or at least act that way. Here are some helpful tips you can use:

- **Wear a long, loose-fitting jersey.**[20] A long, loose-fitting jersey will hide both your behind and your belly. This will make it *impossible* for others to recognize the fact that you are overweight. Because you are the only person who has ever thought of wearing loose clothes to camouflage extra weight.
- **Spare no expense in making your bike light**. If you can find a way to reduce the weight of your bike by 20 grams, it's worth the cost. Period. And don't think about the fact that dropping ten[21] pounds from yourself would be much safer and less costly. That's not relevant.
- **Get a triple chain ring on your road bike.** It's not because you don't have power in your legs, it's because you want to spin a higher cadence up the hills.
- **Obsess endlessly about equipment and technique.** These are the keys to going faster. Those who would say that it's riding with more power simply don't understand the complexities of riding.

---

19 At least, until we start sending our kids to college. Or getting them braces.
20 Not so long that you wind up sitting on that jersey, though.
21 Or twenty. Or thirty. Or forty. Depends on what year you ask me.

- **Buy a helmet without many vents**. If they can't see through your helmet, they can't see your male-pattern baldness, can they?
- **Learn the fine art of anti-trash-talk.** Describe your potential ailments at the beginning of each ride. Be careful not to be too concrete about what's wrong, because it's always possible you'll have a good day and won't need to refer back to your pre-ride excuse.
  Correct: "We'll have to see how long I can ride; I'm still recovering from a cold."
  Incorrect: "I may have to break off early; I had a lung removed earlier this week."
- **Corollary to anti-trash-talk rule**: All ailments are things that have happened *to* you, *not* things you have done to yourself. For example:
  Correct: "My tendonitis is acting up."
  Incorrect: "I failed to stretch and am paying for it now."
- **Start riding your road bike more and your mountain bike less.** Explain that this is because you like the rhythm of the road or because it builds your fitness better. Do not acknowledge that you feel completely pounded after mountain bike riding and are afraid you'll break your hip if you fall.[22]
- **Stop shaving your legs**. Describe it as a "silly custom, and I've got better things to do with my time."[23] Under no circumstances admit that you can no longer reach down to your ankles, nor that shaving your legs underscores the fact that you have varicose veins.
- **Let everyone know that "I'm just taking it easy today."** All cyclists know that some days are for going out hard, some days are for resting. When you ride with someone else, tell them you're just resting. Then ride at 80%. If the group still drops you, well, you were just resting. If you manage to hang with the group, then you're a strong rider even when you're

---

22   I wrote this before I was middle-aged; none of my friends had broken a hip mountain biking. Now that I *am* middle aged, I have two friends who have broken their hips. I hate being right.

23   So far, I have not stopped shaving my legs, even though I'm 45. I've begun wondering, however, what the outside age limit is on leg shaving.

resting. And — trust me on this — nobody else has ever used this excuse, so everyone will believe you.

- **Dispense advice to younger riders.** Tell them their seat is too far back. Tell them they're pedaling squares. Tell them they need to ride with their hands in the drops. Tell them to stop accelerating during their turn leading the group. Kids love to be taught and never get tired of hearing your wisdom. Really, it's the main reason they ride at all.

Finally, I'd like to point out that I have discovered these tips purely by observing other cyclists. None of these apply to me.

Nope. Not even one.

COMMENT FROM GOURD

Unfortunately I didn't get the tongue-in-cheek right away. Good thing I kept reading before I invested in an oversized jersey and a tiny bike.

COMMENT FROM PETE

You left out "buy a Serotta."

HOW TO NOT SELL THE CYCLING LIFESTYLE

Cyclists feel misunderstood, which is quite surprising. What's not to understand in a sport that takes three times as much time to do as most exercises, requires skintight clothing and a restrictive diet, costs thousands of dollars (before maintenance), has shoes which do not allow walking, and shares a playing field with people who are three times as fast and/or twenty times as heavy?

Thus, it's a special experience indeed when you successfully recruit someone over to the world of cycling. For, in spite of all the remarkably sound arguments against this sport, you have opened their eyes to something that will change that person's life.

*Sharing the lifestyle of cycling in such a way that the other person sees the light feels **incredible**.*

Or so I hear.

About fifteen[24] years ago, Stuart convinced me to buy a mountain bike. He described the rush of speed, the incredible trails close by, and the challenge of climbing. I was getting tired of rollerblading (yes, really) to stay fit, and so bought a Bridgestone MB5. It cost $350, which seemed excessive at the time, and immediately after buying it, I called Stuart to take me on a ride.

I should have known better.

Stuart took me to the top of Squaw Peak, an incredibly steep, rutted, dusty, loose, downhill, primarily used by ATVs. Then he vanished, flying down the hill at a phenomenal rate.

I stood there for a moment, looking into the abyss. Then I sobbed a bit, took a deep breath, and headed downhill.

I made it down the first ledge. Made it past the first switchback. Made it over the first jump.[25]

It was the second jump that got me.

I am told that I hit the jump, flew over the handlebars, and landed square on my noggin. I am told that horseback riders found me lying

---

24   OK, now it's more like twenty. I've stopped keeping track.

25   I've never been back down that route, picturing it as an awful, steep mess of a trail. I suspect that if I were to ride it today it might not seem so terrifying anymore. On the other hand, maybe it would still kick my corn.

in the trail. I am told that eventually Stuart came back up the trail and took me to the hospital, while I jabbered on about how I couldn't remember my own name, didn't know how I got where I was, and had a very bad headache.

I have to believe what I am told, for I have no recollection of the next six hours.

I didn't get back on that bike ever again. Eventually it was stolen and I've never been so glad to have something stolen in my life.

TRY, TRY, AGAIN

Five years later, another friend, Dug, convinced me to buy another mountain bike, this time a Specialized Stumpjumper,[26] for $800, which seemed excessive at the time. When he took me out on my first ride, we went to a dirt road. It was steep in spots, forcing me to get off and walk, but I was able to ride about 75% of it on the first try. There was no downhill on that first ride, nothing that posed a crash-and-burn risk.

I was instantly hooked.

I remember talking with my wife all the rest of the day about how I had found what I wanted to do, that I was never going to ride my rollerblades again (yes, I was still rollerblading five years later).

Every day for the next month I went out to the trail Dug had showed me, until I could ride the whole thing without putting a foot down.

Is it much of a surprise that climbing became the most important part of bike riding to me or that it still is, ten years later?

I don't know anyone who has turned more people into cyclists than Dug. In fact, a few years ago, we started calling him "Shepherd," because he had built up such a big flock of cycling followers. Which is not to say that Dug's a wonderful person. Depending on whether he needs something from you he is either:

- Snide, mean-spirited, impatient, and irritable

OR

- Cloying, saccharine, and sycophantic

But he's a remarkable bike evangelist.

---

26 To give you an idea of how much things have changed, this Stumpjumper was fully rigid, because *all* mountain bikes were sold fully rigid back then. How odd that now I'm back to riding fully rigid. Or maybe it's not.

MY TURN

A couple[27] years ago, Jeff told me that he wanted to try mountain biking. We talked through dozens of different bike options until he settled on a bike he liked: a full-suspension Trek Fuel.

Conscious that this was my chance to give him a great first impression of mountain biking, I picked out one of my favorite easy trails. Not too much of a climb, no frightening descents, nothing very technical, lots of places where you can bail out.

Jeff had a miserable time.

The trail was too narrow, it twisted and turned with numerous blind corners, and there was a nasty, deep, rocky ravine on the left into which he tumbled.[28]

To his credit, Jeff wasn't a baby about having a bad wreck on his first ride like I was. He'd caught the bug and is riding more and more. He's even shaved his legs and bought a road bike.[29]

WHAT HAVE WE LEARNED?

I write all this as a reminder to myself, because this weekend I'm taking a friend to look for bikes. Once he's found a bike and is ready to take it out for a spin, I will remember the following:

- What I consider an easy ride is not an easy ride.
- What I consider slow is not slow.
- What I consider an easy climb is a hard climb.
- What I consider a fun downhill is terrifying.
- What I consider a short ride is a long ride.
- If I give him more than two or three tips on how to ride, I'm a dork.
- If I take off to show how fast I am, I've completely blown it.

I don't know any cyclist who doesn't get excited at the prospect of bringing a convert into the fold. The trick is remembering to share it on the new guy's terms.

---

27   Maybe seven or ten or even more now. Weird.

28   Unfortunately, this predates the days of point-and-shoot digital cameras, or at least I didn't have one. If I had, you can bet that I would have gotten a photo, after checking to make sure Jeff was all right, naturally.

29   I am pretty sure this creeped his wife out.

COMMENT FROM TIMD

I remember taking my friends Joe and Alan up to Rivington for what is really an easy ride. The first big descent meant riding over the lip of a dropoff and, although it was a fairly gentle slope, you couldn't actually see that from the top. Alan chose to walk. Joe followed fearlessly. By the time he reached the bottom he had his belly on the saddle and his legs trailing out behind him, screaming all the way. He was hooked. He pushes me up the hills now.

COMMENT BY LIFESGREAT

I still ride my Bridgestone MB5. Got it at a bike store near the old Bamboo Hut in Provo in 1990. So no, I didn't steal it from you.

COMMENT FROM ROCKY

This one resonates. I took my manager from Texas on a "Colorado Experience." We were headed to a trail that is, by all accounts, the easiest trail in western Colorado. We were almost ready to ride; he was getting used to the bike on the road before we started the trail. He was returning on the road on slight incline when he grabbed an enormous handful of front brake. Six months later he is still in physical therapy. Can you say greenstick fracture? From his elbow up to the middle of his humerus bone was split — nearly 1/2 inch at the widest point — requiring six screws, and, well, you get the picture. My point: profile the newbies before you take them out. Unless of course, you are a little sadistic like Dug and enjoy the misery of others. Had I done so, I would have found out the following: "I hadn't ridden one of those bike with hand brakes."

HOW TO FALL DOWN

I really wish I'd kept track of certain things since I started riding. For example, how many PowerGels have I managed to keep down? How many times have I flatted? How many times have I won races? Actually, that one's pretty easy: one.

Or, here's one that I think would yield a staggeringly impressive number: how many times have I fallen?

Now that I think about it, actually, I've decided I don't want to know.

I managed to get a concussion the first time I ever rode a mountain bike, which put enough fear into me that I didn't try again for several years. Really, I suppose I should thank Stuart for saving me from all the crashes I would surely have had during that time period, had I been on a bike.[30]

LEADVILLE FACEPLANT

The second time I tried the Leadville 100, I did something very stupid: I tried jumping my bike[31] 85 miles into the ride. This is stupid for two reasons:

- It's stupid because 85 miles into a race, I didn't have the coordination or strength to do a jump properly.
- It's stupid because I *never* have the strength or coordination to do a jump properly.

So I landed hard on my front wheel, bounced off the side of the road, and plowed a furrow with my face. The effect was horrific and I admit I loved the attention.

DISLOCATED SHOULDER

A few years ago at the Leadville 100, I was very close to getting the sub-nine-hours time I've wanted so badly for so long.[32] I was coming

---

30 Instead, I just kept rollerblading, which is about as dorky a way to get around as is possible. On the plus side, by doing so much of this during my formative years, I developed an enormous set of quads that continue to serve me pretty well on the bike.

31 Nothing big, just a little hop on a whoop-de-do.

32 Not as close as I'd like you to think, though.

off of some lost time due to a 45-minute bout with the barfs, but I was beginning to feel better on the descent and I was pushing myself. I took a gravel patch with too much speed, washed out, and went down. I caught my full weight plus some momentum on my right arm, which dislocated with a nasty-sounding *schkrukkk*.

I sat up, yelping in pain, and then in fright at the fact that I could not move my arm at all. I was convinced my race was over.

Not having any idea of what I was doing, I used my left arm to lift my right arm, which settled back into place with a *fwop*.[33] The sudden and complete transition from agony to relief was so intense I started giggling and couldn't stop.

OK, maybe there was a little shock and a lot of adrenaline in there too.

In any case, I finished the race (9:20), and my shoulder swelled up impressively before the end of the day.[34] It's never been the same since.

FALL AT GOLD BAR RIM

I was tired of being the guy who couldn't do technical moves, so I took a shot at a double ledge drop on Gold Bar Rim in Moab, Utah. I knew I shouldn't try this. Everyone I was *with* knew I shouldn't try this. And yet, I tried it.

I approached too slow, hit with my weight too far forward, my front tire blew, and I flew forward over my bike, landing about six feet below on my face, wrists, ribs, palms, and forearms.

For what it's worth, I surprised everyone by finishing the six-hour ride. I may be clumsy, but I'm also remarkably stupid. Plus, if I hadn't tried that move, I wouldn't have this, my all-time favorite photo of me:

---

33   I don't know if that sound would have been audible outside my body, but I promise you I heard it.

34   There's no way that injury cost me twenty-one minutes. Though if I ever tell you the story in person, I might tell you otherwise.

UNEXPLAINABLE FACEPLANT

This next wreck is hard for me to talk about because I don't have a legitimate reason for why it happened. I was just zipping along downhill — alone — on a trail I ride more often than any other. One second I'm consciously happy, actually thinking something like, "I'm so happy riding my bike on a perfect trail on a perfect autumn day."

And the next moment, I'm sliding on packed dirt, gravel, and embedded rock on my face.

Later, I would explain to friends that scree[35] washed into the trail from a recent rain was the cause of my fall. They didn't believe it and I don't either. The simple truth is, I just fell off my bike at 20MPH.

So, back to the crash. I'm stunned, I'm bleeding profusely, and I don't know what I ought to do. OK, I should get home. What's the fastest way home? I don't remember. No, the best way home is to just keep going the way I was going anyway and finish the ride.

The bike was OK, so I got on and finished the ride, my face bleeding onto my top tube. The whole way home I never checked to see if I had all my teeth, because I was certain I had lost some (I hadn't). I got home. Nobody was there. I looked in the mirror. My lip was split all the way up to my nose. I called my wife and told her to come get me, but to drop the kids off at the neighbor; they would be freaked out if they saw me this way.

Several stitches later, I was all fixed up, though the resulting scar means I will never look quite as good in a goatee again.[36]

FALL COMING DOWN ALPINE LOOP

This crash is different from the others, in that it was not my fault and it's the only time I've fallen while on a road bike.[37] I was flying downhill on a mountain road, the Alpine Loop, above the Sundance ski resort in Utah, when a Geo Metro trimmed a corner, coming into my lane and forcing me off the road into a ravine.

Luckily I was wearing gloves, because now they, instead of my palms, were shredded. I was bruised and bloody and my front wheel

---

35   "Scree" is an actual word and a darned useful one at that: "An accumulation of loose stones or rocky debris lying on a slope or at the base of a hill or cliff (*Merriam-Webster*)." See, this book is *educational*.

36   Now that there's a considerable amount of grey in my beard, I don't like growing a goatee as much as I used to anyways.

37   Six years later, this is still true. Knock on wood.

was tacoed. To his credit, the guy in the Metro was horrified at what he had done. He apologized over and over and insisted on giving me a ride back to town. This meant, sadly, his girlfriend would have to wait on the side of the road for him to come back; the car was not big enough for the three of us and my bike to fit.

On the way down, the guy apologized several times more, then confided he was distracted on the road because he was taking his girlfriend up to a scenic spot to propose to her. I had him drop me off at Sundance so he could get back to his proposal appointment.

My wedding gift to them was that I never took him up on his offer to pay for the damages.

FALL ASLEEP, FALL OFF BIKE

When Brad and I did the 24 Hours of Moab as a two-man team, I was cooked by the final lap. I didn't realize how completely cooked, though. Although I had noticed as I rode that my head kept drooping and snapping back up.

Then, suddenly, I was skidding on the sand and my bike was 20 feet ahead of me. I had just fallen asleep and fallen off the bike.

Of all the places to fall asleep on this course, I had picked a pretty good one. I was unhurt and my bike was fine too.

As a bonus, I was once again fully awake.

ONE BEAUTIFUL MOMENT

From the accumulated clumsiness, one could reasonably conclude that I have no business on a bike, or at least that I should have very high insurance premiums. And yet, one time, just once, I did a move nobody else would try and I stuck it.

We were at the Timpooneke parking lot, about an hour southeast of Salt Lake, after a great ride. Everyone was jousting, fooling around. People had been eyeing a drop — about two feet — between two levels of the parking lot. But you couldn't just drop it, you'd have to jump over the curb, *then* land on the flat pavement below. People rode up, then turned away. Finally, everyone went back to their cars to start putting their bikes away.

That's when I rode up to it, jumped, and landed perfectly. (Okay, really I landed front wheel first, but it was no big deal.)

Nobody could believe it. The cautious guy who nevertheless stacks it up regularly had just casually done a high-consequence move. Better yet, nobody followed my lead after I showed it could be done. It stood unchallenged.[38]

And that, the hope that I will once again, some day, surprise everyone with a moment of agility, is why I keep trying the technical moves.

> COMMENT FROM BIKE MIKE IN OZ
>
> Your crashes are precisely the reason I don't own a mountain bike. When I go down I want people watching. Not so they can laugh, but so they can get help. FAST. Over 20% of all events involving me, the ground and the bike vacating the space in between, have resulted in one bone becoming two bones (or many shards). Congratulations on staying alive and mostly in one piece despite your dubious record.

> COMMENT FROM UNKNOWN
>
> We were up in the Lakes once, about six of us riding along a fairly easy grassy track, when suddenly the guy in front sank to his brake in a bog. He flipped over the handlebars and landed face down just beyond his bike. Fortunately for us, he and his bike made a nice bridge over the boggy bit and we rode on (and over him). We did stop on the other side and help him out, honest!

> COMMENT FROM LEROY
>
> A couple of weeks ago, I fell on ice on the Brooklyn Bridge right after passing a guy standing next to his bike taking pictures. Later that morning, I'm Bike Snob's lead-in to his post. Thankfully, years of wearing bike clothes have done away with any sense of shame I may have once had.

---

38   I've been back to that parking lot several times, each time thinking maybe I'd try that move again. I never have. I get queasy even looking at it.

HOW TO RACE FASTER

*OK, this is going to freak you out. This piece may be **actually useful** with **potentially good advice**. It's also advice with which you may disagree, although the people with whom you disagree are probably a lot faster than you, so maybe you might want to reconsider your position.*

Or not. I don't know. Because truthfully, I have not yet gathered the courage to follow this advice myself.

Not yet, anyway.

When I'm in an endurance race, I'm constantly doing math. How much more time do I have if I want to finish in my goal time? How far do I have to go? How fast do I need to be going to complete that distance? I swear, I have been on some of the most beautiful trails, looking over some of the most incredible vistas in the world, yet finished the ride with my odometer as the prevailing image in my mind.

Hey, when you're racing, you've got to keep track of how fast you're going.

Except, apparently, you don't.

SAGE ADVICE
Back in August, the day before the 2005 Leadville 100, Kenny, Chucky, Bry, and I were sitting together in the afternoon sun, talking about the next day's race. Kenny usually finishes in well under nine hours, Chucky is a semi-pro racer, and Bry had been training hard, hoping that on this try (his fourth, I think), he'd break nine hours.

Naturally enough, Bry wanted some advice from the fast guys.

"What do you have targeted for your split times?" asked Bry, who is, by the way, a veteran of the Kona Ironman.

"I don't have any," said Chucky.

"I don't check my splits," said Kenny.

Bry was amazed. So, in truth, was I. "How do you know whether you're on target to finish at your goal time?" Bry asked.

"I don't have a goal time," Chucky replied. "I just go out riding as hard as I can for as long as I can. If that means I win, cool. If that means I finish fifth, cool."

"I don't even wear a watch or ride with a bike computer during races," Kenny added. "Just give it everything you've got."

BUT...BUT...

Bry said what I was thinking: "But what if you miss your goal time by just a couple minutes? Won't you wish you had brought a watch?"

Kenny said, "When you ride with a clock, you demoralize yourself. Let's say you're ahead of schedule and you decide to ease up a bit. That's going to slow you down. If you're behind schedule, is knowing your time going to speed you up? If it does, you weren't going fast enough in the first place."

Kenny continued, "I have ridden with a clock and missed my goal. Three quarters into the race, I was having this battle inside my head whether I should go hard and try to make my goal, or ease up and stop the pain."

"By not *knowing* your time or if you're making your splits, you just go *as hard as you can for as long as you can*. You'll always do your best on that day. Some days your best will be fast. Some days, not so fast."[39]

Chucky added, "Look, a watch will never make you race faster. It can only slow you down. If you've got a watch and see you're dropping behind your target, you accelerate for a minute and fry yourself. Then you lose more time than you would have lost in the first place. Just race as hard as you think you can all the time, and you'll get the best time you can get. If you think you could go faster to pick up a couple minutes at the end of a race, *you should do it*,[40] whether it gets you in under nine hours or not."

AFTERMATH

Bry rode with a watch and a bike computer the next day anyway and he did in fact finish in under nine hours. Chucky, meanwhile, finished fourth *overall*, moving up four places in the final 20 miles because he

---

39   Kenny's like Yoda. But really fast on a bike. And not as short. And he doesn't have that annoying second half of predicate/object/subject/first-half of predicate syntax thing going on. But he is sage, like Yoda. And he's bald, too.

40   This is the part that's difficult for me. I *always* think I'm going as fast as I can.

stayed on his bike where everyone else got off to push. Kenny finished in 8:08, more than an hour faster than I ever have.[41]

I still rode with a bike computer that day, too. It's hard to let go of the mindset that if you know how fast you're going, you can go a little faster. But part of me sees a beautiful logic in just pouring everything I've got into a race, without knowing the numbers and then just dealing with the result.

The other part of me, of course, says, "Yeah, but what if you do that and get a 9:01? You'd kill yourself."

> COMMENT FROM HAMISH
>
> I feel the same about my wearing a heart rate monitor at times. If I'm wearing it, I can give myself permission to slacken off ("I'm working hard enough."). If not, I'll just give it everything. I'm mostly interested in the stats at the end of the session. Perhaps I should wear it such that I can't read it during the session. Like your racing, I can't usually do much about it if I'm not happy along the way.

> COMMENT FROM MIKE ROADIE
>
> I want the money back for all those cycle computers I wasted MY money on!

> COMMENT FROM CALOI RIDER
>
> The only thing worse than finishing a race and knowing you missed your "goal" is finishing a race knowing you didn't empty your tank completely while you were out there. My solution is this: quit setting goals and just empty the tank. Whatever you do, finish with a smile on your face. Leave goals and times for training. I find that I enjoy races much more when I do.

---

41   I'm very happy to say that this is no longer true. Now it's ten minutes faster than I ever have.

HOW TO NOT GET INVITED ON THE NEXT GROUP RIDE

I've probably been on only ten or fifteen big group rides in my lifetime. You know the ones: the bike shop organizes a weekly ride and everyone shows up, the fast guys drop everyone and those of us who are really slow get left alone to battle a headwind home, starting from approximately 72 miles south of the county line.

Now, small group rides with a clutch of close friends...well, that's a different story. And it's also how I collected this list of ways you can avoid getting invited to go on the next group ride.

Specifically, I'm pretty sure that I have been the culprit for every single one of the infractions listed here.

Want to be "accidentally" left off the email list the next time a ride is organized? Of course you do! Here's how you can ensure that, no matter your riding skill, other cyclists avoid you like the plague.

PULL "THE ELDEN MOVE"

OK, let's get this one out of the way first, since, in some circles, it's apparently been named after me. For reasons which I cannot fathom, some riders don't like to have the first guy to the top of the climb turn around, come down to where they're climbing, and climb back up with them.

Well, humph.

To those people, I defend myself by saying that I'm not doing this to show that I'm a superior climber, I'm doing it because I just don't like hanging around forever at the top of the climb. I figure I'd rather come back down part way and keep riding, even if it is at your snail-like pace.

Oh, wait. Now I think I see your point.

SURGE AND FADE IN A PACELINE

Some people don't have the knack of riding at the speed of the group. They drop back a little, maybe fifteen feet, and then surge forward to catch up. If you are the person who is lucky enough to be behind the surge-and-fade rider, you know that it completely kills any drafting effect you get from riding in a paceline. The best thing you can hope for is an opportunity to switch the riding order up.

I have ridden behind a surge-and-fader for more than four hours once.[42] It was the most draining week of my life.

BE THE TIPSTER

If you've been riding for a while — or perhaps you've read a bunch of cycling magazines and books — you no doubt have valuable advice to offer those with whom you're riding. And no doubt they'll want to hear it. All of it. Even to the exclusion of any other possible conversation.

I remember vividly when I was new to mountain biking, there was a particular person who gave me tip after tip after tip on riding, every time we rode together. Finally, I shouted, "No more tips!"[43]

Here's a tip for those who love to give tips: No more than three tips per ride no matter what, and a maximum average of two per ride.

BE THE GEARMEISTER

Almost all serious cyclists, road or mountain, have a certain amount of gear geek in them. But some people want to debate the virtues of Shimano versus Campy,[44] or Ti versus carbon, or tube versus clincher endlessly. This is not just annoying, it's dangerous: this kind of talk can hypnotize other riders, causing terrible accidents.

Here's a good rule of thumb to help you recognize whether your chatter about gear is boring: if you're chattering about gear, it's boring.[45]

BE CONSISTENTLY LATE

This one probably applies mostly to riding groups of middle-aged people with jobs, kids, and lots of responsibilities. If you're late to every group ride, it's not funny or endearing. It's indicative that you

---

42 I don't remember his name, but it was in the Seattle to Portland ride. He was (still is, I'm sure) a great guy, but he just couldn't maintain a consistent speed.

43 For *years*, everyone else in the group would, from time to time and apropos of nothing, suddenly shout, "No more tips!"

44 Or, now, Shimano vs. SRAM vs. Campy. I've got my own thoughts on this matter, which are of course the correct ones.

45 Unless, of course, it's not. Like when I talk about gear.

need some time management training or that you're living in Stephen Covey's Quad 3 (urgent, but not important)[46] or something like that.

HARP AT OTHERS FOR BEING A LITTLE LATE

Same thing applies in reverse: if you're riding with a group of people who have jobs, kids, and responsibilities, you've got to accept that everyone has three-minute emergencies[47] from time to time. You're just ruining the ride for yourself and others if you get in a twist about it.

BE STUPIDLY CHEERFUL

If I'm bonked, or I think the weather's bad, or I don't like the ride, I expect everyone else to have the same reasonable outlook I have: that everything in the world sucks. If I'm not having fun, there's no fun to be had. If we can agree on that, we can all get along.

BE A CRYBABY

If I'm having a great time — feeling strong, enjoying the weather, liking the course — then clearly everyone else should be having a good time. Please don't pretend like you're tired or hot or hungry or bonked.

STICK TO YOUR TRAINING REGIMEN, NO MATTER WHAT

I know people who only rarely ride with the group because Chris Carmichael himself has taken time off from coaching Lance Armstrong to give them explicit instructions on how and when they ought to ride. Those instructions don't make provisions for actually enjoying yourself. After a while, you stop inviting those guys, because what's the point?

By the way, I have noticed, in race situations, that I pass guys in Carmichael Training System jerseys much more frequently than I am passed by those guys. I'm just saying.[48]

---

46   This is a totally non-subtle jab at a friend of mine who shall not be named (Rick), who, though he once worked for leadership training firm Franklin-Covey and therefore knows all about the seven deadly habits of highly mercenary people, is always late to everything. But this doesn't bother me. At *all*.

47   I wrote this back when my typical emergency lasted three minutes. Those were good times.

48   Check me out. I just called out CTS. By the way, Chris Carmichael's jerseys say "Train Right" prominently. So when you pass people wearing one of these jerseys, you should feel free to say, "On your *left*, Train *Right*." Make sure you emphasize the right words to get the full effect of the jab.

MAKE EXCUSES, BEFORE, DURING, AND AFTER THE RIDE

If you're not feeling well or you've had an injury, it's OK to mention this before the ride. Once. You do not get to repeat it for the benefit of those who didn't hear the first time, and you do not get to elaborate for those who did not really understand just how bad your case of consumption really is. Everyone has a bad riding day sometimes. We understand that. Let's move on.

WEAR YOUR BADGE OF HONOR TOO PROUDLY

If you've chosen to ride a singlespeed mountain bike or fixed-gear road bike, that's super. However, you do not get to point it out and you do not get to use it as an excuse for doing badly.

If someone points out your gearing choice, you may acknowledge it and, if so prompted, even elaborate. But you do not get to call out your absence of derailleurs any more than someone gets to call out that they *do* have derailleurs. You've made your choice; don't treat it like it was forced upon you.

BE RELENTLESSLY APOLOGETIC

I'm guilty of this one, big time. If I'm slower than the people around me, I apologize over and over for slowing them down. I have been told to shut up. To those to whom I have apologized too often for not being able to keep up, I apologize.[49]

GLOAT ABOUT TRIVIAL WINS IN THE DISTANT PAST

Remember that time you rode up that impossibly steep pitch in the "Toilet Bowl" move at Gooseberry Mesa, and nobody else was able to clean it? Well, the rest of us don't, and yet we press on.[50] Somehow.

---

49 Sorry.
50 I can be downright mean sometimes.

COMMENT FROM UNKNOWN

Wow! I pulled "The Elden Move" and I didn't even know it had a name! This year, I was trying to get two people into cycling. I started taking them on light road loops. After a couple of weeks we tried some hills. I would impressively climb to the top in a flash and then descend to do it over again, "just to get a nice workout." Wow, I had no idea that I was such a dope. They couldn't find the time to ride with me after that and stopped riding altogether, I think. "The Elden Move" is extremely effective.

COMMENT FROM PAUL

Ah, what appears to be missing from the list is the "jackrabbit." Every time when it's your turn to pull, you boost the speed a little. Not too much, just enough to make everyone work harder and the guy who just rotated off gets cracked off the whip. The jackrabbit will of course act sheepish when called on this or comment, "Wow, I didn't know how strong I was today."

HOW TO MAKE ANOTHER CYCLIST CRASH

One of the requirements to be an ultra-successful beloved cycling megastar blogger is that you must surrender your privacy and dignity, and be willing to not just talk about great things you do, but about the embarrassing things you wish you'd never done.

For me, this was actually an easy thing to start doing, because otherwise the blog would have run out of material inside of a couple weeks.

Still, whenever I think about this particular story, I have to fight the urge to hide under my desk.

I am a clumsy oaf who can only barely manage to make a bike do the most mundane things: go straight, turn, go faster,[51] go slower, stop. I was reminded of this recently (um, today) when I sat up to ride no-handed on my fixed gear bike and immediately started veering hard to the right. I just, but only just, managed to put my hands down in time and avoid dropping into a ravine.

Really, this was lucky. It served as a reminder: I am not the guy who can do tricks on a bike. I am not the guy who can pull pranks. I am not the guy who impresses the neighbor kids by riding a wheelie down the street or sitting backward on the handlebars and riding the bike facing the wrong direction.

I am not, in short, the guy who can show off when riding. Because when I show off on a bike, bad things happen.

THE SURGE

The most powerful example of my oafishness happened three years ago,[52] the day before the Leadville 100. Kenny, Mark, Serena, Bry, and I were out on a short ride, just to keep loose. We were joking around, doing five-second sprints, trying to ride our bikes up stairs, and just having a good time in general, enjoying the nervous energy that comes before a big ride.

Caught up in the moment, I forgot that I am incapable of doing anything clever on a bike, and decided to try a prank that Kenny has

---

51 And the "go faster" part isn't all that easy, either.
52 So I guess now it's more like nine years ago. Wow.

played on me once: pass someone on the left, and as you go by, grab their brake lever to slow them down. Finish it all off by pushing off on your victim's handlebar to give you an additional surge of speed.

When Kenny had done it to me, it had worked beautifully. He brought me to a near standstill, and shot on ahead of me thirty feet or more before I was able to get back up to speed.

So, thinking how funny I would be, I passed Bry on his left, grabbed his brake lever, and pushed off, yelling "Surge!"

To say it didn't go off very well would be an understatement.

A *vast* understatement.[53]

I had grabbed Bry's brake too hard; I didn't just slow him down, I put him into a nose-wheelie. And my push-off was way too enthusiastic. It didn't so much as push me forward as crank Bry's handlebar hard to the left.

The result was as predictable as it was humiliating.[54]

Bry's handlebar hooked up nicely with my seatpost. Everyone gasped as Bry tumbled down to the left, landing squarely on top of me. I landed half on the pavement, half splayed on my bike.

It took half an hour and a borrowed pair of the Jaws of Life to untangle us.

Later, the scrapes and bruises from the fall would hurt like crazy. At the moment, though, the only thing I could feel was intense humiliation. I had just caused a good friend of mine to wreck the day prior to a race for which he had been training an entire year. Probably ruined his bike, too.

WHEW

As it turned out, Bry hadn't been hurt much at all. He had landed on something soft: me. His bike had some scratches, but nothing severe. I'm lucky; Bry's an easy-going guy and he didn't get anywhere near as mad at me as he should have.

However, every time we ride together now, Bry shies away from me if I get too close. "Please, Fatty," he begs, "Don't try The Surge."

---

53   A really vast understatement.

54   Really, I need a stronger word than "humiliating" here. I think about the damage that I could have caused, the day before a race Bry had been training for all year, and I get a pit in my stomach. I have one now. I'm going to go hide under my desk for a few minutes.

Don't worry, Bry. I won't try that kind of thing ever again. Or at least not until the next time I forget that I'm a spaz.

COMMENT FROM DUG

My personal favorite is one Stuart taught me. Ride up behind someone, grab the top of their lycra shorts, and pull the shorts back behind and under the saddle. Ride away. The victim is left not only with his (I've never tried this on a woman) ass hanging out, but also weaving all over the road/trail while trying like crazy to get the shorts unhooked from the saddle. Good times, good times.

COMMENT FROM CLINT

Yeah, learning that kind of lesson once is (almost never) enough for me. Good to see someone else can be an oaf, though.

COMMENT FROM AUSSIE KEV

I "surged" in a Madison once, missed the guy's hand then grabbed hold of his handlebars and threw those in instead. Carnage ensued.

COMMENT FROM DI

I'd really like to see the surge executed well. Perhaps you could make a video of Kenny demonstrating this. Then, you could make a video of you showing us how not to do it. I would love to see it. Some people are just so talented and smooth on their bikes. I am not one of those people. It's best if I just leave both hands on the handlebar and keep pedaling.

HOW TO MAKE A PERFECTLY GOOD EXCUSE FOR NOT RIDING TODAY

When I lived in Sammamish, Washington, I commuted by bike. Religiously. Or at least semi-religiously. The thing is, as winter got close, it rained pretty much constantly. And it got light so late and dark so early.

Sometimes, I just didn't want to get out and ride. Not when I had a perfectly good car just sitting in the garage.

Usually I'd go anyway, just out of force of habit or not wanting to break my streak or knowing that it would be my one and only chance to get any exercise in that day.

Once in a while, though, I just couldn't face the idea of biking to and from work in the cold, wet slush. But "I just don't feel like it" didn't sound good enough; I needed an external force.

Hence, a piece on how to make excuses.

In one hour and ten minutes, I will post whatever it is I'm about to write. Then I'll read it online and make a couple edits, usually adding a parenthetical joke or two, and maybe adding a few paragraph breaks.

Then I'll get on my bike and ride to work.

The truth is, at this moment, I'd prefer to drive to work. It's cold, dark, and raining outside, and it'd be nice to just say, "forget it, I'm driving" today.

But I'm going to ride, because I don't have a Perfectly Good Excuse for not biking to work.

Shame on me for being so ill-prepared.

THE IMPORTANCE OF EXCUSES

Really, I'm a little bit embarrassed that I don't have a good excuse for not riding today. In the past, I've generally been able to come up with something that sounds pretty convincing whenever I needed it.

Why do I need an excuse at all? A couple reasons:

- **Others**: I'm noticing, as winter progresses, that an increasing number of people at work are asking me whether I biked in each day. I'm beginning to suspect that an office pool has been started on when I'll stop. If I don't ride in, I need to have a *reason* why I drove or they'll think I've given up. Somehow, if I give these people a good, compelling explanation of why I didn't bike that day, I expect I'll still get credit for being a cyclist. Now that I articulate that thought, I realize how completely boneheaded it is.

- **Myself:** More than convincing others that I'd be biking if — darn it! — I didn't have this Perfectly Good Excuse I cooked up, I need to convince *myself*. This allows me to be a slacker without being a quitter.

THE ANATOMY OF A GOOD EXCUSE

So, in order to avoid the dilemma in which I find myself today — riding into work when I feel more like hibernating than exercising — I need to replenish my stock of Perfectly Good Excuses.

This is not as easy as it seems, because an excuse is nothing but an excuse unless it meets the rigorous entrance criteria necessary to become a Perfectly Good Excuse. These are:

- **It must be fresh**: An excuse that you have used within the past several days is no good. If you use the same excuse frequently or two days in a row, people will think you are just too lazy to fix the problem.
- **It must seem to have caught you unawares**: The excuse needs to be something that came out of left field. If you knew it was coming, you could have probably planned for it and found a way to ride in anyway.
- **It must be convincing**: The excuse must be good enough that the person you are using the excuse on agrees: he or she would also not ride into work under those circumstances.
- **You must sorta-kinda even believe it yourself**: This is the tough one. If you know that your excuse is an outright fabrication, you're not going to have much luck making yourself believe it's true. You need to have a component of truth, no matter how small, in your excuse.

PERFECTLY GOOD EXCUSES UNDER CONSIDERATION

In order to avoid finding myself in today's dilemma I am currently developing a new stockpile of Perfectly Good Excuses. They are:

- **General achiness/approaching illness**: I don't *ever* feel great first thing in the morning. In fact, if I went strictly by how I generally feel about the world when I first get up, I could probably make a case for calling in sick on any given day.[55] The thing is, though, I know that this "blugh" feeling (a medical term) passes on its own within about five minutes and I'm not very good at nursing it into a sense of impending illness. There's also the problem that when you feel sick, a ride is more likely to cure it than make it worse.

- **Can't find my helmet/shoes**: This is actually a really good one; there's no way I'm going biking without my bike shoes or helmet. And with the forgetfulness that seems to be accompanying middle age,[56] this is an easy one to pull off, too. It just takes a little planning. If I put my helmet or shoes down anywhere besides the space I have reserved for them in the garage, I will not be able to locate them the next time I want them.

- **Broken bike or part:** As long as you've got only one bike, this one's bulletproof. It's been a long time since I have had no serviceable bikes, though.

- **Need my car:** This is a good one. If you've got to go pick up someone at the airport during the day, there's nothing you can really do about it; you've got to drive in. The problem is, these excuses generally don't coincide with days I don't feel like biking. In fact, they seem to most often happen on days that a ride sounds really, really good.[57]

- **Rest day to avoid overtraining:** Oh, this is a fine one indeed. Not only does it give you a reason to skip riding that day, it carries an implied *boast*: "I skipped riding today because I am so fit it's dangerous." (*Interesting note: did you know that*

---

55   I suspect that my manager would eventually get tired of this behavior.

56   I think I might have just turned 40 when I wrote this. Does that count as middle-aged?

57   I'm pretty sure there's an axiom here. Something like, "The probability of your needing your car at work is directly proportionate to your desire to ride your bike to work that day."

"overtraining" is something that only very few pro-level athletes are even capable of? 99% of the people in the world couldn't overtrain even if it was their fondest desire.)

- **Weather**: Since most people won't ride their bikes if it even *looks* like it *might* rain, you can almost always use the weather as an excuse.[58] The problem is, the weather is a slippery slope. If you use it as an excuse today when it's drizzling, you'll wind up using it tomorrow when it's raining again. Soon, the season's over, and all that's happened is you've become an expert on rain.

COMMENT FROM UNKNOWN

Since I am down to only two days a week that I can ride to work, excuses become harder to come by. So this morning, when my alarm went off and I looked at my wireless thermometer that read −14°F, I decided −13°F was the cutoff for what's considered safe riding weather. That's the best I could come up with. Then I laid awake and wasted my extra hour of sleep that I get when I don't bike in beating myself up for being a wuss.

COMMENT FROM LOES

I can never convince myself with excuses, although I try to say to myself that I already train enough and can afford some rest, but I'll always feel lazy and guilty. It even troubles me to take rest days when I've trained too much and can hardly get my cranks around. Bad weather does always work as a good excuse though.

---

58 If you live in the Northwest, anyway.

HOW TO TRASH TALK

I am excellent at trash talking. Sadly, I also have an "awesome trash talk comment" time delay mechanism of approximately three hours. I am pretty sure I have never made a great remark at the moment it would have any impact whatsoever.

This time delay mechanism extends to other parts of my life as well, which is probably why I'm a blogger instead of a stand-up comic.

Yesterday,[59] I bought a ticket to Salt Lake City. So now there's no backing out. I'm going to Fall Moab 2006. Fall Moab is an annual event where an increasingly large group (close to 20 this year, it looks like) of mountain biking buddies gets together and goes riding for three days in and around Moab, Utah, the desert mountain bike capital of the universe.

This means I need to get a mountain bike, pronto. It means that I'm going to have to shave my legs again. It means I'm going to get banged up, and cut up; it happens to every single one of us, every single year.[60] And it means I'm going to have more fun than I do at any other event of the year.

Most importantly though, it means I need to brush up on my trash-talking skills.

WHY IS TRASH TALKING IMPORTANT?

Know this: When a group of cyclists gets together for what they call a "friendly group ride," they're speaking in code. What they actually mean is, "We're getting together to bare our teeth and snarl at each other for fifteen minutes, after which we will climb on our bikes and see who is the alpha cyclist: the dominant rider of the pack, the one who chooses the course, who picks the pace, who keeps the other wolves in line."

You see, the group ride isn't just a group riding together. It's an important ritual, an essential component of which is trash talking.

---

59   This is 2005's yesterday. Now that I live 20 miles south of Salt Lake, purchasing a ticket to Salt Lake City would be downright counterproductive. In fact, I'd go so far as to call it an unnecessary expense.

60   It's a strange thing, to go somewhere with the plan to do something that you know with absolute certainty is going to hurt you at some point. The only question is, "How much?"

It's during the pre-ride trash talking that you discover other riders' intentions. Who is in contention? Who is weak? Who can be damaged psychologically before the ride, making them more susceptible to a bluff attack during the ride?

It's a beautiful dance, really. And I'm sadly out of practice.

TECHNIQUES FOR BEGINNERS

I've done some research into cyclist trash talking behavior and have uncovered some patterns even novices can use to good effect.

- **Feigned concern**: "You've had a hard time keeping up lately. Are you ok? I can tell the group to go easy today if you want." Or, "Man, that's a pretty technical move; I don't think I clean it more than six out of ten tries. You may want to skip it; you don't want to get hurt."[61]
- **Cloaked boast**: "Dude, that is a seriously nice bike. Every time I ride with you, I can't help but admire that thing. How much does that thing weigh, sixteen pounds? Sheesh, that's light. I wonder how I manage to keep up with you, what with my bike weighing around twenty pounds and my goiter acting up."
- **Anti-trash talk**: "Could we go easy today? I just had a kidney removed and am still a little sore. Plus, you guys look like you're really strong. I'm not sure I can hang." **Important note:** Do *not* use this technique unless you are certain that you *can* hang with the group, even if they ramp up into the red zone and stay there. If you miscalculate and your anti-trash talk turned out to be an accurate prediction of the day's events, you will be known as a hangdog, whiney, weakling complainer.[62]
- **Question and follow-up**: "So, how are you feeling today?" (Wait for response.) "Seriously, you feel good? Because you look like you've gained some weight. I'm sure that's just because you're wearing a padded jacket, though." (Wait for response.) "Oh, really? No padding at all? Well, that's weird."
- **Power play**: "I look out at this group, and I see nothing that impresses me. Oh well, I guess I can treat this as a recovery

---

61   I've lost count of how many times I've heard that one. Doesn't even bother me anymore. In fact, I now just take it at face value and say, "OK, I'll sit it out."
62   It could be worse. You could be known as...no, never mind. It couldn't be worse.

day." **Important note:** This is a risky technique. If you use this, be aware that anything apart from *absolute domination* will be perceived as failure.

TIPS FOR ADVANCED TRASH TALKERS

There was a time when people used to remark that I was the meanest person they knew, once I actually started saying what I was thinking. In days of yore, I have shut people down, so completely dumbfounded them with my trash talk that backing it up with performance on the bike seemed beside the point.

That, alas, was years ago. I am now so out of practice with advanced trash talking (I have young children who don't exactly thrive on that kind of feedback), that I must rely primarily on other, more skilled trash talkers for these advanced techniques. Thanks, I guess, to Dug, whom I no longer consider a friend.

- **Get personal**: If someone has a gut, use the gut to your advantage, even if man-with-gut is kicking your butt and dropping you. Ask probing questions: "Does your gut get in the way of your legs on the upstroke?" or "Do you think you'd go faster if you lost some weight?" If your target does not respond, you can be confident that he hears you and that you are being effective.
- **Do not back down**: If your target appears to be sensitive, this is not the time to back off. Run up the score. This is a good time to get experimental. Try some techniques you've been keeping until they're ready.
- **Exploit admitted weaknesses:** If your target acknowledges an actual, diagnosable problem that will slow him down, it's time to lean in. For example, if he says, "Well, jeez, I just had a heart attack this afternoon and am taking beta blockers that slow me down quite a bit," he has just made your job easier, not harder. Immediately respond by rolling your eyes and saying, "Oh, playing the heart attack card. Nice. You know, I have technically been a corpse for three months now. It's never slowed *me* down."

With all of these techniques, it's important to realize that, if your opponent comes up with something ridiculously good, you have to recognize it. It's a community effort.

And then immediately incorporate the learned technique into your own arsenal.

COMMENT BY ROBERT

Whew, sometimes it's good to be reminded why I don't do those Moab trips. I almost made the horrible mistake of coming this year.

COMMENT BY BOB

Glad you're coming to Fall Moab this year, Fatty. Remember, it's about friendship, not competition. We'll work with you. We'll start out slow, like maybe the Slickrock practice loop. We'll give you some pointers, remind you to stay hydrated, that kind of thing. You'll be fine.

COMMENT BY ERICGU

A couple more, though I will admit to being an amateur at these: "I had to work hard to catch up with you (but I did, despite the fact that you were ahead)." "You almost dropped me on that (but you didn't)." The best, however, was related to me from somebody who rode with the late Larry Kemp up Zoo Hill. Larry was riding next to him, looked over at his bike, and said (I'm paraphrasing here), "You know, (Campy) Record would be overkill for you. Chorus is better. Good choice!" And then he rode away up the hill.

HOW TO PEE WHILST RIDING YOUR BIKE

Bob Bringhurst wrote this story; in return I wrote a story for his now-defunct Bob's Top 5 site. Little did he know that I would one day take his post and use it in a book.

I should also mention that Bob is a better writer than I am. I apologize for the rest of this book not being as good as the following entry.

Today was going to be the day that I peed while riding my bike. I know what you're thinking: "Why?" In case I ever get called up to ride in one of the tours, that's why. The last thing I want to have happen is to be riding for Team Phonak during one of the six-hour stages of the Giro d' Italia, only to realize that I didn't know how to urinate while bicycling. I just know what would happen. I'd overhydrate and then try to hold it in. Soon, I'd drop to the back of the pack, clenched and sweating, and then I'd just let go.

Riders would make fun of my soggy shorts and I'd start crying.

No, I want to be ready.

But how do I go about this? On the bathroom wall of my favorite bike shop is a poster of a rider holding another rider's seat; a third rider is holding the second rider, and the first rider is making a beautiful stream away from his bicycle. Getting help seems like a good option. Should I ask someone to hold the back of my seat? If so, what accent should I use? I do an OK breathless old man impersonation[63] ("Young man, I'm about to soil my trousers. I need *help!*") and my Spanish accent is OK, but I think the British dandy would be the best approach, given the awkward nature of the request. Oh, or maybe go back a few centuries to Elizabethan times:

"Good sirrah! I am ill at ease! My full bladder bespeaks a most disquieting pain, a pain at once nightmarish and exquisite. My body cries out to me as if bedammed for nigh this fortnight. Were that it were not so! Perchance thou

---

63   Whenever Bob calls me or I call Bob, we both do our old man impression. He does breathless old man, I do Jimmy Stewart. This goes back to the days when Bob had an office with a phone number one digit different than the local hospital's phone number. Bob would get many, many calls from old men, asking for help, and refusing to believe they had just reached a technical writer instead of a medical establishment.

couldst hand my seat whilst I heed the beckon of nature's most insistent call. Prithee, answer man!"

No, I knew I had to be realistic. I wasn't riding with a buddy and I wasn't about to ask a stranger to help me, accent or no.

If I was to go through with this, I needed to do it alone. Besides, you know those urinal troughs in seedy downtown bars and old baseball parks? Those make me nervous, especially when there's a line. No one wants to hear the guys muttering behind him: "How long has that guy in the green fleece been standing there? I don't see a stream. Hey pal! What's the problem? Maybe you should step aside and figure it out while the rest of us go about our business." This was going to be awkward enough without dealing with performance anxiety. I needed privacy.

I also needed some advice. So I went to the library. Ha! Just kidding. Here are the three rules I learned from the internet:

Rule 1: Make sure you're safe from legal repercussions. Urinating in public may violate indecent exposure, public nuisance, and/or disorderly conduct laws. In some states, you can become a sex offender for urinating in public. You don't want to have to knock on your neighbors' doors and notify them of your status. It's awkward.

Rule 2: Make sure you're riding on a slight decline. If you're going too fast, you don't want to lose control of your bike. If you're going too slow, you don't want to have to pedal midstream. You might as well just stop and get off your bike.

Rule 3: Learn the proper technique. Extend one leg and rotate the opposite hip towards the extended leg. Free your member from the top or bottom of the shorts, and let it flow. Tap as necessary.

After doing my research, I decided it would be easy. On the way into work, I found a nice, remote location with a slight decline and got ready to go. That's when I learned one more rule to successful relief on a bicycle.

Rule 4: Make sure you really need to go. The first time you try this, understand that Nature doesn't just have to be making a polite house call, ding-dong. Nature needs to be banging on the door with an oak cudgel, shouting and threatening to break windows.

After work, I didn't stop by the bathroom on my way to the bike cage and I downed two bottles of water. I was good and ready. Almost too ready. After a painful twenty-minute ride through traffic, I finally got to a trail where I could get on with my business. I don't want to go into the details of my experience, but let's just say I learned two new rules.

Rule 5: Account for shrinkage. You may not have as much capacity for extension as when you started the ride.

Rule 6: Once you start, don't stop until you're done. It doesn't matter if you think you see the lights of an approaching car or an oncoming cyclist. Stay committed. Otherwise, you'll finish your ride with a soggy bottom.

And if You're a Woman... I have neither information nor advice for you.[64] I'm sorry.

> COMMENT FROM SFCGIJILL
>
> I am shocked. Guys pee while riding a bike? I'll never watch the Tour de France the same way again. I am disgusted. And a bit jealous.

> COMMENT FROM LEAKY
>
> I've wondered for years how cyclists and other athletes manage this necessity. Whenever I asked, I was made to feel like a perv! Thanks!

---

64   I don't either.

HOW TO SPIT

This is a post I wrote to a certain person whose name rhymes with "Doug."
Which is to say, my friend Dug, a man better at most everything than I am,
is a terrible spitter. It was my hope originally, that Dug would read this and
learn to spit. Or if he didn't learn to spit, maybe he'd learn to stop spitting
when anyone (i.e., me) is behind him.

I now re-publish this post in the hopes that perhaps this time my idea
will actually work. Because it's possible, you know, that Dug just needs
reminding.

I was sixty miles into the Brian Head Epic 100 and I was blind. Or, more specifically, there was so much dust in the air that I may as well have been blind. All I could see was a light brown fog.

I was riding a downhill stretch on dusty doubletrack, taking it as fast as I could, which was not particularly fast, since I could not see more than fifteen feet ahead of me. I was squinting, blinking rapidly, trying (and failing) to keep the dirt out of my eyes. I could feel the grit caked on and between my teeth. For the millionth time that day, I cleared my throat and spat over my right shoulder.

And hit the guy passing me right on the neck.

"Dude!" He shouted.

"Oh, dude.[65] Sorry," I replied. I had not seen him.

"It's OK, dude," he said, generously, and continued on ahead. I was dumbfounded at his kindness, for by all rights he should have punched me in the face. Dust clouds or no, I had broken the First Law of Spitting: **know what/who's behind you.**

WHY DO WE SPIT?

When biking, mountain or road, you're going to need to spit and often. The reasons are myriad. To clear the sports drink taste out of your mouth. To get the fly out. To clear your windpipe. To get rid of the gunk that's constantly draining from your nose into your mouth when you're

---

65   Normally, I don't call people "Dude." But I thought the safest thing to call him was what he had just called me. Of course, this strategy would have backfired if he'd have just called me what he was probably thinking of me at the moment.

biking. (Note to whatever gland it is that makes mucus: I don't really want or need that stuff in such great quantities. Please feel free to cut production by about 90%. Thank you.)

Also, you spit to look tough and to mark your territory.[66]

HOW TO SPIT

Unfortunately, just because everyone *needs* to spit while biking doesn't mean everyone's *good* at it. I am an excellent spitter, however, and can offer some advice.

- **Assess the spit.** High viscosity or low? Is it going to hold together or is it frothy? These are ugly questions, but you must consider them in order to spit properly.
- **Assess your surroundings.** Are you alone or riding in a group? If in a group, are you in front of anyone?[67]
- **Aim.** How you aim depends on what you discovered in steps one and two. If you've got a high viscosity payload and nobody's near, you're clear for a high-arc spit. Low viscosity and/or people nearby? Point it at the ground, buster.
- **Fire.** You spit with a "Too!" mouth motion, meaning you do *not* start the spit with your mouth closed. If you are spitting with a "Poo!" mouth motion, you are in serious danger of dribbling on yourself, sounding ridiculous, and — worst of all — breaking the spit up into a fine mist.[68] And that's just gross.

SPITTING ETIQUETTE

As important as knowing *how* to spit is knowing *when* to spit. As you spit, please keep the following in mind

- **Move Over:** If you're in a paceline, you are required to move out of the line.
- **Mind the Headwind**: If there's someone behind you and you spit to the side, you stand a good chance of hitting the person to the side. **Bonus Tip:** No wind is the same as a headwind, if you happen to be riding your bike forward.
- **Careful of Shrapnel**: As all experienced spitters know, even

---

66 It's possible I've got my body fluids mixed up here.
67 I'm looking at you, Dug.
68 Still looking at you, Dug.

the most cohesive payload may have some incidental spray. So even if you have high confidence in your spit, don't go for distance unless you are alone.

CLEARING THE NOSE

Dust and mucus conspire and congeal, clogging your nose as you ride. This is unfortunate, because consensus among cyclists is that it's better to be able to breathe than not.

The solution is simple. Use a finger to close off one nostril, then blow out through the other with all your might.

When doing this however, please observe all the above rules, plus this important additional one: **For the love of all that is good in the world, please do not do it *anywhere near me*.**[69] I have ridden with people (by which I mean "a certain person") who think they are far enough in front that they are OK to clear their noses. They are not.

That nose-clearing blast creates a mucus cloud, which is only slightly heavier than air. It drifts and hovers, right in the way of the following riders. The result? Everyone (by which I mean "me") behind the nose-blower gets treated to a mucus mist in the face, after which they go into paroxysms of revulsion.

I, unfortunately, am completely unable to clear my nose in this manner, for I have teeny-tiny nasal passages. Any time I have tried to do the nose-blow, my eyeballs pop out.[70]

This is inconvenient.

COMMENT BY JIM

I laughed out loud at your description of what I call "The Farmers Blow." Imagining you trying that maneuver and popping an eyeball made me laugh so loud my co-workers now think I smoke crack.

---

69   Dug, if I was ever *not* looking at you, please be assured that I am now looking at you, with purpose and a massive amount of displeasure and disgust. Has anyone who rides with Dug *not* ridden through his fine mist of snot? I shudder.

70   Okay, that's not strictly true, but it is true that I have never successfully blown a snot rocket. My nostrils are tiny; any time I try to blow a snot rocket my eardrums pop instead. And it *feels* like my eyes are going to pop out.

COMMENT BY DUG

Um. Sorry. I think I lose about a kilo in expectorant every ride. I regret that you gain some of that.

COMMENT BY CRAIG

Wow FC, you can't fire a snot rocket? I don't know what I would do if I couldn't do that. Maybe I would scrape the piles of mucous out with popsicle sticks or something. I guess I would have to think about it, especially during the winter season. A thought I was having while reading this: 'Snot Rocket' launching should be its own three-credit course and not a sub category of how to spit.

COMMENT BY KELLY

This made me laugh out loud. I'm so into bathroom humor. I'm proud to say that not a man, but a woman, taught me how to properly blow a snot rocket. It's one of my favorite things about myself that has no place on a resume, but is highly valued anyway.

HOW TO CRASH WITH PANACHE

I have written around 1,500 entries for Fat Cyclist. Some, I'm really proud of. Some I honestly just phoned in.

This one's a curiosity, though: I really like it, but have no recollection of writing it. Surprising, because it's a pretty hefty piece of writing.

Anyway, you'd think my partial amnesia on this essay, would make introducing the piece and giving it a little bit of extra context very difficult indeed.

Except that's what I've just done.

You want to know the fundamental difference between mountain biking and road biking? If you crash frequently while road biking, you're doing it wrong. If, on the other hand, you *don't* crash from time to time while mountain biking, you're doing it wrong.

So, if we take it as given that you will occasionally crash while riding your mountain bike, what can you do to get the very most out of the experience? How can you turn your wreck from a display of clumsiness and negligence into the kind of story that gets told around campfires and office coolers?

By following these simple steps, that's how.

PLAN AHEAD

Think of some generic injuries you can claim when the moment is right. Here is a brief list, to help you get started.

- **Internal bleeding:** Keep this one in mind for the occasions when you're hurt — no, seriously, you really are — but don't have an injury that actually *shows*. Insist that you need to be taken to a hospital immediately. Once you've made this demand, however, you cannot back down. Follow through, even though you'll probably feel just fine by the time you get to the hospital. When you finally get out of the waiting room, though, slip the doctor a $20[71] and say there's another $20[72] in it for her if she'll play along and tell your friends it is one of the most harrowing examples of internal bleeding she has

---

71   You know what? Better make that $50.
72   Yeah, another $50. Doctors aren't cheap.

ever seen, and that they're lucky they listened to you.

- **Ruptured diaphragm preventing breathing:** If you get the wind knocked out of you, you can claim that you actually ruptured your diaphragm, and now have only moments to live before you suffocate to death. Explaining later why you're alive may be difficult. I leave that to you.
- **Torn ligaments:** Good general-purpose, believable injury, and practically impossible to disprove in the field. Highly recommended.
- **High Altitude Pulmonary Edema:** Use this if you've been riding clumsily the whole day. It's best not to say you have this ailment if you're below an altitude of 500 feet.
- **High Altitude Cerebral Edema:** Use this if you've been riding clumsily and saying stupid things. Again, it's best not to say you have this ailment if you're below an altitude of 500 feet.
- **Total amnesia:** Save this one for an accident you'd rather forget. You may want to consider downgrading this to **concussion**, which allows you to say you don't remember the events surrounding a certain time period. Which you choose should depend on how bone-chillingly stupid and predictable your crash was.[73]

DURING THE CRASH

Sometimes, a crash is so instantaneous you have no time to react whatsoever. I once, for example, was riding along on my own when I suddenly found myself sliding on my face.

Other times, however, you may be luckier. You may see a crash coming and have time to add some theatrics. In this case, I recommend the following steps:[74]

- **Unclip** from your bike, if at all possible. Separate from it to whatever degree you can.
- **Flail**. Wave your arms while you're in the air. Flailing looks good on camera, and increases your chances of winning in America's Funniest Videos.

---

73 Don't you love the way I'm writing this in second person, as if it were really you — not me — who is having all these crashes?

74 Disclaimer: All of the following ideas are really stupid and you should not do any of them. Ever.

- **Twist.** If you're in the midst of a good long fall, take a moment to try to do a 360.
- **Keep your arms and hands close to your torso, post-flail.** As your landing approaches, bring your arms and hands in close, so as to not snap them like twigs. It's very easy for me to type this, although I have never successfully *done* it in my entire life. You would think that now that my right shoulder sometimes separates just for the fun of it, I'd learn. But no: I still reach out to catch my fall every time.
- **Roll.** Roll once on impact at a bare minimum. If you feel you've got sufficient momentum, keep rolling. As you roll, ask yourself, "Am I badly hurt?" If the answer is, "No, not really," try finishing the roll by standing up with your arms held high. Bow smartly.

AFTER THE CRASH

Immediately after the crash, you have to make a snap decision. Will you go for comedy, stoic resilience, or drama?

- **Comedy** is a surprisingly good choice, if you aren't badly hurt and you've got an audience. Try saying, "Nothing to see here, move along" in your best Monty Python voice. Or, "I was pushed! I accuse you!" Or my favorite, "Ladies and gentlemen, the candlesticks are *still standing!*" Your audience is likely to laugh, even if you're not funny, out of gratitude that they're not going to have to perform first aid.
- **Stoic resilience** is risky. If, after you crash — especially if it looked bad — you get up as if nothing happened, you will gain respect from your peers as being tough, though perhaps not especially bright. However, this severely reduces your options. If you start out as stoic right after the crash, but then discover ten minutes later after the adrenaline rush fades that the bruises, lacerations, and compound fractures are hampering your ability to enjoy the ride, *you still must be stoic.* You can't go from stoic to drama queen. That's ten times worse[75] than starting out as a drama queen in the first place.

---

75   Scientists have actually measured this as being eleven times worse, but I rounded down.

- **Drama** is my default choice. It's the safe bet. For one thing, crashes really do almost always hurt. For another, if I start out acting like I'm badly hurt and then discover that I'm actually just fine, it's not difficult to make the conversion to comedy. Just sit up and say (Monty Python voice again), "I'm not dead yet...I think I'm getting better...I believe I'll go for a walk." Or you can grab for the brass ring and do a drama-comedy-stoic transfer: suddenly go from rocking and screaming to standing up, dusting yourself off, and deadpan, "I now choose to internalize my pain."

If you decide to go for the drama option (good choice!), you have a few moments after a given fall to think about what you will say to your riding companions. Use this time wisely.

First, choose your injury. If you are unsure which injury you are going to trumpet, go into the fetal position. The fetal position is a good universal symbol of pain and gives you time to think.

Next, play it up. Don't trivialize your pain. Never *ever* immediately say, "I'm OK." Make them wonder for a couple seconds.

As you lay, moaning and dying, memorize your surroundings. It's best if the wildly exaggerated tale you will tell later has some basis in fact. Your surroundings can help you find a good external cause for your crash, which is almost always preferable to, "I'm a bumbling fool and briefly forgot how to ride a bicycle."

- **Ledges:** Going over an unforeseen ledge is a great cause for an accident. Highly recommended. Unfortunately, if you did this, you're probably really injured. Sorry 'bout that!
- **Roots:** Roots are tricky things that cause your wheels to change directions. Nobody will ever dispute the root reason. A suggestion: If you're going to use a root as the reason you fell, always intensify it. Roots must always be slippery, slimy, wet, twisty, gnarled, or knotted.
- **Scree:** Scree is dirt and rocks on the trail. Most mountain bike trails are constantly covered with dirt and rocks, so scree is difficult to disprove.
- **Rabbits with big, nasty, pointy teeth.** Monty Python again. Sorry, can't help myself. I'm definitely going to watch the Holy

Grail this weekend.[76]

- **Too much speed:** You're a victim of your own mountain bike prowess and bravery, not to mention your outrageous athleticism. Very good.
- **Gear:** Chainsuck or a blown tire are great crash causes. They are verifiable, however, so don't use them if they aren't real, or at least if you have witnesses present. My best gear-related crash had me thinking I had actually been shot in the chest. It was back when Rock Shox Judy SLs were all the rage. The Judy used an elastomer stack for damping, which was inserted through the top of the fork, then secured with a screw-in cap. Coming down Mud Springs one day, I suddenly saw a flash of red, felt a sharp pain in my chest, and then crashed. I was sure some kid had shot me with a paintball. It turns out that the cap over one of the elastomer stacks had come loose during the downhill, and the stack had ejected, popping me right in the sternum.
- **Despair** over the state of _____.[77] Hey, why not turn your misfortune into a political or moral statement?
- **Ennui:** "I was tired of being on my bike, and thought I'd mix things up a little."

Later, you'll have time to craft a fine story about your crash. As you do this, remember: what was going on internally is as important as what happens externally. And it's much more difficult to disprove. Say things like:

- "Time slowed down."
- "I thought to myself, 'I am about to die,' yet remained strangely calm. I was at peace with the world, almost eager to meet the earth as it rushed to embrace me."
- "The pain was exquisite."
- "My spirit left my body. I remember hovering over my carcass, asking myself, 'Do I want to go back into that vessel, to endure the suffering that comes with reuniting with my body?' Believe me, it was not an easy choice."

---

76   I have seen this movie 24 times. Really.

77   The economy, political gamesmanship, and the proliferation of reality television are all solid perennial choices.

- "No, seriously. My diaphragm was totally ruptured. I'd be dead if it weren't for my quick thinking and a fairly unorthodox use of a patch kit."

COMMENT FROM YOKOTA FRITZ

My good friend Randy chopped off all of his fingers in a shop accident, which I think qualifies for "badly hurt." In the ER, Randy was cracking so many hilarious jokes about his mishap and his pain that the doctor and nurses were going hypoxic from laughing so hard. Randy's wife was bawling and laughing at the same time. Today, when small children stare at Randy's hand he tells them, "This is what happens when you pick your nose! It's a bad habit."

COMMENT BY UNKNOWN

I always laugh and joke first, before I have the time to look things over and go through the internal systems check. I do so in a Pygmalian attempt to ward off bad karma, and injury. I am completely convinced that if I don't see it, it doesn't hurt. Unless, of course, it is the obvious compound fracture, in which case a bone jutting through my skin simply makes me faint, eliminating the need for any further conscious reaction.

COMMENT BY TIM

My own favourite is to jump to my feet and throw my arms in the air like a gymnast who has just completed a particularly complicated tumbling routine.

HOW TO BE LAST

I spend a lot of time fretting over whether I'm too slow or unskilled to be riding with the people with whom I'm riding. Considering that I'm more than six years into a blog founded on being excessively self-conscious, that's probably no surprise.

Shortly after moving back from Washington, where I lived at or a little below sea level, to Utah at 4800 feet, I found myself overweight and under-trained. I was in no condition to hang with my faster, lighter, stronger friends on one of the steepest trails in an area filled with steep trails.

So, in short, there's no irony in the title of this essay.

Last Saturday was my 40th birthday ride, held — as is traditional — on Tibble Fork. We went up Tibble, down South Fork to Deer Creek/Joy, up to the Ridge trail, down Mud Springs back to Tibble, and then back down Tibble to the reservoir. Dug, Kenny, Brad, Sunderlage, and Dan joined me for this ride. The weather was perfect and the trail was in good condition.

Sadly for them, Kenny and Dug were both injured. Kenny had broken his back on the mountain two days earlier (Dan and I puzzled over the right "broke back mountain" joke for the occasion, but neither of us ever really nailed it); Dug couldn't lift his right arm higher than elbow level due to a high-speed downhill endo earlier in the week.

And yet, I was the slowest guy of the group.

By a lot.

Fortunately, I kept my wits about me and therefore avoided the embarrassing mistakes usually made by the slowest guy in a riding group. I emerged at the end of the ride with my dignity intact, or at least with my dignity as intact as a fat, balding, middle-aged guy wearing a Reese's Peanut Butter Cup jersey is likely to.

How did I do this? By remembering and observing the Three Rules of The Slow Rider.

RULE 1: STAY BACK

You would think that because you are the slow guy, you would automatically always be sorted to the back of the group.

You would think that, but you would be wrong.

Fast riders want to take pity on slow ones. Riding with the slow guy shows that they're nice, for one thing. And it gives them a reason to rest for a minute. And, perhaps most importantly, it gives them a chance to look casual, comfortable, and maybe even just a little bit bored while riding at the slow rider's absolute redline.

As a slow rider, it is critical you deny them this opportunity. Decline all invitations to "go on ahead." Remember, if you consciously go ahead of someone who is faster than you, you accrue all of the following deleterious circumstances:

- You have taken a position you have not earned.
- You are now officially being baby-sat.
- The guy behind you will have plenty of wind, and will want to use the extra wind for light-hearted banter. You, on the other hand, will have no such oxygen surplus.
- Know that you will have someone right on your rear wheel, which means that if you have to put a foot down you make the other guy stop, too. Further, having someone right on your rear wheel isn't exactly pleasant on its own merits.[78]
- You have set yourself up to be the stumblebum[79] in the story your good buddy will tell at the end of the ride about how easy this ride is when you don't really push it, and how it's sometimes nice to go out and ride easy, and that this is the first real recovery ride he's had in ages.

So how do you decline the "after you" invitation? Simple. Use these words: "No, you go on. I'm riding sweep today."[80]

Do you see the beauty of that statement? By saying this, you are taking charge. You are accepting a mantle of responsibility. You're ensuring the safety of all other riders. And you are not admitting that

---

78   This was originally a pointed jab at a notorious wheel-rider in the group. He would ride two inches behind my rear wheel on mountain bike climbs and then let out an exasperated sound whenever I put a foot down.

79   I just checked; "stumblebum" is a word. And it means pretty much exactly what you'd expect.

80   This phrase graced the front of one of the 2011 Fat Cyclist t-shirts.

you are going slow just because...well, because you are slow.

99.4% of the time, that's all it takes. The other 0.6% of the time, you'll be riding with some former (or worse, current) scoutmaster-type who has some deep-seated, twisted need to take care of the group. This person will assert that he wants to ride sweep.

In this instance, it is within your rights — nay, it is your duty — to push the other rider into a ravine. Or, if that's not your style, you can always trick them into going on ahead. You do this by stopping immediately after getting on your bike to pretend to twist a barrel adjuster on your rear derailleur. If they slow, just say, "Go on. I'll catch up." Even though you won't. Can't.

RULE 2: SHUT UP

The most overwhelmingly powerful sensation you will have when you are the slowest rider in the group is shame.

The second most powerful will be a searing of the lungs.

The third most powerful and the one I choose to talk about right now, is the urge to explain yourself whenever you catch up to the group, as they wait for you.

Picture this: You ride up to the group. Clearly, they're just chatting, waiting for you to catch up so they can continue on. Judging from how well-rested they all look, you sense that they've been waiting there for a while.

What's your inclination?

Why, to explain yourself, of course. To tell them how hard it is to do this ride when you're so out of shape, or to apologize for being so slow, or to thank them for waiting up.

Do. Not. Do. Any. Of. Those. Things.

Instead, roll up to the group, smile, put a foot down, and join the conversation already in progress. Convey a sense of well-being. Exude peace and pleasure that you're on your bike. Your entire being should tell your co-riders that you're happy to be on the trail.[81]

Hey, it's not a race, after all.

---

81   If I had a top-ten list of the most useful and wise things I have ever said on this blog, this little piece of advice would be on that list. Probably very close to the top.

RULE 3: NO EXCUSES

This is the most important rule of all: do not explain why you are slow. Everyone already either knows, or doesn't know you well enough to be interested. Yes, you're busy at work. Yes, you've had an injury. Yes, you're middle-aged, and it's not as easy to unload the weight as it once was.

No, nobody wants to hear it.

Unless you've got a really good self-deprecating joke. In which case, bring it on.

COMMENT FROM TIM D.

While you are catching your breath, out of sight, take a bit of time to rub some dirt into your arms, legs, and clothes. Make it look like you crashed. When you ride up to the group, don't say anything. If anyone asks if you are OK, just smile in a slightly dazed way and nod.

COMMENT FROM CRAIG

"Hey, it's not a race, after all." Ahhhh, the rationalization that takes place after the searing of the lungs and pegging the heart rate in the first minute.

4.
Wherein I Talk About *Actual Bike Rides*

ONCE IN A WHILE, I TRY TO OBJECTIVELY CONSIDER MY OBSESSION WITH BIKING. I STEP OUTSIDE MYSELF AND LOOK AT THE DRY FACTS: IT'S A person, going slowly, on a two-wheeled personal transportation device. Sometimes that person goes to new, interesting places on that device, but much more often, he starts at home, rides one of a few loops he has traveled many times before, and ends up back where he started.

Often, because that person has ridden the same loops so many times, he hardly even notices the environment through which he is passing.

It seems, well, stupid.

But biking isn't about what's going on around you. Not really. Biking, somehow, does something remarkable and unexplainable:

It makes you happy.

This section is about some rides I've taken, and how they've made me happy.

THE BEST PLACE IN THE WORLD

As I went through the 1,500 or so stories I've written for FatCyclist.com over the past six-ish years, I've been startled by the fact that there are at least a few I don't remember writing. Which makes it really hard for me to write a clever introduction explaining where the post comes from.

This is not one of those stories.

I remember this one all too clearly. I was riding to work at Microsoft in Redmond, Washington, when I was hit by a huge wave of homesickness. I was homesick for my friends, homesick for the mountains, and homesick for my favorite trails.

What I wanted, at that moment, more than anything, was to be riding my favorite trail — Tibble Fork — with my favorite friends: The Core Team.

That night, when I got home from work, I sat down and wrote this. While most stories I write for the blog take about ninety minutes for me to write, this one just tumbled out. It took less than an hour, and I knew when I was finished that I had come closer than ever before to writing why I like mountain biking.

I like living in the Northwest. I like riding in green countryside. I like the incredible forests. I like the big evergreens that surround my house. I like all the lakes around me. I like that it never really gets unbearably hot, nor unbearably cold.

But today as I rode my bike to work, I started thinking about Tibble Fork and now I miss Utah something awful.

Tibble Fork, the reservoir and the trail that starts at the reservoir, is at the North end of American Fork Canyon, in Utah County. It is all singletrack and is, from a purely objective analysis, the best mountain bike trail in the entire world.[1]

WRONG WAY

Most people, in fact, everyone I've ever seen, except my own little group, rides Tibble incorrectly. They take a shuttle to the summit of the Alpine Loop and ride their mountain bikes down.

There should be a law against that.

---

1   And by "purely objective," I of course mean "totally subjective." Which is to say, if you think your hometown trail is the best one in the world, it is.

In fact, I hereby decree: henceforth, all descending on mountain bikes must be earned by corresponding climbing on said mountain bikes. So let it be written, so let it be done.[2]

There, I feel much better now.

FIRST MILE: OW

That said, there's a reason most people ride Tibble Fork down, not up. It's because it's unbelievably steep. The first mile, in particular, is pure agony (but it's the good kind of agony). It's steep and often loose, with a couple of near-impossible switchbacks at impossible angles,[3] followed by a quick maze and climb over roots and rocks. When/if you clean that first mile, you haven't had just a good day. You've had a red-letter day, the kind of day you talk about in your Christmas letter to friends and relatives.

Please, allow me to illustrate. A few years ago, my college-age niece told me her boyfriend would like to go out mountain biking. I tried to get a sense of what he could do as we drove out toward the Ridge Trail network (of which Tibble is a part). When he said, "Oh, whatever you can handle. I don't want to put too much hurt on an old guy like you," I made up my mind: Tibble.

Instead of riding *behind* my guest and letting the guest set the pace as a good host normally would, I took off at race speed up Tibble. I was seeing purple spots, but it was worth it, because "the boyfriend" as I now called him, was dropping off the back, fast.

I got to the end of the first mile, which is where we usually regroup and rest.

I waited. And waited some more. After about five minutes — remember, I had only gone a mile — he rolled up, got off his bike, knelt, and threw up.

It was my proudest moment ever.

---

2   Everyone of approximately my age or older knows exactly where this quote came from. Back before you could record TV, TV just kept showing you a half dozen movies over and over. *Wizard of Oz. Sound of Music.* And, more than any others, *The Ten Commandments.*

3   Just this last summer, those switchbacks have been eliminated by a re-route of the bottom of the trail. In their place are...equally-impossible switchbacks. I'm cool with that.

A BRIEF RESPITE

The next third of a mile is about as severe a climb as can be ridden on a mountain bike. It's also very muddy in the spring. Horses tromp through it, churning up the trail and leaving postholes with every step. And they say it's the *bikes* that are ruining the trails. When the mud dries, this section of trail is pretty choppy for the rest of the year. And there are a couple of logs and waterbars you've got to wheelie over. And some boulders.

Once you make it past that climb, though, you're in for a treat: a beautiful mountain meadow, with a beaver pond at the far end. A thin line of singletrack cuts through the meadow, and your legs stop burning for the first time since you got on the bike. And that's one of the things that makes Tibble great: intense climbs are always followed by a little flat spot where you can get your air back.

I've snowshoed up to this meadow in the winter at night, during a full moon. I was the first person up there since a big snow. I tromped out to the middle of the meadow, flopped onto my back, and for a little while was the only person in the entire world. I apologize for any inconvenience I caused by making the rest of you disappear.

Anyway, a couple hundred yards later and you're climbing again. In fact, you've got two more miles of climbing. It's still small-ring climbing, but you can ride parts of it in second and third gear.

THE BLAIR WITCH MOVE

Next up, the Blair Witch Move. This is a jumble of embedded rocks and a big root ledge. There are basically two ways you can try to ride up: the rocks or the ledge. The jury's out as to which is better. Sometimes I can clean this on my first try, sometimes I can't clean it no matter how many tries I have.

But why is it called the "Blair Witch Move?" A group of us were riding at night, trying this move, when we heard the most hideous screaming/yelling/dying-by-murder-most-foul sound I have ever heard. Human? Animal? We couldn't tell.

It sounded close, though.

"It's the Blair Witch," someone said. We finished our mandatory three tries at the move, and got out of there.

Afterward, we decided it must have been elk calling, or something like that. The thing is, I've heard lots of elk in my day (my dad's big on hunting), and this sounded *nothing* like elk to me.

CRUX OF THE MATTER

Immediately after the Blair Witch Move comes the Crux Move. It's a brutally steep hill, about fifty feet long. You can't bring speed into this move, because the approach is littered with loose dirt and fist-sized rocks, followed by an off-camber left turn. From there, you've got to pick your line and keep enough weight on the front wheel to steer, while keeping enough on the back to not spin out. Adding insult to injury, it gets *steeper* at the top. If you clean this, you have earned the privilege of thumping your chest and standing at the top of the move, shouting bad advice to the poor saps below.

In the hundreds of times (have I really ridden Tibble hundreds of times? Maybe not. I'll bet I've ridden it close to 100, though, and you get three tries at any move)[4] I have attempted the Crux move, I have cleaned it exactly *once*.

You know where I said earlier that making The Boyfriend barf at the top of the first mile was my proudest moment ever? I'd like to take that back. Cleaning the Crux Move was my proudest moment ever.

ENDLESS MOVE

A quick zip through another meadow brings you to the last move of Tibble: Endless. This move isn't especially technical, though there are parts that will throw you off your line if you're not careful. But it is long. And since you've been climbing an unbelievably steep mountain for 2.5 miles, you're probably not at your strongest anymore. I have never measured it, but I believe you are climbing in the red zone for just about a quarter mile.

And then there's a little more climbing, a few switchbacks, and you're at the top of Tibble, the best climb in the world.

JOY

At this moment, you could turn around and go down the way you came up. I've done this dozens of times. Or you can go down the other side, down South Fork of Deer Creek trail, which is the most unimaginative name for a trail ever. Instead of using this clinical name, we call the trail "Joy."

You'd have to ride this trail to really understand why it's called Joy. It's a little like being in that scene in Return of the Jedi where Luke and

---

4   I believe there may be an essay elsewhere in this book on this topic. See *Three Tries*, p. 232.

Leia are being chased through the forest on their motorcycle-esque land-speeders. Except it's real, and it's downhill, and the trails are banked to perfection, and you're threading through the aspen and evergreen trees knowing, but not caring, that if you fall right now you will wrap around one of them, and then there's a little jump on the side of the trail (you need to know to watch for it), and you're pedaling in your big ring, not quite spun out but oh-so-close and then you're suddenly in sagebrush, still flying, and the trail's banked just where it needs to be so that you can just open it up on your mountain bike like nowhere else in the world.

And then it's over. It ends at a little campground, where everyone regroups and tries to describe what just happened. But it always comes out just giggles[5] and big grins to match.

Joy is the only trail that has ever brought tears to my eyes.[6] It is perfect.

MUD SPRINGS

Now you've got to go up to the summit of the Alpine Loop, and then across the Ridge Trail (in other words, more climbing) in order to get to Joy's opposite: Mud Springs.

Actually, "opposite" is a poor word choice here, because both Joy *and* Mud Springs are spectacular descents. It's just that they're spectacular in very different ways. Joy is smooth, open and fast: a perfect ride to teach someone to love mountain biking. Mud Springs is twisted, technical, and treacherous:[7] a perfect ride for someone who is already hooked and is ready to be challenged. Rocks, ledges, roots, chutes: Mud Springs has them all, in such a perfect combination that one is forced to conclude that God is a mountain biker.

Or at least that the Forest Service guys in Utah care deeply about the trails they maintain.

BACK WHERE YOU STARTED

I've said before that I'm terrible with maps and location in general, so it shouldn't surprise you to know that I'm still a little surprised[8] every

---

5   At least, I think they're giggles. They may be chortles. I have a hard time telling the difference sometimes.

6   Without falling, I mean.

7   I swear, that alliteration was not intentional.

8   I'm not surprised to see that you are not surprised that I am surprised. Is that surprising to you?

single time Mud Springs drops me back onto Tibble, about two thirds of the way up. I mean, I've just been riding all over the place and I'm here again? How is that possible?

And yet, it is. You're back on Tibble Fork, and get to fly down as fast as your courage will let you go. Usually, we would race it. Dug and Rick would give me a head start, because I'm the slow guy going downhill, and they'd catch me with about a half-mile to go.[9]

Flying downhill Tibble is totally different than going up it. (Yeah, well, *duh*). What I mean is that you see different things, get a different perspective of how long a certain part of the course is, think of different parts of the trail as the "good" stuff.

If you consider it, the people who shuttle, not just Tibble, but any great mountain bike trail, only see half the trail.

Climb it, and you get to see it *all*.

WRAPPING UP

Whenever I get to the bottom of Tibble Fork and am packing up, I feel like I'm one of very few people who knows an incredible secret. Ponder: everyone in the whole world was doing *something* right then. But only a few of us were mountain biking at the best place in the world.

COMMENT FROM ROBERT

This is the single greatest description of the joy of mountain biking that I have ever read in my whole entire life.

COMMENT BY UNKNOWN

In California, we have a trail that sounds a bit like that with eleven-plus miles of technical downhill singletrack. Keep in mind though, that some of us have lightweight XC bikes *and* downhill gear. So while I might be the guy on Sunday that is shuttling with a 42lb bike and a single 38-tooth chainring, I was also the guy on Saturday who climbed it on a 25lb XC bike. Next time I shuttle it, I'll be sure to wear a sign on my jersey that says, "I climbed this yesterday!"

---

9   I'm happy to report that, five years later, this is no longer the case.

NO ONE RIDES ALONE

Part of why I like biking is that, from time to time, I'm struck by a moment of clarity. I'll just be riding along, minding my own business, watching sweat drop off my nose and onto my bike's stem, when — wham — I'm struck by the solution to a problem I had previously considered unsolvable.

I've actually told managers, with a straight face, that I was going to head out on a ride in search of just such a job-related epiphany.

More often than lightning bolts of brilliance, I'll have weird background chatter in my head. A running commentary, as it were. And not a very nice one.

I know some people who will not ride unless they have company. I am not one of those people. I like riding with another person, a small group, or even, occasionally, a large group, but I'm also happy to go riding by myself.

And yet, I never ride alone. There's always that stupid voice in my head, right there with me, providing a narrative, giving advice, and making remarks about my riding ability.

Frankly, I don't care for him much.

MEET THE VOICE IN MY HEAD

He (yeah, he's male) doesn't talk *all* the time. In fact, sometimes he'll go for long stretches without saying a word. And the times he chooses to talk actually says a lot about him. It's always when I'm right at my limit. I could use some encouragement. And that's when he says things like:

- "So. This is all you've got, is it?"
- "Any time you'd like to step it up, feel free."
- "Come on. Go. Seriously, it's time for you to stop holding back."

And, sometimes, he doesn't say anything at all. He just laughs.[10] Man, I hate it when he does that.

NO COMFORT, NO HELP

As near as I can tell, the voice in my head lives to motivate me exclusively through the medium of sarcasm and derision. Why is this the case? I mean, this is just a voice in my head. It's me, talking to me. Why

---

10   It's a dry, humorless laugh.

can't I say nice things to myself?

For example, I'd love to hear me say to myself:

- "Hey, you're headed for a personal best. Keep up the good work!"
- "Don't worry about fading. You've done your best."
- "You can do it! I have complete confidence in you!"

Come to think of it, never mind. That guy sounds like a motivational speaker. I think I prefer the sarcastic snide guy.

MAYBE IT'S JUST ONE GUY?

I did extensive research for today's post, consisting of instant messaging with my friend Dug for a few minutes. First off, I should point out that it's not easy to broach this topic. Asking a guy if he hears voices in his head is similar to accusing that guy of being insane.

Dug said that of course he heard a voice when he's riding hard. As near as I could tell, it's the same guy I hear. Condescending, disappointed, and curious as to why you're even bothering, if this is all you've got.

I developed the theory that perhaps everyone has the same voice. That there's just one snarky, ethereal jerk, wandering the earth and whispering mean-spirited remarks into our ears, a disappointed, cynical, and smart-alecky spirit guide for cyclists, if you will.

OR MAYBE IT'S NOT

Then, because I am an extremely intrepid journalistic-type who always wants to get my facts straight, I conducted even more research, this time in the form of an instant message conversation with my brother-in-law/friend Rocky.

It turns out that Rocky has got a voice, too. But it's a way different voice. His voice tells him, in a matter-of-fact way, to cut it out. "This is stupid. You are not getting paid for this. And this is not fun," it says to him.

And when Rocky really dials it up, a completely new voice barges in. This one doesn't even talk. It just belts out a primal yell.

I'm pretty sure my inner voice has never yelled. Maybe that's why Rocky makes all the technical moves and I clip out at the first sign of danger.

FINAL REPORT

Based on my exhaustive research, I make the following assertions about cyclists and inner voices:

- All cyclists hear voices when they ride hard.
- The type of voice you hear corresponds to the type of rider you are.
- None of the voices are friendly.
- We are therefore all either equally sane or equally insane.

I am of course, interested to know what kind of voice you hear, what it says, and under what conditions.

Also, I'd like to know if mine is the only one that speaks with an outrageous French accent.[11]

> COMMENT FROM UNKNOWN
>
> My voice is female. I'm pretty sure she's Kathy Bates. Not the nice Kathy Bates either, but the Kathy Bates from *Misery*. I ride faster to get away from her.

> COMMENT FROM DANIEL
>
> My Bike Voice generally just mocks my appearance while expressing vague shame at being stuck in the head of someone so slow. I placate it by telling it about the next team-sponsor-knockoff jersey we're going to purchase. I have a Running Voice, too. The Running Voice tells me that what we're doing is really, really boring, and can we stop now, please?

> COMMENT FROM ANDREW
>
> I used to hear them voices but the Seroquel makes them go away.

> COMMENT FROM UNKNOWN
>
> My inner voice doesn't talk. It sings Depeche Mode songs at me.

---

11   Only sometimes, like when he's taunting me. Something about elderberries. Weird.

INTO THE FIRE

I become personally attached to trails. When I ride, I tend to think about events that have occurred along the section I'm riding: moves I've completed (or not), conversations I've had, crashes.

So when my backyard trail, known simply as Frank, was threatened with fire, it felt like someone was burning family pictures.

I had to see it, one more time.

Five years ago, by which I mean "between three and seven years ago,"[12] Utah was in the middle of a serious water shortage. This crisis deeply affected me in several ways, including (but not limited to):

- I watered my lawn only once per day, instead of the normal twice.[13]
- I stopped going to Lake Powell, because it had dried up completely. Just kidding; it was easily still 15–20 feet deep in some places.
- My favorite mountain bike trails became incredibly loose and dusty.

These problems, however, suddenly seemed trivial when my favorite bike trail[14] in the world, Frank, got caught up in the path of a fire that chewed up and spat out mountain after mountain near my home.

PERSPECTIVE

Just so you understand how important Frank (yes, everyone I rode with spoke of this trail as if it were a person named "Frank") was to me, I should also point out that this same fire also threatened my house. But while I was concerned about my potential property loss, my

---

12   When I was younger, I was able to remember much more accurately when things had happened. Now, it's all kind of jumbled together into "pre-hair loss" and "post-hair loss."

13   When I originally posted this, I knew this sentence would make some folks mad. So why did I write it (especially since it wasn't true)? To make some folks mad. What a strange person I am sometimes.

14   I know, earlier in this section (see p. 94) I refer to Tibble Fork as the best place in the world, and it is. But because Frank was so close to home, I had a lot of memories tied up in the place; it maybe wasn't the best trail, but it really was my *favorite* trail.

indignation, my hate-filled rage, was reserved for the likelihood that I was about to lose my trail.

And then the day came: Fire trucks and firefighters were stationed at the trailhead. Helicopters were slurry-bombing burning trees just a few hundred yards away from the ride I had done hundreds (no exaggeration, for once) of times.

There was no question about it. Frank would burn.

I WAS A BLAND YOUTH

I'm now going to shift focus, both for a break in this story's incredible dramatic tension and to give you a little bit of my personal backstory.

I think we can agree that most teenagers express their individuation via some sort of rebellion. Here are the things I did to rebel:

- I grew my hair so far down it very nearly touched my collar.
- I listened to Oingo-Boingo and DEVO, occasionally at volumes of which my father did not approve. I also wore out (literally) a copy of Pink Floyd's The Wall.

I bring this list up by way of demonstrating that, in general, I am a law-abiding type, one who does not cause waves.

DOING WHAT MUST BE DONE

Knowing that Frank would never be the same and knowing that access was both blocked and forbidden, I did the obvious thing: I got on my bike and got on the trail anyway, using a lesser-known trailhead that had three essential benefits:

1. It was not blocked by firefighters.
2. It was not on fire.
3. It was easily accessible, if you happen to know the trail so well that you can close your eyes and imagine the whole thing in perfect detail.

I wasn't thinking about the fact that I was breaking the law or putting myself in danger or about anything else, really; I just wanted to ride my favorite trail one more time before the fire took it.

THE RIDE

I expected the smoke to be a problem, but it wasn't. In fact, Frank seemed perfectly normal during the climb. Two switchbacks, both of which I had mastered. I cleaned the next section, a hard scrabble up a loose, rocky bit, maybe half the time (I can't remember whether I cleaned it this day). Then, a nice, steady singletrack climb through scrub oak. Then I got to the top of Frank, a rock cairn where the fastest guy gets to sit and wait for everyone else to regroup. As such, it's more of a throne than a simple pile of rocks.

This time, though, I was riding alone, so didn't care about the rocks. Also, I didn't care about the rocks because there was a fire coming down the mountain, about 300 yards (I'm guessing so wildly that I may as well be picking a number at random here) away. I couldn't see beyond the fire to what it had done, because the smoke was so thick.

Better keep going.

Before the fire, the first part of the descent down Frank was a group favorite. How could it not be? You're blasting through a tunnel of brambly trees. The trail, which had been nothing more than a deer track before we started riding it, was smooth and fast. There were embedded boulders and trees to dodge, but you could really open it up and fly.

And that is the real reason why this last pre-fire Frank ride is one of my favorite memories. Because after the fire, the tunnel would be gone. And then, a little while later, several days of rain would come, and without the thick brush and grass on the mountain to slow it down, the water would briefly form a running stream along this part of the trail, turning it from a hang-on-let's-fly section of downhill to a rocky riverbed: a bumpy, rattle-your-teeth-out section.

Nobody rides that trail anymore. In fact, I don't think there's a trail there at all now.

For some reason, I get tremendous satisfaction that I was the last person to ride this trail as it was, before it got turned to a charred, stark, naked-looking thing that smelled of smoke for years afterward.

Finishing my ride, I dropped off the trail near the water tower. There were several firefighters and vehicles there, getting ready. I didn't look at them, employing the "I don't acknowledge you, therefore I don't exist" technique.[15] Amazingly, it worked. I just rode by them.

There were a couple kids straddling bikes on the side of the road, looking at me as I came off the trail. "Are you that guy?" one of them yelled at me as I approached.

15　I think I was using The Secret, though I didn't know it at the time.

"What guy?"

"The firefighters were talking on the radio a little while about some stupid mountain biker, riding up into the fire, about half an hour ago. Dude, they said you're an idiot."

A fair point.

And yet, this stands out as maybe the only very stupid thing I have ever done that I do not regret at all.

COMMENT FROM JAMES

Did people look at you funny when you asked them "Hey, you wanna go ride Frank on Saturday?"

COMMENT FROM LARS

I have to admit FC, I think it's worse that you watered your lawn twice a day than to have ridden a trail about to burn.

REPLY TO LARS FROM FATTY

Lars, I see where you're coming from, but please try to see my point of view. The ferns were getting a bit dry, and the palm trees weren't producing coconuts quite like they were when I was watering five times a day. Even dropping down to twice a day was a real sacrifice.

BEST. CRASH. EVER.

Whenever I tell this story, the part I have a hard time with is convincing people that it happened, really and truly, without exaggeration.

I guess that's the problem with making stuff up and exaggerating all the time. When you eventually do have something bizarre-yet-true happen to you, nobody believes it.

Someone should write a fable about that or something.

The details leading up to the crash are fuzzy. Was it five years ago, or seven? Was it spring, summer, or autumn? I don't remember.

I do remember the crash, though. Perfectly.

Our riding group was pretty large: Dug, Rick, Bob (visiting from Seattle,[16] therefore turning the ride into an event), Jeremy, Gary, and me. There were a couple others, too.

We were doing a semi-epic ride, beginning ~~the ride~~ by climbing up Frank. That's about 1,800 feet right there. Then, instead of hanging a left and going down, we were going to keep going up Francisco. That's another thousand feet[17] or so. And then there's the Five Fingers: five climbs out of five ravines of varying difficulties. That's probably another 1,500 feet[18] of climbing.

Which brought us to the Terraces.

LEFT OR RIGHT?

The Terraces are strange. Created as part of the WPA program back in the '30s (ostensibly to stop erosion, but really just to give some people work), these giant stairsteps are now a more-or-less permanent feature on the grassy slopes of several mountains in Utah.

When we got to the Terraces, we had an option. We could turn right, toward Little Baldy, and keep climbing for another twenty minutes, then drop down into Pleasant Grove Canyon. Or we could turn left and begin descending immediately, riding the ridges of the Terraces,

---

16   This was after Bob had moved to Seattle, but before I moved to Seattle. I have, however, moved back from Seattle. Bob has not.

17   Possibly 500 feet.

18   Or, again, maybe 500 feet.

eventually winding up in Dry Canyon.

Either way promised to be a fun ride, but when presented with the option of *climbing* now or *descending* now, well, what do you think the group decided?

Of course, we turned left. We'd ride the goat trail along the Terraces, then hook up to Dry Canyon.

UNFOLDING DRAMA

I'm the acknowledged slowest downhiller of the group, so I generally don't even volunteer to ride sweep; I just wait to ride until everyone else has started; that way I don't hold them up. Ordinarily, this means I'll watch everyone else disappear as they distance me.

This time, though, it meant I got to watch something extraordinary.

Just about the time I got a full head of steam, Dug, riding first, hit a dip that had been well-hidden by the deep grass. That dip wasn't bad enough to knock him off his bike, but it was bad enough to throw him to the left, off his line. And since we were riding on the lip of one terrace, that meant he got shot suddenly and immediately down the steep slope to the next terrace level, at which point he endoed,[19] flying high over his handlebars and landing on his back.

And then, a quarter-second later, Rick did the exact same thing. Ride. Dip. Jerk. Flip. It's like they were synchronized swimmers.

Then, as fast as you can read this, Gary, Jeremy, and Bob did the same thing. Flip flip flip. Each person landed with his own special sound effect. Each separated from his bike in his own way. And they all went down so close together that things started getting crowded. One would be wise to pick one's landing spot carefully, which one would obviously do if one were at all in control of oneself whilst being thrown ass over teakettle.

I WILL NOT FALL DOWN

Of course, I'm writing this with clear hindsight. I now *know* what caused everyone to get flipped off their bikes. While it was happening, though, it was the strangest thing I had ever seen. When one guy goes down, it's no big deal. But *everyone* was going down.

---

19 I'm pretty sure "endoed" (past tense of "endo," i.e., to go "end over") is a real word. Right?

I swear, it looked intentional.

I slowed down, cautious. Already, I was forming a plan. I would pull alongside all these fallen riders, shake my head in mild amusement, make a "tsk-tsk" sound, and then continue ahead, in a most dignified manner.[20]

Then, just like everyone else, I hit the dip, jerked off course, flew off the terrace, and flipped over my bike. Just like everyone else had.

To my relief, I landed in a clear spot.

I had made it unanimous. Every single one of us had crashed in the exact same spot. Lemmings on mountain bikes.

BACK ON YOUR BIKE, SOLDIER

So now, like everyone else, I was lying on my back in tall grass. I sat up, startled to find I was completely unhurt. It had been the rarest of crashes: a no-cost endo.[21] I looked over at Dug, who was just now stumbling to his feet, unaware, I think, of what had happened to everyone else. Then he looked around, seeing the around a half dozen bikes and riders scattered on the ground.

Dug sat back down, laughing. And within moments, we were all laughing, sitting where we had landed. A passerby, had there been even a remote possibility of passersby up in the Terraces, would have certainly suspected substance abuse.

But it wasn't.[22] It was just a bunch of guys caught up in the moment of what was without a question the Best. Crash. Ever.

Eventually, we'd finish the ride.

COMMENT FROM UNKNOWN

I get this image of catapulted cows from another Monty Python bit, piling up in the meadows below and you above shouting: "I wave my private parts in your general direction," with a goofy, haughty French-ish accent.

---

20   Really, I should have known better. I'm the least accomplished rider of the group. What are the odds that I would be the one to *not* crash where everyone else has?

21   Actually, it was more rare than that: it was a whole *group* of no-cost endoes.

22   Not that I know of, anyway.

RACE REPORT: THE NEWARK HILTON STATIONARY BIKE CYCLING CHAMPIONSHIPS

If you're a cyclist, you hate traveling for business. It's as simple as that. Because while you're traveling, you're either going to have to skip exercising (which you don't want to do, because you know you're going to be gaining weight already, thanks to near-impossibility of keeping to your diet), rent a bike (almost impossible to do, since work travel doesn't usually include enough time to pick up a bike, fit it, ride it, and then return it), or you're going to have to use one of those horrible exercise bikes.

So I've ridden my share of exercise bikes.

Only once, though, have I raced one.

I didn't want a contest. I just wanted to work off the QDoba Molé Burrito, the Delta Snack Box, and the TCBY Frozen Yogurt with mini M&Ms I had eaten before, during, and after my flight.

I just wanted to try to do *something* right, food-and-training-wise, during my trip.

So as soon as I arrived at the hotel, I dug out some shorts and a jersey, put on the running shoes — I figured there was no way the hotel's gym would have SPD pedals — and headed to the second floor.

There were only two stationary bikes: one upright, one recumbent. And both of them were taken. Both the treadmills were taken, too, which is good or I would have been forced to run. Ick.

So, confronted with the options of either lifting weights or skulking menacingly near the stationary bikes, I skulked.

It worked. Within a few minutes, someone got off one of the treadmills, and the woman on the upright stationary bike hustled over to it. Clearly, she had been riding the bike just to kill time.[23]

I got the seat to something approximating the right height for me, which is not easy when the saddle only adjusts in one-inch increments, and started pedaling the Lifestyle 2000, or whatever it was called.

---

23   The question remains: if the recumbent had been the first machine to become available, would I have taken it, or continued to skulk?

HILL WORKOUT PLUS

I'm pretty sure that in 1983, some very good salesperson sold the same exercise bicycle to every hotel in America and that nobody has sold any exercise bikes since then. Meaning, yes, I've been on a bike like this before. I started pedaling, pressed the "Hill Workout Plus" button, and started pressing the "Level Up" button over and over, until I felt some resistance.

Then I turned on the iPod, put my head down, and tried to switch off my brain.

I did not succeed.

Here's the problem with hotel exercise bikes. They're poorly maintained (mine had a sticking point at the 8:00 position on the left crank), they have short crank arms[24] to monkey up your spinning motion, and their built-in programs are specifically designed to bore you to death and back again.

OK, technically that's more than one problem.

I endured the Hills Plus workout program pretty well, keeping my cadence right at 100, my heart rate right at 145. The hills never lasted more than a minute, so I didn't really feel like they should be called "hills." More like "moderately sized molemounds."

FOE

As I rode, I occasionally looked over to my right. There, on the recumbent, spun a guy about my age, who looked like a triathlete. You know the type.

Now something I've noticed in hotel gyms many times: nobody stays very long. I arrive, start pedaling, and by the time I've done a half-hour workout, there's been a complete turnover in the gym.

But not this time. The guy was still pedaling a nice 95-plus RPM cadence by the look of it.

So, when the workout ended, I immediately dialed up another one. This time a "manual" workout: a half-hour long spin where I got to specify the resistance at will.

A BRIEF CONTEMPLATION ON SADDLES AND SORTING

As I pedaled, I devised a simple and foolproof test to tell whether someone is a cyclist. Here's how it goes: Offer a person identical bikes, except one has a narrow saddle, and one has a big, padded saddle. The

---

24   I'm going to guess 120mm, just for fun.

person who picks the big, padded saddle is the one who doesn't know better, i.e., the non-cyclist.

The reason this simple test occurred to me is that the saddle I was sitting on was big and padded, and I was rapidly discovering how awful such a saddle feels — the thing was cutting into my butt in any number of painful ways.

On a good bike with a good saddle, I can ride all day. I could not, however, ride a bike with this saddle for more than two hours if my butt depended on it.

And it was while I was thus thinking that second half-hour workout ended.

And still, the triathlete (for I was increasingly certain he was a triathlete, though we had not yet spoken) pedaled on.

So I dialed up another half-hour workout.

It was official (in my head, anyway): it was a contest of endurance.

CHAMPION

An hour and seventeen minutes into my workout, the triathlete finally spun to a stop. I contemplated saying each of the following things:

- "Done already?"
- "Better luck next time."
- "Good effort."

Instead, I said none of these things. He, however, walked up to me and asked, "So do you ride mountain or road?"

Oh, so he was going to try the *friendly* approach. Fine. I can play that game. "I like both. How about yourself?"

"Oh, I'm a triathlete."

I knew it. *Knew* it.

"Hey, enjoy the rest of your workout," he said, and left.

I continued spinning, at a renewed pace.

Until he had been gone thirty seconds and I was confident he wasn't coming back. Then I got off that stupid bike and promised myself I'd never ride on a hotel exercycle again in my life.[25]

---

25   I have reneged on that promise, though rarely.

MY 9/11 STORY

I'm not at all certain that this kind of post belongs in a goofy cycling humor book, but it is a story about riding, as well as how riding can help.

Of course, this was all back in 2001. Susan was alive and well; the prospect of cancer hadn't even occurred to us. The twins hadn't even been born. The financial tailspin of my employer hadn't even begun.

But here started a pattern that I have found to be true countless times, during some very hard times: a bike ride can help you feel better. At least for a little while.

A PROGRESSIVELY BAD DRIVE TO THE AIRPORT

Back in 2001, I worked at Fawcette Technical Communications. I lived in Orem, Utah, but made frequent trips to Seattle to meet with Microsoft. On the morning of September 11, I was driving to the airport for just such a trip, listening to the morning show on an alternative music radio station. I had only gone a mile or so and I wasn't even on the freeway yet when the DJ said a twin-prop airplane had hit the World Trade Center Towers.

That barely registered with me. I don't think I thought anything more than, "Stupid pilot," and continued on.

Then, during the next traffic report, the woman said a second plane had hit the WTC. "We already talked about that," said the DJ, thinking she had her story mixed up. There was no *way* two separate planes had hit two separate towers.

They finished the traffic report and then went on to their "Really Stupid News" segment.

I changed the channel, surfing for a real news station on the radio. Turns out there wasn't anyone with a better idea of what was going on. Lots of conflicting reports, lots of confusion. No real concern.[26]

So I finished my drive to the airport.

---

26 Why would there be?

AT THE AIRPORT

By the time I arrived at the airport, parked, checked in, and found my gate,[27] it was obvious that something was going on, though I had no idea what. Flights were being delayed, but not technically canceled. Everyone was standing around the TV monitor at an airport bar, transfixed.

And that's where I saw Dug. He also worked for Fawcette and was also scheduled to travel that day from the adjoining gate.

So at least I was standing by someone I knew when I saw the first tower collapse.

I called Susan, who I knew for sure would not be watching the news at that moment — eight months pregnant with twins and getting two boys ready for school, she'd have her hands full with other things. "Turn on the TV," I said. "Doesn't matter which station."

I went to the gate counter to confirm what I assumed was obvious: flights would be canceled for the time being. I was behind a woman who was completely panicked. She was demanding a refund immediately; she was never going to fly again, she had to get out of there. I remember feeling bad for her, but also a little bit amused. If my flight had been available, I would have gotten on without concern.

Things hadn't really sunk in yet.

BACK HOME

I drove home, switching radio channels. Now they were all talking about what was going on, but the quantity of misinformation was incredible. Cars were exploding. The White House was on fire. No, the White House *wasn't* on fire, but *something* in DC was. Another plane had crashed, this time into a field.

I got home, and my wife was crying, watching the towers collapse, over and over.[28] We watched the smoking hole in the Pentagon, we wondered what the deal was with the plane crashed in the field. We wondered what was coming next.

After a couple of hours of watching, I said I may as well go to work; we weren't going to learn anything else. I got there and an hour or so

---

27   What's weird is that I can't even exactly remember what the check-in process was *like* back then. I know it was a *lot* easier and shorter, though.

28   Eventually, we'd stop even turning on the TV. The horror was too much, and it's not like we were learning anything new.

later, Dug got there too.[29] Like me, I think, he didn't have the stomach to watch any more.

Of course, neither of us got anything done. We either surfed for news — I remember that news sites were slow because of being overwhelmed with traffic — or talked about what we knew. Which wasn't much.

GET AWAY

Eventually, I had had enough. "How about we leave early and go ride Timpooneke," one of us suggested. I don't remember which of us it was, but it sounded good. Of course, we channel-surfed the radio as we drove toward the mountain. Of course, we didn't learn anything new.

We got to the parking lot, got dressed, and got our bikes ready without saying much of anything. Then we started the four-mile dirt road climb.

And I started feeling better. Somehow, getting away from the media, being in the mountain, on a mountain bike, on a beautiful late summer day, helped things. I started going faster. Dug did too. I don't think we were racing but we were both going for it.

By the time we got to the top, I felt clear again. I hadn't forgotten what was going on, but I no longer felt like I was in shock.

Then came the downhill. The descent down the Timpooneke single-track requires your full attention. Hairpin turns come out of nowhere. Water bars surprise you. You've got to descend through gauntlets of loose, fist-sized rocks.

It was just what I needed. Forty minutes of insanely good singletrack downhill, punctuated by three gut-bustingly-difficult climbs, is a fine reminder that life is good. When Dug and I got back to the parking lot, we were both smiling.

We put away our bikes and started driving home. I didn't turn on the radio and Dug didn't ask me to.

---

29 We worked in subleased offices, so were the only ones from our company who were there.

COMMENT FROM UNKNOWN

I remember going out for a ride that day, too. I wanted silence, and I got it. In fact, the silence was so deafening that I almost lost it. I became abruptly aware of no airplane noise in the sky. For the next three or four days, the skies were eerily silent. I couldn't escape, even in my best places for escape.

COMMENT FROM KEEPYERBAG

An airliner crashes into a field in Pennsylvania. Another one crashes into the Pentagon. It's still unfathomable to think that these were the sidebar stories on that terrible day five years ago. Your last paragraph sums up my feelings regarding the anniversary. I'm staying away from the news today. It's just too gut wrenching to re-live.

I remember the days of eerie silence, too. At the time, we lived right under the approach path for the Bountiful Skypark, so we had a non-stop stream of Cessnas and Pipers flying overhead. Normally it was annoying, but I actually took comfort hearing them again once the flight ban was lifted.

COMMENT FROM UNKNOWN

Funny, I thought the same thing. I was just getting up and my now ex-wife says a plane crashed into the World Trade Center. Being a United pilot, I assume it's just some little airplane that crashed and I think, "What an idiot." Then I go downstairs and turn on the news. Today I won't be watching much news, but tonight as I fly to Sydney, I'll be thinking about it. Glad I got my ride in today.

COMMENT FROM BARRY1021

One of the best "Why We Ride" stories ever.

5.
Open Letters

PERHAPS THE MOST USEFUL THING I CAN SAY IN INTRODUCING THIS "OPEN LETTERS" SECTION IS THAT WHEN I WRITE THESE, I HEAR A DIFFERENT voice in my head than when I write pretty much everything else.

OK, it may sound just a little bit odd that I hear voices in my head at all,[1] but hear me out.

As I write any given sentence, I'm also kind of speaking the sentence aloud, just under my breath. That way, I can hear if it sounds right, like something I would actually say, instead of just write.

For most of the stuff I write, the voice I write is in my own voice. I'm trying to write just the way I would talk with you. Or at least, how I would talk with you if I had the ability to go back and edit my spoken self so that there aren't any ummms or ahhhs or sentences that begin but never end.

But when I write open letters, most of them, anyway, I hear John Cleese in my head. There's no preventing it. So, if you'd be so kind, I'd appreciate it if, when you read these letters, you'd do so aloud, in John Cleese's voice.

Just to keep the experience authentic.

---

1   See *No One Rides Alone*, p.100.

AN OPEN LETTER TO TRIATHLETES

This post was an experiment. I had heard that triathletes are humorless and thin-skinned, so thought I'd write an absurd little post making fun of triathletes. Then I'd make an even more absurd contention that triathlon isn't even a sport.

At this point in my blog's life, I normally got around 15 comments per day. For this post, I got an even hundred. Mostly from irate triathletes.

To this day, I have never ever ever enjoyed the comments section in my blog as much as I did on this post.

Dear Triathletes,

First off, I want you to know that I admire you. I really do. I admire your tenacity and determination. I admire your intensity. I admire your endurance.

And it's a darn shame you waste all those admirable qualities on the most ridiculous activity (yes, "activity," not "sport" — I'll get to that in a moment) that has ever been created.

I will explain.

SWIMMING IS MIND-BLOWINGLY AWFUL

Consider some of the things that make biking wonderful. You get to see beautiful terrain. You're going somewhere. You can use it both for entertainment and as a practical means of conveyance. You can talk with your friends while you're doing it. The variety of the terrain means that you get interesting new challenges on a moment-by-moment basis. And perhaps most importantly, you are unlikely to drown or be eaten by a giant fish (see Jonah 1:17).[2]

None of these desirable attributes can be said of swimming.

Here, on the other hand, is what *can* be said of swimming:

- **It is insular:**[3] When you're swimming, you are isolated from everything. You don't get to look at anything, except where you're going (and that's only kinda-sorta). You don't get to talk

---

2   This was the line I put in to tell everyone, "Hey, this whole thing is just silly. Don't take it seriously." Quite a few people missed the message.

3   I was being pretty much honest in my description of this part.

with anyone, should the mood strike you. You *do* get to listen to the environment, I'll give you that, but the environment is always making exactly one sound: "splash." That loses its charm after a bit. Triathletes, consider: people are currently facing court martial for using many of these same tactics to extract information from prisoners in Guantanamo.

- **It is crowded:** While swimming doesn't allow you any normal human interaction with your competitors, it does allow uncomfortable, *abnormal* interaction. Specifically, while you're swimming in a race, especially open water courses, you're constantly being kicked and elbowed.[4]

- **It is gross:** Triathletes, I'm sure *you* never pee in the pool. And your nose never starts running while you're swimming. And you never need to clear your nostrils. And you never get a mouthful of water, then spit it back out. And of course you're not sweating while you swim. Right? Right? Oh. Well, in that case, I'm sorry, but a swimming pool is absolutely the most grossifying place on planet Earth. I just had an involuntary shudder thinking about that stew of fluids in which you swim back and forth. Ew.[5]

- **It is mind-bogglingly boring:** You swim and swim, exerting incredible effort with your entire body to go approximately the speed a child can easily skip. You don't get to see anything. You don't get to hear anything. You don't get to feel anything, except water (and elbows and feet as you're kicked and knocked about). This is actually the same point I made at the beginning of this bullet list, but I feel strongly enough about it to make it twice.

- **I am no good at it:** Okay, this may be more my problem than a problem with the sport itself.

- **It is dangerous:** There are giant fish out there. And they're

---

4   Eventually — as a result of my having made fun of triathlons in a different post many years later — I wound up doing an Ironman. In the swim portion of that event, another person literally pushed me under water and crawled over me. That has never happened to me while cycling. Which is good.

5   You know what's gross? The fact that everything in this paragraph was/is true. In order to swim in a public pool, you pretty much just have to set aside the part of your mind that is grossed out by this kind of thing.

hungry. Do I have to remind you of the story of Jonah? Or Pinocchio?[6]

RUNNING IS PURE MISERY

Giant fish notwithstanding, swimming at least is good for you. It works your whole body out without busting you up. Running, on the other hand, is just plain evil. I've covered the problems of running before, though, so won't go into it here. Trust me, though: Running is bad.[7]

TRIATHLON IS NOT A SPORT BECAUSE IT DOES NOT FIT INTO THE WAY I CHOOSE TO DEFINE "SPORT"

As far as I'm concerned, a sport is a physical activity you can do for fun or competition. By my very authoritative and comprehensive definition, a sport is not legitimate unless you'd go out and do it just for kicks, even if there weren't a competition coming up.[8] So biking's a sport. Running's a sport. Even swimming's a sport. But doing all three in succession? No, that's not a sport. That's a stunt, or self-imposed punishment, or a statement. It's not a sport.

You do all three events in a row only during a competition or to prepare for a competition. And while you may be having fun during some of those events, you are not having fun *because you are doing all three of the events in a row.*[9]

So cut it out.

TRIATHLON IS ARBITRARY, AND NOT EVEN IMAGINATIVELY ARBITRARY

Let's imagine for a moment that none of the points I have made so far stand up. I know, I know: my arguments are so compelling they brook no dissent, but still, for the sake of argument, pretend.

Here's my final point: Triathlon is silly because it takes three random

---

6   Me, once again, being absurd, so as to remind people that I'm just joking. Ha ha!

7   I guess it's only fitting that I eventually married a runner and now participate in several running races per year. Poetic justice hurts. Quite literally, in my case.

8   I was really disappointed that nobody commented that by my criteria, cyclocross isn't a sport either. Because then I would have said, "Agreed!" Even though I kind of want to start cyclocross racing.

9   Now that I read this several years later, I find myself surprised at how convincing my logic was.

events, pins them together, and calls them a different event.

Why three events? Why not five? Or eleven? And why always the same three events, always in the same order?[10]

If you absolutely *must* cram multiple events together, why not get creative about it from time to time? Here are some suggestions:

- Bike, football, poker
- Bike, horseshoes, log-rolling
- Bike, snowshoe, line-dancing
- Road bike, mountain bike, velodrome, cyclocross (as I type this, I suddenly realize this would actually be a really interesting event[11])
- Bike, nail-driving, yodeling[12]

I could go on.

A HEARTFELT PLEA

Triathletes, please. Stop it. The rest of the cycling world would happily welcome you into our arms if you'll only join us. We'll teach you how to draft. We'll teach you how to pedal circles.[13] We'll teach you how to ride a bike that's both comfortable and efficient.

Just admit you have a problem. We'll do the rest.[14]

Sincerely,

---

10   I've actually spent a little time contemplating the order of triathlons, and have realized that if, in an Ironman at least, the events were in any order *besides* swim, bike, run, there would probably be deaths at every race. Especially if you went with bike, run, swim as the order; I expect the casualty rate would be right around 50%.

11   Someday, I'm going to make this event happen. Mark my words.

12   I think I could do pretty well at this event. I'm an excellent yodeler and a fair driver of nails.

13   Since I wrote this post, I've done two triathlons: an Ironman and an Xterra event. In both cases, I'd say that the bike riding skills were, on average, about the same as I've seen at pretty much any other event.

14   Note that in the comments section for this story, I've left the spelling and grammar as they originally appeared. Why? To support my theory that triathletes are bad spellers. Just kidding. Actually, my theory is that when people are angry they spell badly, and triathletes get angry easily, because they're tired of always being picked on.

COMMENT FROM WATRBG2

Well, Fatty, I used to like you but I'm not so sure now.... The only reason I can think of for today's horrible blog is that you just got back from a longer than normal ride. Sitting on your brains that long can lead to a reduced blood supply and oxygen depervation. I hear a nice swim or run can help!

COMMENT FROM ROBERT

Your logic is flawed. You claim that swimming is boring because you can't see anything, but so is sitting in a dark closet. You also claim that swimming in a pool is gross because people pee and spit and sweat, but that's nothing compared to jumping down into the bottom of an outhouse. Nice work, Aristotle.

COMMENT FROM UNKNOWN

Make up your mind fatcyclist, are you proprosing to swim in a pool (ometimes crowded just like traffic on the roads, ditto fumes that are bad for you and high risk of injury caused by others) or in the ocean (pick a nice bit and admire the aquatic scenery — fish, coral etc), peaceful (ie well away from my 4 screaming children) insular (it gives the mind time to ponder questions that get overlooked in day to day life).

COMMENT FROM UNKNOWN

Running — I guess you have never run REALLY fast — it is a joy to experiance, so much so that some of us have been doing it for 20 years in the hope of reexperiancing the euphoria.

COMMENT FROM UNKNOWN

By most definitions of a sport triathlon is one eg our state govt has a definition that separates activities from sports for grants purposes: A sport must involve physical activity, be competitive, be organised, have defined rules of competition, a defined field of play etc.

COMMENT FROM UNKNOWN

One last thing Poker you consider that a sport?

COMMENT FROM UNKNOWN

Dear fatty cyclist,

From a swimmer (which by the way I find melts my stress away while Im getting fit & HAVING FUN) I sure hope I never come across you while im driving my HUGE SUV while having a fit of road rage & feeling like tony stewart because then you'd find out why swimming isnt nearly as dangerous as cycling.

COMMENT FROM JUELS

I do find your list of possible sports quite interesting though but again, I would go for Dodge vehicle. Meaning of course, Im on some sort of gas powered vehicle (ATC, Motorcross, 4 wheeler, etc...) and its your job to keep the hell outta my way before I run your fat cycling backside over. We could also call it ROADKILL!!

COMMENT FROM UNKNOWN

That was very rude. Just because you aren't good at something doesn't mean you have to put it down and everybody else who does it. I know that it is your own opinion and I respect that. But in my opinon a triatholon is a sport. My defintion of a sport would be something that gets you physically and mentally healthy. It should also be fun and swimming is. Even if you are doing it in a competetion it is still fun because its heart racing and its a challenge. A challenge is something everyone should want. If you keep winning all the time because its too easy its not fun. Also all sports are dangerous. In cycling you could trip, fall, or collide with someone. Every sports has its risks but that's something you assume to be able to do it.

COMMENT FROM ERIKA

Well at least with your attitude, I know there will be one less person getting in my way.

COMMENT FROM LAURA

lol, sport is already defined. no matter how you 'choose' to define what it is, won't change the actual meaning.

AN OPEN LETTER TO DUG, WHO EVIDENTLY DOES NOT REALIZE HE IS SLOW AND MIDDLE-AGED, AND THEREFORE HAS ANNOUNCED HE IS RIDING NEXT YEAR'S LEADVILLE 100 ON A SINGLESPEED

My friend Dug was the one who introduced me to riding. For years, he was much faster than I was. Then I got obsessed and started making it my life mission to be faster than Dug. Eventually I succeeded, but by then Dug had stopped caring about racing. At all.

So when I publicly called him out for his not-all-that-ridiculous idea of doing the Leadville 100 on a single speed, it was at least, in part, retaliation for his not really giving a damn that I had become faster than he.

Dear Dug,

I take no pleasure in what I am about to tell you. No, that's not true, because I guess I do take a little bit of pleasure in it, but my somber tone of voice is meant to convey the seriousness I want you to think I feel, regardless of whether I actually feel it.

I know that you have chosen to ride the Leadville 100 on a singlespeed next year, Dug, and it's important for you to know what everyone who knows you knows:

Dug,[15] you don't have a snowball's chance in hell of finishing the Leadville 100 on a singlespeed.

It's questionable, in fact, whether you'd finish the race on a geared bike. But that's not the point I'm trying to make.

POOR MEMORY

Dug, I can see why you might think you could do a 100-mile mountain bike race on a singlespeed. After all, you have ridden White Rim on a singlespeed and that's 100 miles, right? And you've ridden the Leadville 100, so you should be able to do it again, right?

Unfortunately for you, they're vastly different rides. White Rim is a

---

15   It really irks Dug when I call him by name over and over in text. Which is why I do it.

mostly-flat basin with two short, steep climbs. Leadville has 11,000 feet of climbing, with five excruciatingly long, steep climbs, each of which is miles long, one of which is about ten miles long.[16] You'll have to walk all of those climbs, Dug. And don't forget that the whole ride happens at or above 10,000 feet.

Night will have fallen before you roll into town, Dug.

If you don't believe me, try to dig back into your own recollection. The best you've ever done at this race is 9:45. And that was when you were much, much fitter than you are now. Do you really think that with your decreased fitness, increased weight, advanced state of male-pattern baldness, increased age (your best time happened eleven years ago, man: eleven!), and your haphazard training style, you can do this race in only two more hours than that? On a singlespeed?

Let me give you an example, Dug: the Powerline trail. Remember how, after 80 miles of riding, riding that in your granny gear was all but impossible? How are you going to do that on a singlespeed?

How are you going to ride St. Kevins, Dug? How are you going to ride SugarLoaf? How are you going to ride eight miles of Columbine?

If you're serious about riding the Leadville 100 on a singlespeed, Dug, I have a piece of training advice for you: bring a bike you're comfortable pushing. Because that's what you'll be doing the whole day.

POOR FITNESS

Let me ask you a question, Dug. When we rode together this past summer, did you find yourself holding back for me? No sir, you did not. In fact, did you perhaps notice that you had to push yourself pretty damned[17] hard to stay with me?

And what was my finishing time at Leadville? Ten hours, more or less. On a geared bike.

I figure you would have been an hour behind me, had you raced. Or, if you had been on a singlespeed, you would have finished the following Tuesday.

It hurts me (though not much) to tell you this, Dug, but I must: you are middle-aged, out-of-shape, and feeble.

---

16   It's generally agreed that White Rim is 70% as difficult to ride as the Leadville 100.

17   You can tell here that I'm trying to be very emphatic, because I just used the word "damned."

IN SUMMARY

Dug, I want to see you succeed, but you can only succeed if you give yourself attainable goals.[18] The Leadville 100 on a singlespeed is something Kenny and Brad can do. You, my friend, are no Brad. And you're even less of a Kenny.

Don't be a fool, Dug. Know your limits, and race the Leadville 100 on a geared bike.[19] I look forward to cheering for you at the finish line (which will happen, I suspect, roughly ninety minutes after I finish, shower, change, have a nice meal, and return to the finish area to watch for you).

Kind Regards,

COMMENT FROM EUFAMIANO FUENTES

Dug, do not pay this 'so-called' Fat Cyclist any attention whatsoever. We will come up with a 'training' plan for you not just to finish, but to finish strong, with the energy of twelve Dugs. Well, maybe not that strong, but really strong. But not so strong as to raise suspicions. Just strong enough to finish in whatever time you want to. Like maybe, I am thinking, 20 minutes or so less than one so-called Fat Cyclist. Keep in touch.

COMMENT FROM RICK SUNDERLAGE (NOT MY REAL NAME)

Dug, when you get home tonight, you will see a half used 5lb container of protein drink on you front porch. It's my way of saying you can do this.

---

18   The following year (2008), both Dug and I would do the Leadville 100 on singlespeeds. We both finished.

19   Doug would eventually challenge me to a wager, where if I were more than an hour faster than he, I would get to keep his bike. Otherwise, he'd get to keep mine. Or something like that. To be honest, the specifics were too complex. Anyway, I finished in 9:14, and Dug crashed out. So theoretically I won, but I never collected on the bet, because what would I have done with a bike two sizes too big for me?

AN OPEN LETTER TO THE PASSENGER IN THE GREEN SUV WHO SCREAMED AS HE WENT BY YESTERDAY

I wrote the following piece three times.

The first time was right when I got home from nearly being startled into an accident. I was so outraged that what I wrote was practically incoherent. It was full of threats and rage and showed a side of me that most people never ever see. Heck, even I don't see it that often.

After cooling down, I knew it wasn't the right way to approach this. I deleted it, though I now kinda wish I would have at least kept the draft, just to show off what I'm like when foaming at the mouth.

The second time I wrote this, it was all sober and lecture-y, as if I were this kid's dad or something.

I deleted that draft too...and I don't really wish I would have kept it.

Finally, on my third attempt. I think I got it just about right.

Dear Passenger in the Green SUV,

Yesterday, as I was riding my bike home from work[20] your SUV pulled alongside me, at which point you, the passenger, screamed at the top of your lungs, startling me and making me swerve and nearly hit a guardrail.

I'd like to take this moment to congratulate you on a couple of things:

1. **The quality of your sense of humor.** Everyone knows that startling someone who is two feet away from heavy rush hour traffic without any protection whatsoever is simply brilliant. I only wish that you had videotaped it to show to your friends. I must have looked *so stupid!* And the thing is, this joke's got legs. I can imagine how you might get a similar effect by suddenly screaming at people as you walk by them in hallways, or perhaps at the dinner table. How about in business meetings or, in your case, during your lunch break

---

20   I was living in Sammamish, Washington at the time, working at Microsoft. Traffic on this road was always very heavy this time of day, but the shoulder was wide; I didn't slow anyone down. And motorists were, in general, really courteous.

while you sit with the others in your work-release program?[21]

2. **The originality of your sense of humor**. I haven't conducted a survey or anything, but I'm pretty sure you are *the absolute first* person to ever scream at a cyclist from a moving car.[22] And I'm sure other cyclists will verify that they, like I, have never:

    - Had a car swerve at them as a joke
    - Had a car honk at them as a joke
    - Had someone throw a beer bottle at/in front of them as a joke.[23]

As a fellow humorist — though of course my sense of humor doesn't compare with yours; I just *write* jokes and "amusing" anecdotes — I would again like to thank you for taking the time to share your unique and stylish brand of comedy with me.

Finally, I would like to share with you that since you weren't going that much faster than I was, I had plenty of time to memorize your license plate. We were both going in the same direction on East Lake Sammamish Parkway, so our destinations can't have been too different. I'd say it's almost inevitable that I will find your green SUV parked and alone someday. At which point, I look forward to continuing our tradition of sharing practical jokes with one another.[24]

Kind Regards,

---

21 Originally, this joke had him in a school for the mentally-challenged, but then I thought about the fact that mentally-challenged kids are generally the quietest, least-obnoxious kids around. To have lumped this dork with those kids would have been to insult those kids.

22 It's happened to me several times before and several times since this guy did it. The difference is, this guy did it right in the middle of heavy traffic.

23 I haven't been hit, but I know guys who have.

24 I did, in fact, eventually find the SUV. Just a couple weeks later, in fact. But by then I realized that if I acted on the plan I had when writing this story — letting all the air out of all the tires — I would more than likely be inconveniencing this dork's friend's parent. So I didn't do anything. My anger doesn't burn very hot for very long, apparently.

COMMENT FROM SONDRA

That was brilliant. It makes me want to write an open letter to construction workers about their unique perspecitve on the female anatomy.

COMMENT FROM OTBROE

I bicycle commute every day rain or shine and I have yet to understand the "funny" part of shouting at someone on a bike. It happens about once a month and it is never people who are angry at me for riding a bike. It is *always* people trying to startle me, and comes across as a truly random act of violence/aggression. I have trouble understanding what the ideal outcome is of this behavior.

Incidentally, I have had people throw things at me twice (one small piece of metal and one apple), but both times were less than a week after the highly publicized critical mass demonstrations that ended with snotty cyclist-on-motorist aggression. I can't help wondering what the critical mass folks ideal outcome is also. They're certainly not making the road safer for me.

COMMENT FROM UNKNOWN

Hate those people. I'm riding to work at 5:00am and hear this car coming. Had a bad feeling about it and sure enough, *BAM*. I manage to stay on the bike, only to look up and see a guy hanging out of the back of a VW bug with the diving fins he just hit me with. It was a car full of surfing ham-bones laughing at me. At another time I had a guy in a passing van throw a brick at me. Dude was actually trying to HIT me too. This all happened in California. In North Carolina I had a passing car of punks throw a Big Gulp full of gravel at me. I hope you find that car.

BOTH SIDES OF THE WINDSHIELD

Yeah, I know this piece isn't an open letter. You'll have to forgive me for that. The thing is, the "Open Letter" story right before this one resulted in a comment that got me about as indignant as the original incident.

I tried to be fair in my response to her comment. I succeeded maybe a little bit. Maybe.

About a month ago, I wrote a little something called "An Open Letter to the Passenger in the Green SUV Who Screamed as He Went By Yesterday." Basically, it was my reaction to some guy who, as a prank, screamed at me from his car as he went by. This post clicked with a lot of riders and it still gets comments from time to time, most of them from people sharing similar experiences, as well as outrage that someone would do something so dangerous.

Yesterday, though, I got a different kind of comment on that post: *I live in Colorado and every weekend (when the weather is nice) there are cyclists EVERYWHERE!!!! The area I live in has only two-lane roads and NONE of the cyclists are going anywhere near the speed limit much less the speed of traffic. They do not follow the traffic laws, they do not ride near the side of the road, and they do not even move over to the side of the road when there is a line of cars behind them. However, they do weave in and out of cars waiting at stop signals, they do impede the flow of traffic, they do cause drivers to tale unnecessary and sometimes dangerous 'evasive action' just to get past them, in short they're RUDE... I don't condone any violence or retaliatory action... but please, please FIND A F$%*@ING trail or a bike path and get the hell out of my way. — Becky, August 25, 9:53AM*

My initial reaction was to completely tear Becky apart, line by line. It would be easy; Becky leaves herself wide open. I mean, calling *cyclists* "RUDE" right before *you* say "FIND A F$%*@ING trail or a bike path and get the hell out of my way" is one of the most beautiful examples of irony I have ever seen.

OK, I guess I still intend to bust Becky's chops a little.[25] But that's not all I'm going to do. I'm also going to acknowledge that she has some

---

25   Or quite possibly a lot.

valid points and try to see both sides of the story.

I'm going to do my best to look through both sides of the windshield.

WHAT BECKY (AND OTHER PEOPLE IN CARS) NEEDS TO UNDERSTAND ABOUT CYCLISTS

Becky might not be such a strong candidate for anger management counseling if she considered the following:

1. **You'll see things differently if you try riding a bike.** Most cyclists have a pretty good idea of what's going on in drivers' heads, because most cyclists *are* drivers sometimes. The reverse isn't true, however. Becky, your perspective might change a little bit if you got out of your car and onto a bike. You might notice different things about the road. You might perceive speed differently. You might even find that cars break laws and endanger cyclists as often as (or maybe more often than) cyclists break laws and endanger cars.

2. **Some people act stupidly, whether in a car or on a bike.** The people who do stupid things on bikes — and yes, Becky, I know they're out there, because I've seen them too — also do stupid things when they're in cars. Or when they're at work. Or whatever. Some people are just stupid. Don't go applying the specific to the general, OK, Becky?[26] Saying that no cyclist obeys traffic laws because some idiot nearly got himself killed by shooting out in front of you is like me saying all SUVs are populated by teenage homicidal idiots because one tried to startle me into the guardrail. Or like me saying all pickups are populated by homicidal cowboys because a few have tried to swipe me with their side mirrors. Or like me saying that all cars are populated by homicidal drunk idiots because a couple have thrown beer bottles in front of my bike as they go by.

3. **Sometimes we have a good reason for being out in the road instead of hugging the side.** It's possible, make that *probable*, there's glass or scattered nails on the edge of the road. You can't see all the crud from your car, but it's there.

---

26   I can't believe I'm trying to explain a logical fallacy to someone who has written a frothing rant. Good thing I gave up on that dream of being a politician.

4. **Cyclists have a right to be on the road.**[27] We have a legal right to be there, and moreover, it's the right place for us to be from a common sense point of view. If road cyclists get on a bike path, we're a danger to pedestrians and cyclists on cruiser bikes — we're just going too fast for foot and slow bike traffic. Try to stop thinking of cyclists as being on "your" road. We're all paying taxes.

5. **We are afraid you aren't looking for us, and that you'll kill us.** My friend Dug has been hit twice by people in cars who weren't looking. I've known two cyclists who have been killed by people in cars who weren't looking. So, some cyclists have adopted the tactic of riding right in the middle of the road, where you can't miss them. You may be inconvenienced, but you won't sideswipe and kill someone. Isn't that nice?[28]

6. **We're not causing you to take "unnecessary and sometimes dangerous evasive action."** If it's unnecessary, it's optional. You're doing it because you want to. Guess what: your unnecessary evasive action you're blaming on the cyclist is really just you being a poor driver. Sorry about that.

WHAT CYCLISTS NEED TO UNDERSTAND ABOUT BECKY (AND OTHER PEOPLE IN CARS)

I believe every cyclist already knows the following, so this is mostly just a reminder. And I should be clear: I don't think the below list is true of every driver. In fact, it's not true of most drivers. But you've got to assume it's true of every driver anyway, because you never know which car is being driven by Becky.

1. **People in cars remember every stupid thing they have ever seen a cyclist do, then assume every cyclist does that all the time.** Becky here has clearly seen some cyclists do some stupid, illegal things, and now, right or wrong, she's got it in her head that all cyclists do illegal things all the time. So, those of you doing stupid, illegal things: cut it out. You're building up road rage in people like Becky, and they aren't

---

27   I wonder if any angry motorist has ever been swayed by this argument. "Oh, you have a right to be on the road? Wow, I had never considered that. Well, have a nice day!"
28   I suspect Becky would not think that this is nice.

really careful about how and at whom they vent their anger. And I'll take it one step further: those of us who have friends who take stupid, illegal risks while riding need to tell them to cut it out; they're souring the automotive world on bikes (That's big talk for me; I have a couple riding friends who I'd need to lecture. So far I never have).[29]

2. **People in cars are bugged when cyclists ride right on the line of the shoulder.** And rightly so. I see this all the time when I'm driving — cyclists have a nice wide shoulder, but they ride right on the line.[30] If you can get over, do.

3. **People in cars think you're much wider than you actually are.** They think they can't pass you, even if they can. Signal them forward to let them know they have room.

4. **People in cars expect you to adhere to laws much more closely than they do themselves.** Cars roll stop signs all the time, but they resent bikes doing it. And they hate seeing bikes worm their way through traffic — it reminds them that they're just sitting there, and that the $45 they just spent on gasoline is just floating up into the atmosphere, not actually moving them anywhere.[31]

5. **People in cars look where they're used to looking for things they're used to looking at.** Cyclists aren't *where* they expect, aren't *what* they expect, and aren't going at a *rate* they expect. If you haven't made eye contact, assume you have not been seen. Seriously.

6. **People in cars aren't enjoying the ride like you are.** They're in a hurry. They resent being delayed *even for a few seconds.* If you can get out of the way and let them pass, do.

7. **People in cars convert their worry about being in an accident into anger.** Lots of people in cars have had near misses with cyclists. That scares them. Most of them don't want to kill us, after all. That fright then turns into anger.

---

29   And to be really honest, I could probably use a good lecturing myself, from time to time. But oddly enough, I'm *never* in the mood to be lectured to.

30   I find myself doing this a lot. The line is mesmerizing. I find myself drawn to it.

31   This is really just snark. I don't think any drivers are actually jealous of us. Unless they're also cyclists, in which case seeing a cyclist when you're driving invariably causes a pang of envy.

OK, I see my attempt to be even-handed about Becky's post wound up a little bit lopsided. Maybe I should have just said, "Hey, we've all got to do our best to get along. You chill out and I'll do my best to be safe and legal."

COMMENT FROM UNKNOWN

Yeah, the old bike/car thing. I've been hit, threatened, and confronted. My approach is take non-busy roads and do it early in the morning when there is less tension in the cars. Good luck.

COMMENT FROM STEVE

Fatty (and Becky),

This speaks to something I see a lot of bicyclists in my fairly bike-friendly midwestern university town doing.

Bicyclists need to obey traffic laws. I am amazed every day by my fellow bike commuters who blow red lights, swerve in front of cars, and generally disrespect traffic law. The thing is, they're usually gone too fast for me to say anything to.

Once in a while, while commuting, I have to take the whole lane, riding in the middle, for safety's sake. When I do so, it's actually as much for motorist's safety as my own. Most of the road riding I have to do for my commute is in no-passing zones which are conveniently ignored whenever my rate of speed (in a 25MPH zone) is deemed too slow. It can be downright dangerous for everyone if I ride the shoulder, so I do not.

Again, thanks for posting this. I hope at least one wayward cyclist takes your advice to heart!

COMMENT FROM CLBLOOD

I gave up cycling my 4 miles to work. With the drivers in this town, it was just a question of time until the charity auction to cover my medical bills. Not interested in martyrdom, thanks.

6.
Epic Rides

BEFORE THERE WAS THE FAT CYCLIST BLOG, THERE WAS A FAIRLY SHORT-LIVED SITE CALLED EPIC RIDES. IN IT, I POSTED STORIES ABOUT LONG mountain bike rides. At first, I just did my own. As other people found the site, I posted others.

This was before blogs. And before comments. And the cost of my own domain was out of reach. Too bad, because I think the idea for such a site is a pretty good one: nothing but people telling stories of incredible rides they'd done.

And I've got to say, I love writing my big ride/race reports. I feel like I'm reliving the ride as I write about it, except remembered pain doesn't hurt as bad as when you're actually experiencing it.

Oh, and also I like boasting about my adventures. I'm sure that doesn't show through in my writing though.

Ha.

MY FIRST LEADVILLE 100

I really don't know why the Leadville 100 has such a grip on me. Maybe it's that I like hanging around for a couple days without anything to do. That's nice. Maybe it's that I have a lot of memories tied up in the event and like to revisit them each year. Maybe it's that I've now done it so many times — fifteen starts, fourteen finishes — that I really can't imagine not doing the race.

Here's my report from the first time I ever did it, way back in 1997, when I was in my early thirties.

Just a young pup.

Nothing — *nothing* — has ever got into my head like the Leadville 100. From the moment I signed on in January '97 until August 9th, the day of the race, I thought about that race every day. Now that it's over, I still think about it.

As early as April, I had written an exhaustive checklist of everything I needed to bring to the race, along with what would go in each drop bag.[1] I bought a new pair of extra-nice biking shorts: the nicer the chamois, the fewer the saddle sores. I bought a wool jersey, figuring that race day would be cold.[2] I experimented with every exercise drink and bar known to humankind.[3]

My most extravagant race purchase, however, was probably my bike: right after signing up for the race, I ordered an Ibis Bow Ti. Though I didn't tell anybody until now, the main reason I wanted an ultra-expensive, radically-designed, hardtail-light, titanium full-suspension bike was that I thought it would be a way cool ride on the Leadville 100.

I wasn't the only one obsessing about this race, though. The other guys I knew who had signed up also couldn't get the thing out of their minds. We'd call each other and discuss every possible aspect of the race, from what we planned to wear, to what we were going to eat and drink, to how many tubes we were going to carry, to what air pressure

---

1   The thought of bringing a crew never even occurred to me back then.
2   Foreshadowing. But not in the way you expect.
3   Back then, that was about three different kinds.

we were going to run[4] to whether we'd ride together for moral support and under what conditions it was acceptable to peel away. We all had the race map and elevation chart pinned up where we could see them often. When we rode our bikes, we all imagined ourselves on the Leadville 100.

Basically, for me, waiting for the Leadville 100 was like when I was a kid, unable to sleep on Christmas Eve. Except in this case, Christmas Eve lasts eight months. And when Santa comes down the chimney, instead of giving you presents he makes you ride your bike 100 miles there-and-back on jeep roads around the tiny town of Leadville, Colorado in twelve hours or less, at an altitude ranging from 9,000–12,600 feet, with a total vertical climb of around 11,000 feet. If you finish in less than nine hours, Santa gives you a gold rodeo-style belt buckle. If you finish in less than twelve hours, you get a silver belt buckle. If you don't finish within twelve hours, you don't get squat. And, of course, Santa charges you $160 for the privilege of riding at all.

On August 7th, Doug, Brad and I piled all our gear and ourselves into my Honda Civic, met my brother-in-Law Rocky in Grand Junction, and drove over to Leadville, Colorado. We did a quick preview ride of what is regarded as the toughest climb in the course (more on that later), then went to bed. I was so excited/nervous, I couldn't sleep.

The next day, the day before the race, we went to what seems like a dozen pre-race meetings, where they gave us our numbers and slapped medical wrist tags on us. We spent the balance of the day wandering around town, looking for other people with medical wrist tags strapped on, knowing that everyone with one of those bracelets on was thinking about one thing only.

Knowing the race started at 6:00AM the next morning,[5] we laid out all our stuff before we went to bed. I couldn't sleep.

THE START

We got up early — 4:30AM, so we'd have time to eat and digest a little bit. The good folks at the Delaware Hotel had been thoughtful enough

---

4   I'm pretty sure I had my air pressure at 45 or 50psi back then. Insane. No wonder I crashed so often. I now ride at 20psi.

5   Now it starts at 6:30. Not that it matters, since you're not sleeping anyway. Unless you take an Ambien the night before, which I recommend. Highly.

to set out a breakfast for the racers. It took a force of will to choke down a bowl of corn flakes. I was that nervous.

We got our bikes and walked over to the starting line. Gathering around were 400[6] bikes and riders crammed together in the darkness. We were all stamping, jumping, shivering, stammering. Both from the cold and from nerves. Doug and Brad moved up toward the front of the line; Rocky and I, considerably slower riders, purposely went to the very back, so we wouldn't hold up real contenders. At 6:00AM sharp, the gun went off. Probably a minute later, the back of the line, where I was, started to move.

The first six miles of the race go by quickly; they're on a smooth paved downhill. I was going as fast as 30MPH, those in front probably were going more like 40–45MPH.[7] As packed as we were, those of us in back didn't need to pedal at all; we were riding our brakes. We were all cold. Then we peeled off onto the dirt and pedaled along for a short way before the first climb: St. Kevins.

CLIMBING ST. KEVINS

St. Kevins is a steep, sandy, five-mile[8] uphill, but not at all technical (there's very little technical riding on this course). Within a couple hundred yards I got into a good pedaling rhythm, was warmed up and all my nervousness disappeared.

Vanity alert: I am about to brag.[9] A quarter of a mile into St. Kevins, I started regretting starting so far back in the pack. The narrow road was jammed with slower riders, slowing me down. I passed dozens of people with perfect, ripped bodies — they looked like they belong in beer commercials. But there they were, suffering, some of them were pushing their bikes already. In my mind, I pictured vultures circling over them. And I, with my little spare tire, am passing them *easily*. I guess it was a good idea to spend the summer concentrating on climbing long distances.

Somewhere on the climb I lost Rocky. I didn't know whether he was

---

6   Crazy that four times as many racers now start.
7   Definitely exaggerating here.
8   OK, maybe it's actually two miles.
9   Kind of weird that I warn you here that I'm about to brag, when I don't warn you about it the other thousand times I brag in this book.

ahead of or behind me. And I didn't care.[10] I felt great.

DROPPING DOWN ST. KEVINS

After that grunt up St. Kevins, we were rewarded with the descent down the other side on hyper-smooth pavement. At least, it seemed hyper-smooth at the time. Those of us who didn't know the trail nearly cried tears of gratitude. I buzzed down, hitting 45MPH.[11] I could have easily gone faster, but didn't see the point. With around 90 miles left to go, why risk the Road Rash from Hell? Besides, it was nice to just coast for a few minutes.

At the bottom of St. Kevins, the course takes an abrupt right back onto dirt — and the only singletrack in the entire race. It was beautiful singletrack, too: packed soft earth, wooded, rooty, interesting technically.[12] Challenging, but not impossible. And I didn't get to ride even an inch of it.

See, when you've got 400 people trying to thread a short stretch of singletrack 15 miles into a 100-mile race, you've got a serious bottleneck situation. As soon as one guy dabs, everything stops. So, with someone a foot ahead of me and someone else a foot behind me, I marched. Since there was nothing we could do about it, most everyone was very cool about the slowdown and took the time to talk and get to know their "neighbor."

While we're talking, someone says, "Wasn't that huge paved downhill *great?*" I'm about to agree when it hits me: That huge paved downhill we just enjoyed ten miles into the race meant we were going to have to endure a huge paved *uphill* eighty-something miles into the race. I said as much out loud and everything got real quiet. Maybe a couple of us started to cry. In any case, I wished I had taken a look at my computer at the beginning and end of the downhill. I had a feeling knowing that distance would be important to me later.

Half a mile later, we came out of the singletrack onto fire road. Time to do Sugarloaf.

---

10 Sorry, Rocky.
11 No way was I actually hitting 45mph, sitting up, on a mountain bike. Just. No. Way.
12 This section of the course is no longer part of the race.

SUGARLOAF

I don't much remember climbing Sugarloaf on the way in. It's just a sort-of-steep grunt, mostly notable because traffic had thinned out enough that you could pass without problem. The drop *down* the other side, though, was a blast. It's super steep, sandy, and rutted, with rocks and turns all over the place. I had had my Bow Ti for exactly a week (Ibis had taken eight months to deliver the bike) and this was the first time I had a chance to really see what full suspension is like.

Now, downhill has never been my strong suit, so this bike made a *huge* difference. I bombed down, passing people left and right (oops, forgot to warn you of the bragging this time). On the way down, I noticed four or five people working on pinch flats, and I was glad I had pumped my tires all the way up to 50psi.[13]

FISH HATCHERY TO TWIN LAKES DAM

Sugarloaf[14] dumps you out at the Fish Hatchery,[15] the 25 mile mark and the first support station. It was 8:05, meaning I had taken 2:05 to get there. I was a little ahead of my goal to finish in ten and a half hours. I still had plenty of food and my CamelBak, filled with half-strength Cytomax,[16] wasn't even close to empty. No need to stop. I rode through the station, a huge crowd of people cheering me on.

Okay, the fact is that this crowd of people cheered *every* rider on, but that didn't matter to me. Throughout the race, any time I came across volunteers or onlookers at this race, their encouragement gave me a *huge* morale boost. And when you're riding 100 miles on the dirt, that boost makes a difference.

It's only fifteen miles from the Fish Hatchery to Twin Lakes Dam, the next support station. This section is as close to flat as the course ever gets. Although you're *never* (well, rarely) on level ground, none of the hills are very steep, nor very long. A few miles into this section, though, my right knee started to hurt. I figured my seatpost on my new bike was too low and adjusted it up about ⅛ inch. It didn't help.

What *did* help, though, was talking to other riders. You would think

---

13 Wow. 50psi.
14 Actually, it's the Powerline.
15 The aid station eventually got moved a few miles down the road.
16 I still shudder at the very mention of Cytomax. I'm not the only one, am I?

that during a 100-mile race people would get pretty spread out. I think, though, that there were only a couple short stretches along the entire race when I couldn't see another rider, either in front of or behind me. As I, or they, would pass, we'd often make a point of matching speed for a minute or two and talking. It was chatter, by and large; most of us were too out-of-breath to have involved conversations. Mostly, we'd just congratulate each other on having made it this far, tell each other how good we were looking, and encourage each other to stick it out. Still, during the monotony of this stretch of trail (and the increasing pain of my right knee), any distraction was welcome.

TWIN LAKES DAM TO COLUMBINE MINE

My stats show that I pulled into the Twin Lakes Dam aid station at 9:15AM — I had done the first 40 miles of the race in 3:15. I was on track with my goals, which I had written on a piece of tape and stuck to my handlebar. In fact, I was a little ahead. I felt unstoppable. I refilled my CamelBak to about halfway, knowing that one of the toughest climbs of the race and of my life was about to begin and I didn't want to have any more weight than was necessary. Thanks to the incredibly helpful and supportive volunteers (I can't say enough nice things about them), I was back on my bike in about three minutes.

A quick, rolling two-mile section brought me to the base of Columbine Mine. I had alternately fantasized about and dreaded this stretch of the race for months. In about eight miles, you climb more than 3,400 feet, to an elevation of 12,600.

The first five miles of this climb is surprisingly easy. It's a well-groomed, wide dirt road. I shifted into my middle ring-granny and started to churn. I, like everybody else, hugged the right side of the road, knowing that it wouldn't be too long before the real contenders would come blasting down the other side of the road. Sure enough, about 9:50AM, by which time I had shifted to something considerably easier than my middle-granny, I saw Mike Volk,[17] who would eventually win, come bombing down.

Soon, others poured down, and I started hating them. "It's just not fair," I thought. "They get to ride *down* this hill while I have to ride *up*. The least they could do is show a little sympathy, maybe get off and walk

---

17   Yep, this is before the beginning of the Dave Wiens dynasty.

their bikes down." I may not have been completely rational at the time.

After five miles, the nice groomed road suddenly ends and I had the remaining three miles to look forward to. Except I didn't look forward to them at all. As far as I could see, people were lined up, slowly *walking* their bikes up a steep, rocky, rutted, sandy doubletrack in rarefied air. The only thing we needed to make the agony complete was pit bulls nipping at our ankles.

"Pansies," I thought. You see, earlier in the year, Rocky and I had ridden up this stretch of the climb, just to see what it was like, and we hadn't had to walk much at all. So, staying on my bike, I spun right by dozens of people, climbing like a mountain goat on crack.

At least, that's what I had *planned* on doing.

The reality is, as soon as I hit a steep section, I realized I didn't have any juice in my legs. I guess there's a difference in riding a section by itself and riding it after you've already turned in 40-plus miles that morning. I got off my bike and joined the march.

This was the longest, most agonizing stretch of the race. Although there were lots of people both ahead and behind me, none of us had energy or breath for conversation. We were all just concentrating on climbing this mountain, our bikes sometimes rolling, sometimes on our shoulders, our stupid biking shoes slipping on the rocks. As riders who had reached the summit came rocketing down, we'd step aside and they'd shout words of encouragement: "Looking good!" "You're almost there!"

Damn them all.

One of those guys coming down the trail was my friend Brad. I don't think he saw me until I called out his name; he looked pretty beat. A minute or two later, my friend Doug[18] came by. Now, ordinarily Doug is the guy who just doesn't bonk. At this moment, though, Elvis himself was riding on Doug's handlebars. Doug croaked out, as best as he could, "Looking good, Nelson!" I gasped, "You too, Doug."

Elvis mumbled, "Thank you very much," and had another doughnut.

Finally, the track leveled off enough that I could climb back onto my bike, and I rode the final mile to the aid station. I had hit the halfway point. It was 11:22AM. I was about five minutes slower than my goal. At this point, though, I was just happy to stop.

---

18   This was before I knew he liked to spell his name "Dug."

I rested for a few minutes, during which I stuffed a bunch of cookies and M&Ms into my mouth, a fistful of free[19] PowerGels[20] into my jersey pocket, and snarfed a couple of Hardbody bars.[21] More than anything else, though, I relished the thought of the exquisite, eight-mile-long downhill in front of me.

COLUMBINE MINE TO FISH HATCHERY

Riding down the Columbine mine was just the break I needed. I coasted down, relaxing, drinking lots of watered-down Cytomax, good-naturedly[22] hollering "Looking good!" and "You're almost there!" at the poor folks limping up the hill.

If you're doing the math, you might have noticed that it took me 2:07 to make it from the Twin Lakes Dam aid station to the Columbine Mine turnaround point. The return trip took 31 minutes.[23] Having had a huge on-bike rest, I didn't stop at the Twin Lakes Dam. Right about at the dam, however, I hooked up with a couple of other guys and we paced each other for the next ten miles or so. One of these guys had clearly taken a bad spill — his shorts were torn up and one of his thighs was a bloody rash. He said that as he rode through the Fish Hatchery aid station, 25 miles into the race, a child had bolted out in front of him; he had dropped his bike and slid on the pavement to miss the kid. This guy (I wish I could remember his name) picked up his bike and kept going, knowing he'd have to do the remaining 75 miles with a nasty road rash. He gets my nomination for the "Never Say Die" award.

I, on the other hand, was giving myself the nomination for the "I Wish I Were Dead" award. Somewhere between the Twin Lakes Dam and the Fish Hatchery, my knee started hurting much worse. My nipples were bleeding (the wool jersey was apparently not such a great idea). It was also during this section that my calves started taking turns cramping. I discovered, however, that by stretching each calf at the end of each downstroke I could avoid going into a full-on debilitating

---

19 If you don't count the entry fee, which I apparently didn't.
20 Fifteen years later, I *still* use PowerGels. Although PowerGel has changed a lot. As in, it's no longer the consistency of toothpaste.
21 Hardbody bars? What? I have no recollection of these. At *all*.
22 By which, of course, I mean "gloatingly."
23 I've gotten slower on this section. Interesting.

cramp.[24] I would ride for the rest of the race — about 35 miles — with my right knee hurting like hell and both calves on the cusp of a cramp.

To add to this, I found I could no longer eat normal food. I was breathing too hard (and the air was too thin) to breathe through my nose, so chewing food meant holding my breath. Plus, my mouth was so dry. Hardbody bars tasted like chocolate-covered particle board.

I knew that without some kind of food, I was headed for a serious bonk. So I decided, as I approached the Fish Hatchery, that from that aid station forward, I would suck down a PowerGel every twenty to thirty minutes. That did the job. For the rest of the race, I didn't feel like I was about to bonk, though since then I haven't been able to think about vanilla PowerGels without triggering my gag reflex.

FISH HATCHERY TO FINISH LINE

I rolled into the Fish Hatchery aid station at 1:36PM, seven and a half hours into the race. Though I didn't know it at the time, Mike Volk had won the race more than half an hour ago. I, on the other hand, was about to start what is widely known as the hardest 25 miles of the course. Imagine: you've just ridden a very hard 75 miles, and now have to climb Sugarloaf Mountain,[25] an extremely sandy, steep five-mile hill. Then you have to climb St. Kevins, the long, steep paved section we had all liked coasting down forever ago. Or, you can quit and pedal along a flat, short, paved road back into town. No wonder so many people bail out of the race at the Fish Hatchery.

Apart from my knee and calves, though, I felt good. Climbing up Sugarloaf Mountain, I even started feeling giddy, elated. I had an addle-brained epiphany and blurted out to another rider struggling up the hill, "Hey, man! We're going to make it! You and I are going to finish this race! Even if we sat down and took a nap right now, we'd still have enough time to finish this race before the cut off time! We are *unstoppable*!" At the time, I meant each and every one of those exclamation points. I rode on in my granny gear, feeling a strange mixture of incredible pain and excitement.

---

24   It's been so many years since I've had bike-related knee pain or cramped muscles I had forgotten that I've *ever* experienced these pretty common maladies at all. So I guess I've learned a few things in the past fifteen years of riding.

25   Ummm...Powerline.

The top of Sugarloaf Mountain led to a bumpy, fast downhill. Once again, I was in love with my Bow Ti. Then a quick jaunt through the short singletrack. This time there wasn't the bottleneck, and I was able to ride it. Sweet.

The singletrack dumped me onto what I thought was the final big climb of the course — the paved St. Kevins section. Because I hadn't checked my computer on the way down, I couldn't remember how long this stretch was, and it seemed to go on forever.[26]

Finally, though, I got to turn back onto dirt. A quick drop down the other side of St. Kevins brought me to the light at the end of the tunnel — just six more miles to go!

I didn't understand, though, that the final six miles don't go along the same road as the *first* six miles. Instead, we were rerouted onto an uphill dirt road known as "the Boulevard." This road has false summit after false summit — very demoralizing. Then the wind started to blow. Then it started to rain. Another racer hunkered down behind me, using me as a wind block. When we got to the top of the hill, he pulled ahead and rode away. Somehow, I knew, I had to find a way to catch this guy. But I didn't have anything left.

Or at least, I thought I didn't.

During the final mile, I recuperated a little, so that I was able to regain a little ground on the guy. And for the last 100 yards (mostly downhill, thankfully), I managed to stand up and sprint. Giving it everything I had, I passed this guy at the finish line, beating him by one second. A race official put a medal around my neck (everyone who finishes gets one) and Doug and Brad helped me off my bike.

I had finished the race in 10:36 — just six minutes off my goal. I felt like jumping up and down, but had to settle for proudly collapsing in a heap.

POSTSCRIPT

Brad and Doug finished the race in 9:44 and 9:45, respectively. Rocky got seriously dehydrated and they pulled him off the course, against his will, at the 75-mile mark.[27] They toted him off in an ambulance, filled him up with glucose, and released him later that afternoon. Meanwhile,

---

26 It's four miles.
27 Thus beginning a long and proud tradition for Rocky.

Doug, Brad, and I kept up our vigil for him at the finish line, totally clueless as to what was happening to Rocky.

That night my right knee swelled up and I kept waking up hungry.

We all still talk about the race.

The 1998 Leadville 100 registration filled up in less than two days. I managed to register in time, so August 15, I'm doing it all again. And, again, I can't stop thinking about it.[28]

---

28   And I still can't.

24 HOURS OF MOAB:
DUO PRO EXPERT DIVISION

Brad Keyes is one of my best friends. He's one of those people who will do anything for anyone, without calculating what's in it for him. He's just nice.

He's also outrageously fast on a bike.

So when he asked me to do the 24 Hours of Moab with him in the Duo Pro Expert division, I was both honored and a little bit freaked out. Honored because I would never have expected he'd consider me fast enough to be on a team with him. Freaked out because "Duo Pro Expert" division sounds a little bit too, um, fast for a guy with the nickname "Fatty." OK, I didn't actually have that nickname back then, but I could have.

Still, we did the race, and I'm glad we did. To this day, I believe it is the most intense race experience I have ever had.

Racing the 24 Hours of Moab in the Duo Pro/Expert division (two guys taking turns racing a technically demanding 15.7 mile course for 24 hours) was just nuts. It's also the most epic ride I've ever done.

I just started a new job,[29] so I don't have any vacation time built up. This means that I had to do this trip on a strict weekend — no taking off Friday or returning Monday. So, Saturday morning, about 6:00AM, I got up and drove to Moab. The road into the camp — which is also the first few miles of the race course — looked even sandier and dustier than usual, and people who had pre-ridden the course said that it was in fact, slower than ever before.

Great.

Anyway, Jeremy, the owner of Frank's Bikes, the best bike shop in the whole world,[30] had set up camp the day before. He was right on the edge of the course, so that his canopy was the first thing you saw as you peaked the last hill and came down the home stretch toward the finish

---

29   I was working with I-Link, which I stayed at for a total of two months. It was the worst job I have ever had. And I'm including my first job, working at Burger King, where I was fired after two months, when I make that assessment. I-Link no longer exists.

30   Frank's no longer exists.

line. Matt Ohran and his crew were there, nervously prepping about eighteen of his Cannondales. I casually mentioned that if Cannondales weren't built so poorly he might not need to bring so many bikes. The Cannondale rep received this comment coolly.[31]

I handed my bike to Jeremy and asked him to give the bike a quick once-over if he had a second. As I got the rest of my stuff ready, nervousness set in. I didn't know if I had prepared well enough for this event, and if I didn't, during the next 24 hours I would pay for it in a big way.

The race begins with a member from each team running, in biking shoes, across desert sand about 100 yards to a juniper tree, around the tree, and back to their bikes, where they can begin riding. The official reason the race begins like this is to spread out the riders — there are 360 of them, after all — a little bit. The real reason is that it makes great comedy. As you may expect, neither Brad nor I wanted to be the guy who does this sprint.

Luckily, I had managed to get Gravity Media,[32] the best darned web design company in the whole world, to sponsor Brad and me for this race. I say it was lucky for two reasons: first, because I didn't have to come with $200 for my share of the entry. More importantly, though, it gave me excellent, compelling leverage against Brad when it came time to decide who would run around the tree at the start of the course. Essentially, it went like this:

> **Me:** *"I arranged sponsorship, so you have to run."*
> **Brad:** *"OK. Bastard."*

FIRST LAPS

Brad and I agreed to do sets of two laps, giving each other more opportunity to rest between turns. That meant I wouldn't have anything to do for at least the first couple hours of the race, except wish that I had worked harder at staying in shape.

I must say, Brad ran magnificently. He was easy to locate, too, resplendent in his blaze-orange Gravity Media jersey. Especially considering he had to run around the tree, Brad put in a very fast first lap, about 1:17, I think.

His second lap didn't go so well, however. Sometime last week, the

---

31 Why do I give Canondales no respect? I'll tell you why: because I cannot for the life of me remember how to spell their name correctly.
32 Gravity Media no longer exists.

pump holder on his bike broke and Brad forgot to replace it. Evidently, Brad had taken race preparation even less seriously than I. So, when Brad got a flat, he was just a teensy bit screwed. He changed the tube anyway, and somebody loaned him one of those tiny little pumps that look really cool in catalogs but have the minor drawback of not being able to inflate a tube. After 1,500 strokes or so, Brad was able to limp his bike to Nosedive Hill, where they had a floor pump. Brad finished that lap in just under two hours.

Of course, I didn't find this out until well after the race was over. While I was standing around in the staging area waiting for him, I couldn't help but think that he must've had a serious injury. And while I wouldn't want Brad to be incapacitated, I have to admit that at the time I could see an upside of having my race partner get injured very early in the race.

If you're going to DNF, DNF early.

Until now, all of my memories of the race course were based on when I did it a couple of years ago. I remembered that the rocky, ledgy descents and ascents were very difficult, and that I had to walk a number of them. I also remembered interminable sand pits you had to walk through. So it was a nice surprise to find that in the couple of years since I did that race, I've improved enough so that I was able to not only ride the technical stuff, but really enjoy it. I cleaned everything but Nosedive Hill, which I didn't even try.

The sand, though, was even worse than I remembered it, to the point that the long downhill section toward the end of the course offered no recovery at all. You had to work constantly to keep momentum, not to mention the right line.[33] Still, I felt pretty fresh as I finished my first lap. I took about 1:20; not as fast as Brad, but pretty darn good for me.

My second lap went a lot like my first, except I didn't clean nearly as many of the technical moves, and I was fully beat when I finished. It was 6:00PM then, giving us an average time of 1:30 — right on track for what we wanted.

Brad must have bungled his math a bit for his next lap, because he went out without lights, even though the very earliest he could hope to come in would be at 7:20PM. So when he finished that lap, it was very nearly dark. He pulled into Jeremy's pit stop, where Jeremy and crew

---

33   Too bad there weren't 29-inch wheeled mountain bikes back then. That would have made a huge difference.

got Brad set up in about one minute, including a quick lube for his chain, and off for his fourth lap.

NO MORE DOUBLES

Brad pulled in from his fourth lap about 9:30PM, looking pretty shot. He said that he wasn't up for doing sets of two anymore. I, still having done only two laps at that point, thought Brad was just being a baby. I took the baton and headed out.

Then, about twenty minutes into the lap (my third lap and first night lap), my handlebar-mounted lights went out. I'm still not sure why. Maybe I didn't charge them properly. Maybe when I disconnected the battery from the gauge something got bunged up. In any case, I had to do the balance of the ride, including all the technical sections, using nothing but my helmet light. I switched it to dim (didn't want it running out, too) and continued.

This was a spooky lap. With nothing but a narrow-focus spotlight, it's hard to tell what's coming up. I walked a lot of the stuff that I had ridden earlier in the day.

Apart from the light debacle, my third lap went fine, and my fourth went great. A fully-lit trail makes a big difference in your confidence. By the end of that lap, though, I understood why Brad wanted to do single laps from that point forward. I was whipped, too.

SETTLING INTO THE ROUTINE

For the remainder of the race, Brad and I turned in very consistent times. We each did 1:40 to 1:50 laps. It was nice being able to show up at the staging area at the right time and have Brad show up within a few minutes every time. Between laps I had a pretty effective regimen going, too. Go back to the camp, give my bike to Jeremy for mandatory post-lap lubing, go back to my car, start the engine, turn on the heater, make a sandwich (Great Harvest bread, smoked turkey, lots of mayo) while the car warms up, climb into the back seat, change into the clothes for my next lap, eat the sandwich, drink about a quart of water, refill my Camelbak,[34] rest for about 20 minutes, go to the restroom, then back to the staging area to wait for Brad.

---

34 I can't help but wonder what I was thinking, riding with a Camelbak. I was out there for an hour and a half. It's cold out. There's no way I'm drinking even one

I should point out that this easy routine I settled into would never have been possible if not for Jeremy. He was taking care of *twelve* riders' bikes (Brad's, mine, a Sport team's, an Open team's, and a soloist's), not to mention their lights — making sure they were recharged in time was no small thing — and often, the riders themselves. He did all this for 24 hours, without a break, and without ever dropping the ball or losing his cool. Thanks, Jeremy.[35]

Okay, now back to the race. Brad says he felt strong up to and including part of his seventh lap. Toward the end, though, I guess he bonked hard. As he handed me the baton, he said that he had done the math and figured that I would finish my next lap (my seventh) about 11:40. He was completely fried, he said, and there was no way he was going to do another lap.

"You have to!" I yelled.

"No way," he said.

"You have to!" I reiterated, just in case I had been unclear the first time.

"No way," he said, just in case I hadn't caught the subtle nuances of his previous statement.

For emphasis, I yelled "You have to!" one more time, climbed on my bike and took off.

DECISION TIME

For the bulk of that lap, I was preoccupied with what we would do when I finished my lap. At first I figured that Brad would see that he was obligated to do one more lap and would be at the staging area ready to go when I pulled in. Then I thought about it a little harder and decided that if Brad said he was cooked, he was really cooked.

I didn't want to hold back, though, and intentionally turn in a slow lap for my final effort. I had treated this event like a race for 23 hours; I was going to finish it like a race.

---

bottle's worth of water. Why am I carrying a big ol' backpack? I sometimes wonder if one of the big reasons I'm faster now than when I was younger is that I've stopped carrying a bunch of gear I don't need for the ride.

35   To this day, I have never seen such an amazing feat of management. Maybe it's no surprise that Jeremy has left the world of bikes and now makes more money than my friends and me put together as an executive bigshot doing something I don't understand at all.

I decided that if Brad wasn't able to do the final lap, I'd do it.

Around 11:25AM I pulled into Jeremy's pit stop and asked if Brad had suited up for another lap. They said he hadn't and that I should just sit down and chill out until noon. Instead, I handed Jeremy my bike and asked him to lube the chain while I filled up my Camelbak.

I don't know if there were really wild cheers all around, but it seemed like it at the time and it drove my morale right through the roof. I took off for lap number eight.

ASLEEP AT THE WHEEL

It was during that eighth lap that I had the most impressive crash of my life.[36] About five miles into the course, there's a steep, sandy descent that ends with a very tall banked curve to the right. Riding high up on that bank is a blast; you feel like a skate rat in a halfpipe (or at least that's what I imagine it feels like).

This time, though, I rode too high up on the bank, snagged my front wheel in deep sand and flipped over the front of my bike at about 25MPH. I flew about ten feet in a Superman position, landed on my hands and rolled onto my back, where I slid to a stop. My bike must have gone over me, because it was another 20 feet down the trail. I just wish somebody would've caught that on film.

It wasn't far into that final lap that I began to feel exhaustion like I have never felt before. Stuff that I had been blowing through in my middle ring now required a granny gear. I walked things that I would never walk. I felt like I was out there forever, but the actual time wasn't much different than my other times for the day: 1:49.

Apparently, that was good enough for a fourth-place finish, which is far and away my best finish ever in an endurance event. I rode a total of 126 miles in that race and pushed myself harder than ever before.

I know this will sound dumb, but I'm excited to do it again next year. Now I just need to figure out a way to make sure Brad does the run again.[37]

---

36   I have since had at least one crash that was much more impressive. That's a story for another book, though.

37   We never raced as a team again, which is kind of sad and something I think we should fix.

THE KOKOPELLI TRAIL RACE

The thing about the Kokopelli Trail Race (KTR) is, it's not technically a race. Technically, in fact, it doesn't exist at all. Word of this race traversing the Colorado and Utah deserts spreads quietly by blogs and email. There is no entry fee. There are no prizes. Time is kept only informally. There are no course marshals or emergency personnel on hand. No help or supplies are allowed; racers must carry food, tools, and equipment to filter water from available sources.

I had thought about doing it for a long time, but never had. I mean, I had actually failed to get that trail ridden, start to finish, at all several times. Racing it just seemed out of the question.

But then I did it. Just because I wanted to be tough. And because, frankly, there was so much going on in my life that was no fun at all to think about that I wanted something big and exciting and adventurous to think about, for a change.

The Kokopelli Trail definitely did that.

The Kokopelli Trail Race is the longest ride I've ever done, in duration or mileage. More importantly, it's the *scariest* ride I've ever done. It begins in the dead of night and continues 142 miles through a brutally hot summer day along an ancient Anasazi trade route. Water is scarce. Signs of wild animals are not.

OK, I'll just come out and say it: it's an unsanctioned and illegal event. And not very smart to do.[38]

And, by far, it was the most epic ride I've ever been on. By a *lot*.

MEET YOUR FRIENDLY BLM REPRESENTATIVES

The race started, or nearly failed to start, with a little bit of drama. At about 10:30PM, about 50 of us gathered at the trailhead in Loma, Colorado to participate in what could hardly be called an organized event.

And that's when the Bureau of Land Management (BLM) agents rolled up.

For the next half hour, everyone in the group argued whether what we were doing required a permit. Our point was that there was no

---

38   But it's also not especially dumb to do. It's just really difficult.

registration, no fee, no list of participants. We were just a rather large group ride, with some, but definitely not all, people hoping to go fast.

The BLM's argument was that we were a little too big and a little too organized to be called a group ride. There was a web page, an organizer, and a name for what we were doing.

The argument went in circles, with no one conceding anything. I stood in the back of the group, torn between wanting to get riding and the weasely hope that the whole thing would get canceled. At least then I'd have an ironclad excuse for not following up on my boast that I would do this ride.

Fortunately (?), the BLM eventually got tired of arguing, wrote Adam — the guy who had sent out the email to the group — a ticket, which we all chipped in to cover, and skulked around the parking lot until midnight, which is when we took off.

THE GEAR

What do you carry if you're planning to ride your mountain bike for 142 miles, completely self-sufficiently, through both the night and heat of day?

Well, I wore bib shorts (bib shorts are like regular lycra shorts, but with built-in suspenders. These have the dual benefit of not binding at the waist and acting as a girdle for those of us with guts), a sleeveless jersey, a short-sleeved jersey on top of it, arm warmers, and knee warmers.

For food, I packed 18 packets of Clif Shot Bloks, six Honey Stinger protein bars, and a gallon of water. Variety and deliciousness were not priorities.[39]

For light, I used a CygoLite Dual Cross 200 I rented from a local sports store, and an LED headlamp, which made wearing my helmet very uncomfortable.

I was keeping it simple.

---

39   That said, the Honey Stinger protein bars are delicious. I eat them recreationally sometimes. Which is a problem, because they have more calories than most king-size candy bars.

TERROR AND PAIN

Starting the KTR at midnight means riding the most dangerous part of the trail at the darkest time of night. I was spooked, thinking frequently that this was the trail from which my sister Kellene had taken an 18-foot drop from a cliff, breaking a leg, an arm, and knocking out most of her teeth while mountain biking in the *daylight*.

And so, unsurprisingly, forty minutes into a 142-mile mountain bike race, I very nearly crashed out of the whole race.

I was finishing a fast downhill section. It emptied into a dry riverbed, which sorta-kinda-but-not-really looked like it was the trail. Fooled, I followed the riverbed for a moment, but didn't see enough tire marks in the sand to convince me I was on the right track. I turned around and followed the riverbed in the other direction.

I couldn't find a trail anywhere.

I was lost. Already.

Perfect.

So I started a slow walking spiral, looking for something that might be a trail.[40] And, in a few minutes, I found it.

Above me.

I hadn't seen the trail before because it was up on a ledge about three feet above me. I had to lift my bike onto the trail to continue.

What a relief. I wasn't going to DNF an hour into a race just because I couldn't find the trail. I hoisted my bike up onto the ledge, then held it in place with my left hand while I stepped up onto what would have to serve as a step.

And then the hard plastic cleats on my new bike shoes slipped. I tumbled backward, scraping up my right knee. Twisting around to the right, I put out my right arm to catch my fall.

Schklopf.

You know, no matter how many times I dislocate my shoulder, it never gets old.

I stumbled around for a few minutes, holding my arm and screaming — yeah, screaming — in pain. I was angry, hurt, and very alone.

---

40   I was scared enough that I started talking aloud to myself, saying things like, "Don't panic, Elden. Just stay calm." The problem is, the rational part of me recognized that only a panicky, about-to-lose-it-altogether kind of person would be talking to himself and so I got even more freaked out.

In the dark.

To make matters worse, my arm wouldn't go back into the socket easily, like it usually does when I dislocate it (I am somewhat of an expert on dis- and re-locating my shoulder). It took several tries and hurt much worse than usual when it finally seated itself.[41]

My shoulder would throb the rest of the day, making ugly, muffled popping sounds at strange, unexpected moments. Every time it happened,[42] I'd yelp.

Once I had myself back together, I hoisted my bike, which had fallen into the riverbed when I fell, back onto the trail. I didn't even look at it to see if it was OK. I just got back on and started riding.

Or rather, I got back on and *tried* to start riding.

The chain immediately got sucked between the rear wheel's spokes and big cog. I got off, got the chain back in place, and started riding again.

Same result.

OK, something was definitely wrong.

Peering at the rear derailleur by the light of my headlamp, I could see: the derailleur — the gizmo that makes it possible to shift gears in the back — was bent and cracked.

My bike was now officially a three-speed. I was screwed.

"OK, fine," I thought. "Now I've got three legitimate reasons to quit the race: a broken bike, a cut-up knee (I knew I could play it up to make it sound like it was more painful than it really was), and a dislocated shoulder."

But first, I needed to get to a place where I could bail out of the ride. I figured that Rabbit Valley, about twenty miles into the ride, would be a good place to quit — it was close to the freeway, and there was a good chance I'd get a phone signal.

Meanwhile, I may as well keep going.[43]

---

41   I kept hoping that someone would show up, so I could tell them, bravely, "I've dislocated my shoulder and am having a hard time re-seating it." Even when I'm suffering, I like attention.

42   Which would be dozens of times.

43   When I want to quit something, I tell myself I need to find a good place to quit, and that place is some distance down the road. By the time I get there, I've reconsidered and no longer want to quit. I've played this trick on myself so many times. I can't believe I still fall for it.

NEW HERO

After I finally picked my way down the canyon and up the other side to the big open frontage road that leads to Rabbit Valley, I started thinking about what it meant to quit. It would be the first time I had ever quit a race. I didn't like the thought of that.

I thought about how my wife was being tough every single day of her life. If I quit this race even though my bike was still rolling, even though my shoulder was back where it belonged, even though my knee injury was purely superficial, how tough would I look?

Not very.

So I revised my plan. I'd keep going until my bike truly could not be ridden. And I looked at my new pink headset — specially put on to remind me of my wife's fight against breast cancer — dozens of times throughout that day to remind me of that.

There was a time when I looked to Tyler Hamilton for an example of being strong through pain.

Now I looked to Susan.

STARS

Rabbit Valley is an ATV paradise, crisscrossed with dirt trails. Some of them are marked. Other times, I had to use my very best Boy Scout skills and try to figure out which way the Kokopelli Trail went. Mostly, I did this by getting low to the ground and shining my light at the trail. The shadows of all those bike tracks showed up more clearly that way.

And, to my credit, I never got lost for more than ten or twenty yards at a time on this ride.

At one of the moments where I needed to stop and assess which trail to take, I happened to look up.

Wow.

I had never seen the stars so clearly. So I took a moment and enjoyed it. Then I rode for a few minutes and did the same thing. I don't get to see the Milky Way so brightly very often, and it was definitely worth taking the time to look.

IRRITATION

By 4:00AM, I was marching my bike up a steep climb out of Rabbit Valley to the plateau that drops to the next big section of the ride: Westwater to

Cisco. While hiking, I noticed that what had started as faint discomfort from my shoes was rapidly blooming into full-blown pain.

If you want to get an idea of how it felt, tape a pencil to the insole of one of your shoes in such a way that the ball of your foot presses on that pencil with each step. It won't hurt at first; you'll just say, "hey, there's a pencil in my shoe." After a while, though, I guarantee that pencil will consume your every waking thought.

For right now, though, I was just marching my bike up. Then, for the second time during that ride, I slipped and fell, my backpack coming off as I tumbled in a backwards somersault.

I stood up quickly, praying nobody saw, and put my backpack back on.

Then I quickly took it back off.

Evidently, my roll in the grass had left the mesh back of my backpack full of goatheads, an especially tenacious and thorny kind of weed.

Nice.

With nothing else to do, I spent ten minutes picking them out as best as I could. Years later, I still haven't gotten them all out.

A GIFT

By the time I was 35 miles into the race, I had made a judgment call on my headlamp: it sucked. I no longer wanted any part of it. So I took it off with the batteries still good, the headlamp in perfect working condition, and hung it on the branch of a tree sticking out into the trail. The next person who comes along that trail gets a free headlamp. Lucky her/him!

I rolled to the intersection where I had to make my first important strategy decision of the day: head to Westwater and fill up with water, or continue on to Dewey Bridge. I had plenty of water, as far as I knew, so I parted company with a couple of guys I had ridden and talked with for about an hour, guys who I could not now pick out of a lineup, because all I saw of their faces was bright headlamps.

It was starting to turn light, which somehow made me more comfortable about getting out the iPod (riding in the dark with one would have eliminated one too many senses). I ratcheted up to the big ring and started pedaling along the fast, rolling, sandy singletrack, singing along with Johnny Cash: "I've Been Everywhere."[44]

Forty miles down, one hundred to go.

MEET YOUR FELLOW RACERS

Now that it was light, it was more natural to talk with others who were doing this race. At least I thought so. The first rider I passed, I said, "Hey, awesome morning, isn't it?" He didn't answer. He had headphones on.

Okay. Here's a rule. If you are on a crazy race where you are going to be spending *hour upon hour alone*, you are *required* to greet each and every other rider in the same circumstance. Take out the stupid headphones for a second. Say hello. Acknowledge that you're both doing something pretty cool/stupid/unusual and wish the other rider lots of luck.

Could I get someone to second the motion on this?

To be fair, this was the only guy the whole day who was too preoccupied with himself and his music to say hi.

And in fact, shortly afterward, I came across another racer, this one very friendly, who was taking a short break, to have a smoke.

Let me repeat, in bold and italics so as to make my astonishment clear: *A racer on the Kokopelli Trail was having a smoke.*

My mind boggled.

Sadly, it wasn't until a few minutes later that I thought to wonder: How many cigarettes does one ration out for the KTR? A pack? Two?

HEAT

Here's a simple way to tell if the day's going to be warm: If it's 8:00AM and you're switching to your sleeveless mesh jersey, it's going to be a warm day.

I jiggled the water bladder in my Camelbak. Not much there. I sucked on the tube and got the dreaded "Shlurrrpp" sound that tells you you've finished it off.

You have no idea how pleased I was with myself: I was ten miles away from Dewey Bridge, the point I had chosen as my first place to replenish my water, and I had two bottles of water left.

Not bad.

---

44   I love it when the iPod picks just the right song for the moment. Of course, "I've Been Everywhere" is the right song for a lot of different moments.

MINOR DILEMMA

It was on this section of trail that I came across my first ethical dilemma for the ride. The rules for the KTR say that everyone takes care of themselves: if you break your bike, you fix it yourself, with stuff you brought. If you need food, you better have brought it yourself.

But see, this rule doesn't work well with my own *personal* rule, which is: if you see a rider on the side of the trail, you ask if she/he needs help.

Anyway, I came across a rider pushing her bike. She said her rear derailleur was broken. That sounded familiar. So, even though it was against the rules, I asked if she wanted me to help change her bike into a singlespeed so she could continue. "No, I'm just going to hike to Dewey Bridge and call it a day," she said.

Wise choice. I continued on.

But as I rode, I asked myself: what if she *had* wanted help? Or what if any of the several riders I saw on the side of the trail that day had wanted help? I guess I would have been disqualifying both them and me to help, in which case I think I'd rather be DQ'd than finish the race.

If a rule precludes me being a decent person, I concluded, it's a stupid rule.[45]

Conundrum solved and, feet hurting something fierce, I saw the Colorado River down below me. The halfway point, in distance anyway.

GETTING READY FOR THE HARD PART

I pulled into the Dewey Bridge campground area, then took about 40 leisurely minutes eating lunch, cleaning my glasses, lubing my bike chain, and filtering a gallon of water from the muddy Colorado river.

I was in no hurry to start, because I knew that the remaining 65 miles, if I remembered correctly, was nothing but steep climbs and fast descents: no easy rolling for the rest of the day.

While I was thus dawdling, a couple of riders rolled in and asked if I planned to go on. Both times I said "yes," then asked if they were going to keep riding. Both times they said no. My theory is that from the looks of me, they figured I was done and would be a good person to commiserate with.

It was 9:40AM when I got back on my bike, fully expecting the

---

45 Not only will I break such rules, but I'll feel all smug and self-righteous while I do so.

steepest, hottest, most painful, most difficult day of riding in my life.

It's kinda cool to be able to talk in superlatives that way.

Before I even started the KTR, I knew there would be three sections that would test my limits: the climb from Dewey Bridge to Seven Mile Mesa, the climb from Fisher Valley to North Beaver Mesa, and the climb up to the La Sal mountains.

The thing is, those climbs come one after another, with descents that either are so technical or are over so fast that you don't have any time to recover.

Consider it: 11,647 feet of climbing, over 64 miles. Which is to say, the second half of the KTR is brutal. And there are none of the easy bailout options that present themselves during the first part of the race.

But at least it's a downhill finish, right?

GREG, PART 1

When you do a big ol' epic race, it's a good idea to set yourself rules for things that matter. My "water rule" was that any time I got down below two full bottles, I would take the next opportunity to find and filter water, completely loading up, just in case it took me a long time to get to the next water crossing or just in case the next water crossing...wasn't.[46]

Following this rule, I began the first big climb to Sevenmile Mesa (look at mile 0–10 in the profile chart) completely loaded up with water. Within a few miles, I felt like a fool. There was a stream: a much clearer, cooler, more convenient water crossing than the muddy Colorado River where I had just filled up. I hadn't needed to pack that heavy (and believe me, it felt very heavy) gallon of water all this way. Oh well.

Incidentally, there was a cyclist lying down in the stream.

I stopped, pulled my earphones out, and said hi. Greg — for Greg was his name — sat up, said hi, then ducked his head in the water one last time and got ready to roll.

Here's a biking axiom: a funny, easygoing riding buddy can reduce the pain quotient of a climb by 35%. Unfortunately for me, I just couldn't keep up with Greg. He tried to slow down for me, but the reality is, when you're deep into an endurance ride it's almost impossible to

---

46   This seems like an overcautious rule, but I never ran out of water the whole day. It's a freaky experience to run out of water in the middle of a hot desert. Believe me, I know.

speed up or slow down your pace. The speed you're going is the speed you're capable of going.

That's why, no matter how many times I plan epic rides with friends, once we get on the trail, everyone eventually winds up riding big pieces of the course alone.

It is as it should be.

HEAT OF THE DAY

So I continued on alone as the day started getting hot. Really hot. I wished, over and over, for two simple things: a lower gear and for my feet to stop hurting so bad. Had I met a two-wish-granting genie, I suspect she would have been so astounded at the simplicity of my wishes that she would have granted them without using one of those "gotcha" clauses that usually come with wishes.

With regard to the latter wish, I finally had a knuckle-headed epiphany: I was packing a full bottle of ibuprofen. Duh. Four capsules sounded like a good number, and half an hour later I was able to beat the pain in my feet into the background of my thoughts.

It was during this climb that the only Bananarama song I have on my iPod — "Cruel Summer" — got shuffled into play. I actually laughed out loud at the perfectness of the song selection.

I passed two cyclists, neither of whom was moving. No, they weren't dead, they were just resting under available shade.

At least I hoped they were just resting.

Then, from nowhere, eight Land Rovers passed me, each with a male driver and a female passenger. Weird. Do Land Rover clubs have a men-with-female-companions-only membership rule?

And no, I wasn't hallucinating.

That came later.

GREG, PART 2

As I neared the summit of Sevenmile Mesa, I finished off the last of the water in my Camelbak. By my rule, that meant I needed to stop at the next water crossing and fill up.

I was hot. I was tired. I was becoming a little thick-tongued and mentally addled. More than usual, I mean. Then I saw another rider trying to get some shade under a bush. He stood up as I approached.

It was Greg.

"How's it going?" I asked, slurrily.

"Oh, I'm just looking forward to getting some water," he said.

"Tell me about it," I replied, and kept going, figuring he'd saddle up and join me.

But when I looked back a few minutes later, he wasn't there.

Half an hour later, it occurred to me: when he said, "Oh, I'm just looking forward to getting some water," he was *really* saying, "Please, I'm dying here. Give me some water before I'm too weak to fend off the buzzards."

But I didn't get it. Like I said, I was thick-tongued and addle-brained.

Greg: If you're still alive and you read this, please accept my apologies. I didn't get the clue, or I wouldn't have left you to die, under a bush, at the top of Sevenmile Mesa. I still had two bottles of water, and if you would have asked, you could've had one.

Honest.

DETOUR

An interminable hike-a-bike down a boulder ravine brought me into Fisher Valley. I was now down to one bottle of water and was beginning to worry. Would I run out of water before the next water crossing?[47] I thought there was one just a few miles away, but couldn't be sure.

On the other hand, I could see that the ranch in this valley was currently watering its alfalfa fields, mocking me.

I decided to take a side trip toward the ranch and pick up some water there, rather than trust there'd be a water crossing on the trail.

The thing is, the longer I rode toward the ranch, the further it seemed to get away from me. And the hoped-for irrigation ditch never materialized.

So, after ten minutes (or fifteen? or twenty? — hard to say), I gave up and headed back onto the trail, figuring I'd trust to finding water where everyone else did.

Nothing like putting in a few extra miles on a 140-mile bike ride.

---

47   It occurs to me that the picture I'm painting of these giant all-day adventures may not be exactly winning you over. The problem is, you've got to actually *ride* in one of these Quixotic races to really get the appeal.

TIME FOR THE BIG CLIMB

Sure enough, after a quick climb (well, "quick" may not be the correct adjective) and descent, I came across the water crossing, just where I remembered it. So the detour really was a waste.

And there were two riders, sitting at the stream. We talked a bit while I filtered water. One of the riders was named Jesper, and he was currently lamenting that he had picked too steep a gear for his singlespeed.

"Oh, and the fun's just beginning," I said.

"Have you ridden this trail before?" he asked.

"Not in this direction, but the trail we're about to climb takes 45 minutes when you go *downhill*."

"How long of a climb is it?" Jesper asked, visibly worried. And rightly so.

"It'll be nine miles before we get any kind of break at all."

As I'd find out later, we'd be climbing pretty much nonstop for about *fifteen* miles.

I DO NOT THINK I SEE WHAT I THINK I SEE

It was during the climb up to North Beaver Mesa that I began to hallucinate.

Yes, really.

I started seeing things on the side of the road that would turn out, as I got closer, to be nothing more than rocks, logs, and flowers.

The following day, as I relayed this to my friends, Adam chimed in, "I was hallucinating on that stretch, too!"

We compared hallucinations:

"I saw a lawn chair," said Adam. "I was so disappointed when it turned out to be nothing but some wildflowers."

"I saw an ice chest," I said. "I had no problem with the idea of raiding it either. I was really ticked off when it turned back into a stump."

"I saw a real estate sign," Adam said. "I was thinking, 'How come North Beaver Mesa is for sale?'"

"I saw people sitting on the side of the road.[48] They always turned out to be trees. And I saw an armadillo. And a hedgehog."

I think I may have hallucinated more than Adam.

---

48 I was hoping they were cheering for me. They weren't.

SO...TIRED...MUST...SLEEP

Amazingly, the climb to North Beaver Mesa eventually ended. At the top, there was Adam, sitting in a stream. Since he confirmed he was really there, I believe I can confidently say this was not a hallucination.

A five-mile descent on pavement (mile 37–42, if you're looking at the elevation profile) brought me to the final big climb of the day, up to the La Sal mountains. This climb was on pavement, has multiple switchbacks, and, frankly, was incredibly boring.

Which was a big problem.

If it's Saturday afternoon, you haven't slept since Thursday, and you've been on your bike for eighteen hours, boring has a peculiar effect: you get sleepy. Verrrrry sleeeepy.

I just couldn't keep my eyes open. I was turning the pedals, but my head kept snapping forward, and my bike was veering all over the road.

The hallucinations were getting more common, too. I saw a train of 8–10 Miatas coming down the road. Once again, each car had a male driver and a female passenger (usually looking bored).

Or were those real? Hard to say.

Somewhere along the way up, it occurred to me: maybe the music on my iPod was making me sleepy. I pulled out the iPod headphones, and that did seem to help.

A little bit.

When I finally got to the top of the road, knowing that it was all downhill (check out the elevation profile) from there, I laughed aloud.

I knew I'd make it.[49]

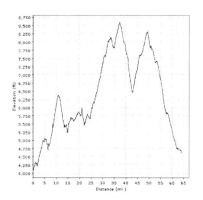

FAST FINISH

After a brutally hard day of climbing, ten miles of fast, easy downhill feels so good. I didn't pedal at all. Just coasted. It was time for gravity to pay me back.

For the first time in eighteen hours or so, my feet felt good.

I coasted downhill, my thoughts turning more and more to ice

---

49   All finishes should be downhill. At least, all finishes *I* do should be downhill.

cream. And Diet Coke. And onion rings. With fry sauce.[50]

And then I was in the parking lot. Dan found me a chair. Mark brought me some ice cream sandwiches, truly the best food I have ever had in my life. Kenny looked relieved and said my wife and sister had been calling, wondering if they ought to send out Search and Rescue.

I finished 25th (or so) out of 60 (or so) starters and 35 (or so) finishers. Mid-pack at best.

And, without question, this was my proudest mountain biking moment, ever.

MISCELLANEOUS STATISTICS

- Distance of the Kokopelli Trail: 142 miles
- Amount the BLM Fined Adam Lisonbee for "Organizing" an Event Without a Permit: $275
- Amount Racers Immediately Reimbursed Adam: $253
- Number of Entries in the 2007 KTR: 60...or so
- Number of People who Completed the 2007 KTR: Around 30.
- Winning Time for the 2007 KTR: 12 hours and change, by Dave Wiens, the guy who has won the Leadville Trail 100 every year for as long as anyone can remember
- My Finish Time for the 2007 KTR: 20:20
- Number of Shot Bloks I Ate During the KTR: 90 (3000 calories)
- Number of Honey Stinger Peanut Butta Protein Bars I Ate During the KTR: 5 (1750 calories)
- Other Food Items I Ate During the KTR: None
- Estimated Number of Calories I Expended During KTR: 16,000
- Quantity of Water I Filtered from Available Water Sources (Colorado River, trailside creeks) During KTR: 2.5 gallons
- Number of Working Gears I Had Access to After Crashing Less Than an Hour Into the Race: 3
- My Pride at Finishing the Most Hardcore Event In Which I've Ever Participated: Not measurable with conventional mathematics

---

50 I recently found out that fry sauce is mostly a Utah thing, so let me explain what it is: ketchup with mayo, and some Cajun spices stirred in. That's pretty much it.

COMMENT FROM ADAM

The Miatas were real! Or perhaps we had the same hallucination? Oh, and I called into a Moab area Real Estate agent to make an offer on N. Beaver Mesa, they laughed at me. I felt like Pee Wee Herman, when he asks to see the basement of the Alamo....

COMMENT FROM BOTCHEDEXPERIMENT

I was at the finish line, watching for 5 hours, as about 20 riders came in. Virtually all of them finished totally wiped out. Most came in and had trouble coherently giving their name and starting time to the woman who was recording them. Some could only lay down on the pavement while cool water was poured over them. Virtually all of them were sick, and none of them wanted any food. That is, until Fatty finished.

Fatty came in looking VERY dirty. He was slurring words, but insisted he felt OK, but he was hungry. Within two minutes of riding up, he was eating. He ate an ice cream bar, cookies, Doritos, and he drank sodas. I already can't remember all the stuff he ate, but literally, it was whatever was in sight. I was in awe. I was dumbfounded. I was flabbergasted. I had just seen about 25 VERY strong riders finish and although some of them nibbled this or that, I don't think any of them were hungry, and none of them had eaten anything even close to what I was seeing Fatty do. The difference was striking.

And so there you have empirical evidence that when it comes to food consumption, Fatty is waaayyy out on the edge of the bell curve.

COMMENT FROM DUG

I say one pack of cigarettes. Two just seems like overkill.

RESPECT FOR THE BONK

The bonk is the common shared experience of anyone who has gone on at least a few really long rides. The complete lack of power. The out-of-body attitude. The slowing of time.

Tell your story about a bonk to someone who doesn't ride, and they'll nod as if they understand. Tell your story to someone who does ride, and they will — guaranteed — tell their equivalent story.

And, strangely, both stories will be told with no small amount of fondness.

Last Saturday, when I did the Issaquah Alps ride outside of Seattle, it didn't occur to me that the hardest climb of the day would come after the event was over. I had used all my food and all my energy in finishing the ride itself, and hadn't left anything in reserve for the eight-mile ride home.

The extent of my mistake, of course, didn't occur to me until I reached the base of SE 43rd Way. This is a fairly moderate climb, one that I do without any difficulty a couple times per week as part of my commute.

As I started to climb, though, I realized: I was cooked. My clock was cleaned. I was out of gas. I had cracked.

I had, in short, bonked.

Now, I don't know if anyone who doesn't do endurance sports really knows what a true bonk feels like. It's actually kind of interesting. First of all, you have only the slightest amount of power. You can turn the cranks over, but just *barely*. Next, you stop caring. You know that you must look ridiculous, riding your bike at three miles per hour (yes, really), but you just don't have the energy to care about appearances. You completely lack the ability to rally; it doesn't matter how bracing a pep talk your friends give you, you aren't going to be able to buck up and go faster.

In a *really good* bonk, I've experienced a disconnectedness between my mind and body: this can't be my body inching along, right? Surely, if this were my body, I'd be able to tell my legs to go faster.

Sometimes I'll feel cold.[51]

All of these sensations, though, are pretty much secondary to the

---

51   Usually when it's cold outside.

main emotion: misery. It's a self-pitying, helpless, weak, beyond-tiredness, beyond-hunger, beyond-thirsty, miserable misery.[52]

And the thing is, as far as bonks go, the one I had last Saturday was pretty minor. I had, after all, a mobile phone; I could quit any moment and call for help. And I knew I wasn't far from home; once I got to the top of the hill, I knew I'd be fine.

A bonk underscored by lack of options, though, is something special. It's something to behold if you're with the guy who's bonking, and something you never forget if you're the guy who bonked.

Here are a few of my favorite — if you can call them that — bonks.

ROCKY AT THE KOKOPELLI

The first time Rocky[53] and I tried the Kokopelli Trail, I believe it was the longest ride either of us had ever attempted. Also, neither of us had ever been on that trail and were just following the map and signposts.

We were, in short, all kinds of stupid.

Early in the day we missed a turn, the only non-obvious turn in the whole route, really, and didn't realize our mistake until it made more sense to continue than to turn around.[54] This added several miles of deep sand to our ride, as well as a few miles of paved climbing.

And it was hot outside. Right around 100 degrees.[55]

And Rocky's a sweater, by which I mean he sweats a lot, not that he's a woolen pullover you wear when it's nippy outside. It's his most obvious trait, really. By the time we got to within ten miles of where we'd be getting supplies, Rocky had gone through all his food, all his water, and some of my water.

Rocky bonked. Hard. He got clammy, his voice slurred, he could no longer ride his bike. Luckily, we spied a ranch and made our way toward it, taking little baby steps because that was truly all Rocky had in him.

Once at the ranch, Rocky drank all the water he could and we left.

---

52   Above all else, self-pitying.

53   Rocky is my brother-in-law. He's a wizard at the technical stuff, and has no capacity at all for endurance riding. He is my exact opposite, really, in mountain bike ability.

54   In retrospect, this is a debatable point.

55   And don't go telling me anything like, "But it's a dry heat." All dry heat means is that you'll be cooked a little bit crispier in the end.

We passed an irrigation ditch; Rocky stripped and laid down in it for about ten minutes.

Yeah, it sounds like heat exhaustion, but it was a heat-exhaustion-induced bonk.

BRAD AT THE KOKOPELLI

Brad does not look like someone who would bonk. Ever. This is because Brad is, to all appearances, the perfect specimen of a man. He bikes, he runs, he does Muay Thai, he eats very much fish.[56]

And yet, a couple of years ago, Brad bonked hard.

A good-sized group of us were doing the Kokopelli Trail, many years after I had ridden this trail with Rocky, and I now had considerable endurance riding experience. Brad was, as usual, riding off the front. Or at least he was riding up in front until over the course of just a few minutes, he imploded and became a husk of a man.

I don't know why it happened, and I don't think he knows why. But Brad was *fully* bonked. Everyone in the group slowed way down — you don't want to leave a bonked rider out in the desert on his own[57] — but Brad still kept dropping behind. He hung his head. He wouldn't talk. A lot of the time he didn't even seem to hear us.

The thing is, Brad didn't have an option about whether to keep going. We were out in the middle of nowhere, and he had to somehow turn the cranks for 30 miles before we next met up with the SAG wagon. I'm pretty sure Brad started crying when he finally saw the car and knew he could quit.

Why did Brad bonk? It's hard to say. Maybe it's because he didn't have an ounce of fat on his body, so had no reserves. Maybe it's because he had been training more for shorter races and the long ride went beyond what he was ready for. Maybe he was just too darn handsome to be riding with the rest of us.

---

56 I don't remember why I went with this weird construction ("very much fish" as opposed to "a lot of fish.") I think I thought it was funny. And now that I read it, I believe I was right. But I still don't know why.

57 Unless that was your plan all along, which might make a great premise for a murder mystery.

FATTY AT LEADVILLE

Three years ago,[58] I was about as fit as I've ever been. I was fit, light, and had been training like crazy. I thought I had a good chance at finishing under nine hours in the Leadville 100. And for the first 65 miles, my split times seemed to show that I was going to do it.

But then, two-thirds of the way through the race, I just couldn't drink Gatorade anymore. The taste of it sickened me. And that's too bad, because Gatorade was all I had to drink.[59]

Before long, I would gag whenever I tried to take a drink. And then, right around mile 78, I lost all power. I rode slowly, frustrated that people were passing me so fast, yet completely unable to do anything about it. I pulled over to the side of the road and vomited. I felt better and was able to ride again — for about two minutes. Then I was weaker than ever. Worse, the final 25 miles of the Leadville 100 have two big climbs.

I had plenty of food, plenty to drink, but every time I tried to eat or drink, the gag reflex kicked in. My world became very small: just me, the bike, and the next turn of the crank (or the next step, since there were big stretches I could not ride).

Eventually, it occurred to me that if I took small sips, maybe I could get something down. It worked. Eventually, I could ride again, and even finished with a respectable time, although not the sub-nine I was hoping for.

The thought of Gatorade still creeps me out, though. I don't think I'll ever be able to drink it again.

BONK RECOVERY

If there's a silver lining to the bonk, it's the feeling of recovering from a bonk. Eating everything in sight, as if it were a contest, as if you have a capacity for an infinite amount of food, as if every kind of food really does go with every other kind of food (ketchup and whipped cream on rye? Excellent!)

And then laying down, knowing that you really are as tired as you can possibly be. And that you survived a bonk.

---

58   So, 2002 or so? I don't know; it all runs together for me now. My memory isn't as good as it used to be.

59   I now think I have a pretty good idea of the problem, and it wasn't what I was drinking. It was the fact that I hadn't been eating.

COMMENT FROM UNKNOWN

Perhaps one of the most disconcerting aspects of the bonk is how quickly it can come on. For me, both times I've really bonked went from feeling fine to wiped out in about ten minutes. The other odd thing about it is the fact that you're going as hard as you can, but your heart rate is like 100 bpm.

COMMENT FROM UNKNOWN

What a great description! I remember, when I was still actually cycling, the last three miles of a 50-mile ride around Baltimore in 95 degree weather thinking "I am young but I can still die." I didn't know it at the time, but maybe that was a little bonk action. Don't want to go there again.

COMMENT FROM DUG

Brad is like Captain America. But he's the best bonker in the world. He does everything all out, including muay thai (is that Spanish for lots of Thai food?). So Brad is either off the front (which is most of the time), or he turns green, shrivels up, and does a full-on impression of a banana left out in the sun. But he does this so rarely (like a cicada) and so well, that when he does it, the "Brad bonk" becomes legend.

COMMENT FROM KRIS

I'm glad to see that there are other riders out there who make complete gluttons of themselves after bonking. This summer after bonking heavily during a five-hour road ride in 100 degree heat, I ate a large meat lover's pizza, two HUGE bowls of ice cream, a half of a box of Triscuits with cream cheese on them (it was actually pretty good), and some 7-layer dip with Tostitos Gold chips. Add about a gallon of water interspersed with that. That's a feat in itself, but consider that it took place in a two hour span! I hereby submit myself for service in the circus.

7.
Fake News

I GENERALLY HAVE NOTHING BUT A HEADLINE AND A GENERAL TOPIC IN MIND WHEN I START WRITING A "FAKE NEWS" PIECE. SOMETHING LIKE, "Professional Cyclist Returns Clean Blood Sample." Then I imagine the setting — usually a press conference, who might be there, and sort of go from there.

If the idea's any good, the whole thing will just present itself to me as I write it. It's really that easy for me. However, I'm always a little bit nervous when I publish these things, because I worry: Have I hurt anyone's feelings? Have I crossed any lines?

And finally: Am I protected by the Constitution, since I'm pretty upfront about the whole thing being satire and fake and everything?

I think I am. I sure *hope* I am.

DONALD TRUMP BUYS TOUR DE FRANCE

I'm pretty sure this was my first fake news piece for the blog. I was frustrated by the way nobody around me knew anything about pro cycling, while everyone seemed to have a pretty good idea of what was going on in a popular reality show. I've still never seen an episode of The Apprentice, *but that didn't stop me from asking myself what would happen if I combined the two.*

TRUMP ANNOUNCES IMMEDIATE INTENTION TO TURN VENERABLE EUROPEAN RACING INSTITUTION INTO U.S.-FRIENDLY REALITY SHOW

PARIS, JULY 1 (FAT CYCLIST FAKE NEWS SERVICE) — In a stunning announcement on the eve of the world's most popular sporting event, Donald Trump has revealed that he has purchased all rights to the Tour de France.

With his usual flair for the dramatic, the Donald declared his immediate intention to overhaul the tradition-rich race.

Speaking from the Trump Building in NYC, Trump proclaimed in a media conference, "The French have had their turn. They've tried to make something of this race, but I just don't think they see the possibilities. The Donald is ready to step The Tour up a notch. I will guarantee you that by the end of Season One, this will be the number one-rated show on television. And by 'number one' I don't just mean in little one-horse countries like Belgium. The Tour will be popular in places that matter. Namely, in America.

"I don't think I'm being hyperbolic when I say that this is going to be the hugest reality show in the history of television, with the exception of *The Apprentice,* naturally," said Trump.

BIG CHANGES TO A BIG RACE

Donald Trump may be the only man in the world capable of turning a century-old race on its head overnight. While cycling enthusiasts across Europe appeared outraged, they were unfortunately outraged in dozens of quaint-sounding languages, reducing their concerns to amusing-anecdote level.[1]

Trump, meanwhile, seems confident. "If you're the world's best surgeon and you come across a patient dying because the local quack has been using leeches on him, do you keep using leeches? Darn right you don't."

Among the changes in the three-week race, which begins tomorrow, the most significant are:

- **Last Man Standing**: Of course, the most important objective of the Tour de France has always been to finish with the shortest accumulated time. "That's an incredibly pedestrian, not to mention, outdated, way of doing a race, kids,"[2] says Trump. In this season's race, the objective will be to be the only one to finish." Racers will be eliminated each day using the following methods:

  - **Last across the line is out**: Between every ten to twenty miles — the exact distance and location will not be made known to the riders, so they will not know where it is until they see it — a black line will be discreetly drawn across the road.[3] The last racer across the line is immediately ejected from the race in a highly visual manner. The manner will vary, ranging from the rider being shot with ten paintballs simultaneously to having a helicopter slurry bomb the racer with black paint to having several burly men tackle the racer from the side of the road.[4]

  - **Grudge Match**: Between traditional stages, any racer can challenge any other racer to a "Grudge Match:" a five-mile bicycle course with multiple hazards (tire fires, broken glass, etc.) strewn along the way. The loser is out of the race. To keep things fair, no racer is allowed to initiate more than three Grudge Matches, and no racer is required to

---

1   I seem to have forgotten here who I'm ridiculing. That's a huge problem I have: staying on target. If a joke occurs to me, I'm going to use it, whether it's on point or not. Usually it's not.

2   I have no idea if Trump calls people "kids," but it seems something he might do.

3   Wow, this sounds a lot like "The Biggest Loser," which, at the time, I had also never seen. Maybe I really should be designing reality TV shows.

4   You've got to admit, that would make good TV.

accept any more than three.[5]

- **"You're Retired**:" Borrowed from his trademark "You're Fired" line in *The Apprentice*, The Donald will tell any racer with whom he was not impressed, "You're retired," for some reason or another, like too much drafting, irregular sprint, tacky outfit, etc. That cyclist is out of the race. The Donald's decision is not subject to appeal.

- **Gear Restrictions Lifted**: Tour de France riders have long been hobbled by stringent gear rules; the type of bike, handlebars, clothing, helmets have all been tightly regulated. No more. "I can't think of a more effective way to limit innovation than all these rules," says Trump. "From now on, ride what you want. Just make sure it's human-powered, all right? Or if it's got an engine, I'd better not be able to see it."[6]

- **Yellow Jersey replaced with Red, White, and Blue Jersey**: "Yellow is the color of cowardice," said Trump. "Let's have the winner's jersey use some colors with which Americans can identify." When told that the French flag uses the same colors, Trump responded, "Whatever."

- **Name Change**: "The Tour de France? What kind of name is that?" asked Mr. Trump at the media conference. "It's long, it's dry, and it has no urgency or tension. In fact, it sounds like a stroll in the park. It's like, 'Honey, I'm in a mood for a European jaunt. Let's take a tour de France,'" said Trump in a derisive tone. "From now on, this is 'The Race.' It's short, it's to the point, and it's got pop. It's not just *any old race*. It's *The Race*."

- **Drug Rules Changed to Drug Guidelines**:[7] "Listen, I'm not pro-drug," said Trump, "but these racers are all adults and I'm not going to be the one to tell them what they can and cannot eat or drink. Just stay away from the hard stuff." When asked what constitutes "hard stuff," Trump replied, "I dunno. Crack?"

- **The Randomizer Roulette**: At the end of each stage, each

---

5   I seem to have thought the rules through here in more detail than is necessary.
6   It'd be awesome to see Trump get in a shouting match with Pat McQuaid. Admit it.
7   Yeah, a *Ghostbusters* reference.

surviving racer will spin a roulette wheel, which will, depending on where the wheel stops, improve his standings, give him a bottle of EPO for use in the next stage, require him to wear a 1980s-style helmet, add ten pounds to his bike, give him the day off, or eject him from the race entirely.[8]

- **Downhill MTB Event**: Noting that several stages in a traditional Tour de France are straight, flat, and do little to change racer standings, Trump is replacing all flat stages with downhill MTB stages. "Sure, these guys can ride fast on the road," said Trump, "but let's see what happens when they're taken out of their comfort zone."

- **Tyler Hamilton Back in the Race**. Tyler Hamilton will be allowed to race in The Race, although he will be forced to ride the entire race as a solo time trial. "Did you see that kid do that solo breakaway with a compound-fracture busted leg a couple of years ago?" asked Trump, evidently meaning Hamilton's hairline collarbone fracture. "That took guts. Let's see if he can do that for three weeks." Oddmakers place Hamilton's chances at 0.00001%, unless he wins the EPO roulette, at which point his odds go to 40%.

- **Human Interest via Heartfelt Accusations and Confessionals**: Between stages, racers will be encouraged to make disparaging remarks about each other, as well as weepily confess their doubts about whether they will be able to even finish the race. "Who're you going to root for, a robot or someone you're emotionally invested in?" asked Trump. "By the time that one guy[9] crosses the finish line, you're going to know him like your own brother."

THE RIDERS REACT

Participants in "The Race" have had mixed reactions to this sudden and dramatic shift in the Tour de France sprung on them by The Donald.

---

8   Is it weird that, as I revisit this piece, I find myself intrigued by the idea and thinking, "You know, I would totally watch this." What is *wrong* with me?

9   I don't think I made it totally clear, but in my mind, The Donald would expect this to be a race that is won by attrition. The person who won would be obvious, because he would be the only one who crossed the finish line.

Several European racers said several things very effusively, but Trump refused to have them translated. "These guys are not the stars. I'd be very surprised if one of them won," said Trump with a wink. "Not that I'm rigging The Race. It's strictly above-board."

Approached for comment, six-time Tour de France winner Lance Armstrong said, "Well, this is a little unusual. But it sounds like fun. Frankly, I was starting to lose interest in the way the race used to be run, so this should make a good change."

Floyd Landis, leader of team Phonak, seemed less certain. "I can't believe they made me shave off my goatee," he said. "This makeup artist said it just 'doesn't work.' I don't get it."

Levi Leipheimer was not available for comment; his publicist said he was being fitted with a hairpiece, to make him more appealing to the highly-sought-after pre-teen demographic.

CHECK YOUR LOCAL LISTINGS

"The Race" premieres tomorrow on NBC at 7:00PM. OLN, which previously had the rights to broadcast the Tour de France in the U.S., will play non-stop rodeo in its place.

SPORT-CLASS MTB RACER
ANNOUNCES PITY FOR ULLRICH

This story, originally published at Cyclingnews.com (and republished with permission here), came straight from a conversation I had with an unknown cyclist I caught up with while mountain biking.

As we were riding along, this guy pedalling at his absolute limit to stay with me, he was telling me about how bad he felt for Jan Ullrich, condescendingly describing how bad it must feel to always lose to Armstrong.

It was so bizarre, and yet, surprisingly typical. I thought to myself, "This would make a great press release."

SANDPOINT, IDAHO, USA (FAT CYCLIST FAKE NEWS SERVICE) — Rick Sunderlage,[10] a mid-pack mountain bike racer, announced today that he feels sorry for Jan Ullrich.

"Can you believe that poor sap's luck?" Sunderlage asked rhetorically about the Tour de France champion and six-time Tour de France podium finisher. "He must cry himself to sleep every night, wishing Armstrong had never got back into the game."

Continued Sunderlage, whose personal best was ninth in his age group (23rd overall) in a regional mountain bike race, about the former German National Champion and Vuelta a España winner: "I wonder why he even bothers trying."

"Look, I'm not saying Ullrich's a bad rider, per se," gasped Sunderlage as he shifted into the lowest gear on his mountain bike. "Just that he never reached his potential as a racer because he doesn't have the discipline." Dismounting to push his bike up the rest of the hill, Sunderlage went on, "Have you ever seen how he packs on the weight during the off-season?"[11]

Reached for reaction to Sunderlage's bombshell announcement, Tour de Suisse winner and Olympic gold medalist Jan Ullrich said, "I

---

10   No, not really the *real* Rick Sunderlage (not his real name). I just like to use my friends' names in my fake news pieces.

11   Let it be known that of all the pro riders there have ever been, I identify with Ullrich more closely than any other rider.

am of course very saddened to know that in spite of my best efforts, I have not been able to earn Rick Sunderlage's respect and I am stricken by the knowledge that I have his pity. His approval means everything to me. I swear to you now, Rick Sunderlage: I will do whatever it takes to be the racer you think I should be."[12]

Upon hearing of Ullrich's pledge, Sunderlage responded, "Yeah, I guess that's cool. But I'm still rooting for Basso in next year's Tour."

---

12   Wouldn't it be strange if pro cyclists really did take armchair critics' advice to heart? Oooh, I believe I just had an idea for a new post.

OLN TO BROADCAST VUELTA A ESPAÑA TO U.S. AUDIENCE...WITH A FEW SMALL CHANGES

(Reprinted courtesy of the good folks at Cyclingnews, which is where this piece was originally published.)

I am not ashamed to admit that I, like a lot of cyclists, first got interested in watching the Tour de France when Lance Armstrong first started winning it. That said, in my case at least, this timing was coincidental. I just happened to get interested in pro cycling the same year that Armstrong came back to the Tour.

I do not think that OLN's (now Versus) interest in cycling was quite as coincidental. And I know for sure that Al Trautwig — who, for the first couple of years OLN broadcast the race, sat opposite Bob Roll in the color commentary role — knew exactly two things about pro cycling: the name "Lance Armstrong" and the race called the "Tour de France."

So, this story is about how OLN would cope with broadcasting a different race. One not in France and without Lance in it.

And don't try to tell me they didn't at least consider some of the ideas mentioned below.

MADRID, AUGUST 26 (FAT CYCLIST FAKE NEWS SERVICE) — On the eve of the beginning of the Vuelta a España,[13] Outdoor Life Network (OLN) today stunned and delighted American cycling enthusiasts by announcing that it would provide live coverage of the final grand tour of the season...although with some unexpected twists.

"In recent weeks, some have said that OLN is only interested in professional cycling for three weeks a year, and that it is interested in one cyclist only — Lance Armstrong," said commentator/OLN spokesmodel Al Trautwig. "Today we silence these critics."

"That said," continued Trautwig, "OLN is a business and we have sponsors to satisfy. Plus, as you've no doubt noticed if you've watched our Tour coverage to date, we don't actually believe that the average

---

13 It took me, like, twenty minutes to figure out how to put a tilde over the "n" when I wrote this piece. After which, for other instances of needing that letter, I simply copied and pasted.

American is any more intelligent than a bar of soap. To please our viewing audience, we have customized our broadcast plans."

WHAT'S IN A NAME?

"First of all," said Trautwig, "We don't think the name 'Vuelta a España' really resonates with TV watchers. I know I've never heard of it. We've tweaked the name to be just a smidgen catchier: 'Cyclism[14] III: Tour de France: Spanish Edition (TdF:SE).' Trust me, people are going to love it."

ADDRESSING THE "ARMSTRONG FACTOR"

Many cycling enthusiasts in the U.S. have contended for several years that OLN focuses too heavily on Lance Armstrong; some have even gone so far as to say that OLN could stand for "Only Lance Network." Confronted with this accusation, Trautwig shrugged. "Look, I'm sure there are other riders out there. Maybe someday I'll even learn some of their names.[15] But one thing I do know is that people recognize the name 'Armstrong.'

"And that's why I'm pleased to announce today," said Trautwig, "that while Lance Armstrong may not be actually riding the TdF:SE, he will be very much a part of our race broadcast."

Here the OLN spokesman paused for dramatic effect, then said, "I'm very pleased to announce that OLN has arranged for the Discovery Channel team to borrow the T-Mobile Pro Women Team member Kristin *Armstrong*[16] as their race leader for the TdF:SE. We've stipulated in Phil Liggett and Paul Sherwen's contracts that they are to reference "Armstrong" frequently, and make it sound like she's winning."

"Um," said Trautwig, momentarily flustered, "But they're never supposed to say 'she.' It kind of destroys the illusion. Sorry I let that slip."

"But I'm just getting started," said Trautwig, getting back into the spirit of the announcement. "We'll also be mixing footage of Lance Armstrong from this year's Tour de France with footage from the current stage of the TdF:SE. Unless you're paying very close attention

---

14 For a while, OLN actually called their Tour de France coverage "Cyclism." Which is a play on the words "cycling" and "cataclysm," I think. I am pretty sure they were hoping this word would give pro racing extra drama. Yeah.

15 I'm pretty sure he never did.

16 I wonder how many times in her life Kristin Armstrong has had to say, "No relation." I'll bet more than two.

— and we're betting most people aren't — you'll never even know that Lance isn't there!"

"Finally, I'm pleased to announce that I've brokered a deal with OLN to allow me more freedom in my commentary. I think audiences will really enjoy hearing my colorful baseball and football anecdotes, and how they relate to biking." Trautwig chuckled. "This is going to be the best Tour de France ever."

Trautwig paused, then said, "I mean, of course, Tour de France: Spanish Edition."

TYLER HAMILTON DEFENSE STRATEGY LEAKED!

(This piece was originally published in Cyclingnews, and is reprinted by permission. Thanks, Cyclingnews!)

I am pretty sure that for many years, there was no bigger Tyler Hamilton fan in the world than myself. I mean, I subscribed to VeloNews for no other reason than to read his "Tyler Tunes" column.

My theory was that he was a victim of bad luck. Terrible luck. And anyone who has ever watched The Brady Bunch *knows exactly where bad luck comes from.*

As to those of you who have never seen the episode I'm referencing, this piece isn't going to make much sense at all.

I apologize.

LAUSANNE, SWITZERLAND (FAT CYCLIST FAKE NEWS SERVICE) — As Tyler Hamilton began his final appeal regarding doping allegations that surfaced almost exactly a year ago, sources close to Hamilton's legal team have leaked his startling defense strategy. "Tyler Hamilton will present strong evidence that this entire blood doping scandal was definitely not caused by Hamilton receiving blood transfusions," said a member of Hamilton's defense team, on condition of anonymity.

"Instead, we will demonstrate that a cursed tiki charm caused these false positives to surface." Continued the source, "Indeed, we will show that it is the exact same tiki charm shown in *The Brady Bunch*, episodes 73–75. We will prove beyond a shadow of a doubt that Hamilton has been in possession of the exact same tiki necklace that caused Greg to wipe out on his surfboard and nearly drown, Peter to be attacked by a very scary spider, and many other dangerous, yet entertaining, incidents in the popular television show in 1972."[17]

---

17 I believe that this paragraph marks the first time I ever did any research for anything I have ever written. Specifically, I had to go and find which episodes of The Brady Bunch these events happened on. A three-parter! Wow.

THE PROBLEMS BEGIN

Pressed for details on how the case will work, the source went on. "It is no secret that Hamilton has been plagued by 'accidents' most of his professional career. What nobody has ever understood is *why*. The fact is, on a family vacation to Hawaii back in 1984, a teenage Tyler purchased what he thought was a harmless tiki charm from a suspicious-looking salesman in a ramshackle tourist shop."

"Since then," said the anonymous source ominously, "his troubles have never stopped dogging him."

TIKI TRAIL OF WOE

"Everyone knows that Tyler began his cycling career only after crashing out of competitive skiing," said this member of Tyler's inner circle. Then, holding up a grainy, highly-enlarged photograph of what looked to be a necklace on a flailing skier, he said, "As you can see, he was wearing the tiki charm when he had this fateful crash."

"Tyler made the same mistake Mr. Brady did regarding the dreaded tiki charm," said the source. "He believed that the charm was actually good luck and had saved him from more serious harm, rather than understanding the tiki caused the accident. Since then, the tiki charm has brought him nothing but trouble."

DEFENSE TALKING POINTS

When told that many athletes, not just Hamilton, have suffered career setbacks, our source smiled. "That is actually an integral part of our defense strategy. Consider the 2003 Tour de France, one of the most drama-filled races in modern history. The morning before Stage 1, Levi Leipheimer noticed Hamilton's tiki charm and asked to see it. Hamilton obliged, but then Leipheimer began a game of keep-away, with numerous racers tossing the charm back and forth before eventually returning it to Hamilton.

"As you no doubt have guessed," he continued, "Every person who touched the charm that day was involved in the crash. And you can see what Leipheimer got for his role in playing with the charm that way."[18] Our whistle-blower had a friend with him, who weighed in on

---

18   Leipheimer crashed out during the first week of the 2003 Tour de Fance. True fact — the first one in this book, I believe.

the point, saying, "On the day Beloki crashed out of the race, he was actually carrying the tiki charm. Knowing that the stage was important to Beloki, the always-friendly Hamilton had loaned the charm to him 'for luck.' Ironic, isn't it?"

"And the day Armstrong got his handlebar hung up on a kid's musette may be the most telling of all," he continued, his eyes wide, his voice low. "All Armstrong did to merit that stroke of bad luck was to brush up against Hamilton's charm on the start line that day."

"Since then," said the source in a hushed, trembling voice, "It's been one bad thing after another. Hamilton wrecked out of the 2004 Tour de France. His dog died. He won a gold medal in the Olympics, but somehow his blood tested positive for a substance I can promise you he did not ingest or inject. Then he tests positive in last year's Vuelta and suddenly he can race no more. At that point, he gave his charm to his teammate Santiago Perez to help give him luck. I don't think I need to tell you how that turned out."[19]

"I tell you, this tiki charm must be destroyed, so Hamilton can begin his career and life again," said our man on the money, his voice shaking with emotion. "Our legal team has top warlocks and sorcerers looking into how to either destroy the charm or otherwise de-curse-ify it."

HAMILTON REACTS

Tyler Hamilton, reached for comment on this legal strategy, rolled his eyes. "That's simply ridiculous," said Hamilton. "This charm is no more magic than the vial of salt I keep with me or the mystical water I drink before each race."

"In fact," continued the man from Marblehead, "I'll be carrying this charm with me during the entire proceedings. I think it'll bring me luck."[20]

---

19 Perez was suspended for two years after failing a test for homologous blood transfusion during the 2004 Vuelta. Isn't this story *educational*?

20 It did not.

PROFESSIONAL CYCLIST RETURNS CLEAN BLOOD SAMPLE!

After reading about yet another doping scandal, I asked myself, "Is there even one clean pro cyclist out there?" Then it occurred to me that it would be really funny if there was, in fact, exactly one clean cyclist. That would be big news.

There are a lot of names in this piece. Most of them are names of friends. I never asked them if they minded. I still haven't.

I wrote this piece for Cyclingnews, but they didn't want it. I don't blame them; doping's a serious issue and I was not being serious about it.

But I still think it's pretty funny.

ELK GROVE, INDIANA (FAT CYCLIST FAKE NEWS SERVICE) — The cycling world rejoiced today when WADA chief Dick Pound, in conjunction with Team Hoosier Directeur Sportif Stuart Talley,[21] announced that heretofore unknown semi-professional cyclist Rick Maddox[22] is, according to all currently available tests, clean.

"Rick Maddox is a bright beacon of hope to the world of professional cycling," said Pound. "If it is possible for a cyclist in a small, non-funded, semi-professional regional team in a farm town in the Midwest to be clean, can the day when we claim total victory over illicit performance-enhancing substances be far off?"

"I am both humbled and honored," added Mr. Talley, "to have Rick Maddox on our team. We believe that he has a great future as a non-doping cyclist and hope to help him continue to be the preeminent non-doper in the cycling world."

"I would like to make it clear," Talley continued, "that the fact that there is no possible way we could afford EPO has nothing to do with why Maddox is clean."

---

21   Stuart is the guy who took me on my first-ever mountain bike ride. It did not go well. You can read about that event in "How Not to Sell The Cycling Lifestyle" earlier in this book.

22   Rick Maddox is a friend of mine. As far as I know, he does not dope.

SCIENCE COMMUNITY WEIGHS IN

While it is still unclear to the general public how a professional cyclist is somehow not doping, scientists and nutritionists from around the globe have been dispatched to study Maddox. Asked what he thought of this phenomenon, Dr. Richard P. Kelly,[23] one of the world's foremost nutritionists, responded, "I have long believed that if one trained, ate, and rested properly, it would be — theoretically — possible to race as a professional cyclist without doping. Here, at last, we have proof."

Other scientists, however, remain skeptical. "Of course I am gladdened that Rick Maddox appears to not be doping," said International Screening Association (ISA) representative Sammakko Miyasaki. "This, however, does not constitute final proof that Maddox has definitively not been doping. We believe the safest course of action is to refer to Mr. Maddox as an 'alleged non-doper,' until we have developed additional tests over the course of the next five years, which we shall then run on his current blood, saliva, and urine samples." At that point, we believe we should be able to say, with 72% confidence, that Maddox either is or is not doping at this moment in time."

"Also," continued Miyasaki, "We're going to need a lock of his hair, a four-inch-square sample of his skin, and one of his kidneys for our tests. You know, just to be safe."

RACERS REACT

As one would expect, the tight-knit community of professional cyclists is abuzz with the news that one of their own is not doping.

As one would also expect, not a single one was willing to speak unless guaranteed anonymity.

"I am very, very happy for Mr. Maddox, of whom I have never heard before today," said one popular-but-currently-suspended professional cyclist, who, prior to his suspension, was well known for winning practically every stage he had ever raced in his professional career. "I wish him great success in the future as he races on the...the...excuse me, on what team did you say he races?"

A recently-retired racer, having raced a long and successful career without a single positive, also offered his congratulations to Maddox,

---

23   Richard Kelly is a good friend of mine from high school (Fruita Monument, in Colorado), and was also my roommate my freshman year of college.

but with a caution. "Don't assume that just because you're testing clean today means you're going to test clean tomorrow, OK buddy? Basically, don't count all your chickens 'til they hatch. And believe me, some of them chickens can take a good long time to hatch. As in *years*."

"Seriously, he tested clean?" asked a third racer, who is currently fighting 29 separate charges of doping. "For everything? Is that even statistically possible?"

"By the way," added this racer, as he sat glumly on the steps of the courthouse, where he will likely spend the rest of his adult life, hastily, "I'm clean, too."

HOW HE DID IT

As one would expect, the public and professional cyclists everywhere want to know how Maddox managed to test clean. "Well, mostly it's been easy, because as a racer outside the limelight, I can barely afford to keep my bike maintained, and the tips I get for waiting restaraunts don't exactly cover $800-per-syringe[24] designer drugs," admitted Maddox.

"Plus, one day I had an idea: what if I just race, and don't start doping?' I know that sounds naïve, but I figured I'd give it a shot. And, well, here I am."

"Also," continued Maddox, "I never take cold medicine, or any other medicine for that matter. And I don't eat cold cereal — have you seen the ingredients lists for that stuff? I wouldn't be surprised if something in those boxes registered on one of the eight or nine new tests they're coming out with every week.[25]

"Also, I stay away from soda. And processed cheese. And I don't use deodorant unless it's been approved by Johan Bruyneel himself.

"And, finally, I cycle my blood through a special chimera-removing dialysis machine on a thrice-weekly basis.

"You know, regular stuff like that."

---

24   I have no idea how much doping costs, really. Of course, that's what I would say if I *were* doping, too. However, if I were doping, I'd hope my racing results would be better than they are.

25   I wonder if Maddox also stays away from beef, too. Probably should.

FUTURE LOOKS BRIGHT

Reached for comment, incoming Tour de France Race Director Christian Prudhomme said, "I wish to personally congratulate Mr. Maddox, who will, by default, be declared the winner of the 2006 Tour de France in a special ceremony this July."

Continued Prudhomme, "This ceremony will last for the three weeks during which we would have otherwise held the race, if we could have found any other clean riders."[26]

---

26 Goodness, how jaded.

TEAM DAVITAMON-LOTTO ANNOUNCES IT WISHES IT WERE DEAD

When alert reader Nathan V. pointed me to photos of the 2006 Davitamon-Lotto team presentation, I felt like I had been given a gift. The awful outfits, combined with the pained expressions on the riders' faces told the whole story.

PARIS, FRANCE (FAT CYCLIST FAKE NEWS SERVICE) — The riders of Team Davitamon-Lotto took the occasion of their 2006 team presentation last week to formally announce that they all wish they were dead.[27]

"While at first, there was a split between some riders wishing we were dead and others wishing we had never been born, we agreed it was important that we act as a team on this issue," said star sprinter Robby McEwan, shown here.

"And so," continued McEwan, "I am both pleased and extraordinarily distraught to announce that my teammates and I all wish we were dead at this moment."

"Or," added teammate Chris Horner, "We might be satisfied with killing the people who designed, approved, produced, and forced us to wear these shirts."

TEAM PRESENTATION SHIRT DESCRIBED

The outfit Team Davitamon was forced to wear has numerous unusual features, including:

- Made of slinky white polyester
- Red and blue trim, including racing stripes down the side, along with blue cuffs
- A red interior collar and a stiff blue exterior collar
- Extraordinarily strange-looking white patch of material that goes over the right shoulder and traverses the chest, logoed

---

27   Seriously. These guys are top pros. They are athletes and have earned respect from anyone who understands cycling. So why not dress them up like clowns?

with, evidently, "Brustor." Note that this patch of material may be modeled after a hunter's shoulder pad, though this is unclear. Further note that Brustor does not get what it pays for, since the "s" in their logo is inevitably tucked neatly into the wearer's armpit.

- Three red straps holding the chest strap in place, each fastened with a snap at the end.
- Blue and black super-fat tie with a Davitamon logo and asymmetrical tip.
- A clip and chain, going from the chest strap to the super-fat tie, and terminating in a red disc which looks like it may have an LED function, or perhaps is a container with a cyanide tablet inside, just in case the mortification of wearing this getup becomes too much.

This shirt is by most counts, a horrible monstrosity. It would, however, be a suitable uniform for workers at a fast-food restaurant or performers in a circus.[28] Until now, nobody would have ever suspected that one could force top-tier professional cyclists — especially in a team that has one of the more conservative jersey designs in the peloton — to wear such a thing.

TEAM PRESENTATION SHIRT EXPLAINED

Davitamon, the primary sponsor of this team, is a vitamin company, and not, as one might gather from the shirts being worn by the team, a manufacturer of circus tents. A spokesperson for Davitamon described the genesis of these shirts as follows: "Well, we wanted something that really popped, something colorful, that really showed off our brand."[29]

When asked by a reporter why the team jersey would not accomplish this purpose, as well as help the public identify the riders during races this season, the spokesperson — who wished to remain anonymous, which is unusual for company spokespeople — said, "Oh. I wasn't aware

---

28   Or for a pet monkey, if you don't like the monkey very much.

29   I was trying to think of how someone could possibly come up with these shirts, and honestly, this was the most realistic scenario I could imagine.

they already had team shirts. I'm not really into motorcycles, you know."[30]

"Anyway," the spokesperson continued, "We just told this designer friend of mine that we needed something big and bright with the logos front and center, and maybe a little dressy, and that he should have fun with it. And as you can see, this is a very fun outfit. Isn't it fabulous?"

TEAM REACTION

Leon Van Bon, shown here, said that when he first saw the shirt-and-tie combination, he thought it was a joke. "I arrived at the presentation with my new bike kit, clean and ready to wear. And then this PR flack hands me this clown suit and tells me to put it on. I thought it was just a gag the others were pulling on me, until I looked around and saw the other riders' faces."

American racer Chris Horner was similarly displeased. "If anyone ever sees a picture of me in this outfit, I will never be able to show my face in the U.S. ever again *(photo shown here)*."

Team manager Marc Sergeant, who did not have to wear an absurd outfit, took the death wish of his entire team in stride. "Actually, they had banded together, saying they would not wear these shirts, until I told them they had to," said Sergeant.

"This goes to show," continued the team manager, "I can make these guys do anything I want. My power over them is absolute."

---

30 Have you ever noticed that hardly anyone associated with a company that sponsors a bike team even knows that the bike team exists? Have you ever wondered how, if the company itself isn't aware of the bike team, the company could possibly expect to have the bike team increase awareness of its brand?

PRO CYCLING TEAMS UNVEIL 2006 HAIR STRATEGY

(This piece originally written for and published in Cyclingnews.com, and is used with permission.)

I am not what you would call a fashion-conscious person. I wear, pretty much always, shorts and a t-shirt.

I'm pretty sure that this lack of a sense of style is pretty common with cyclists and for good reason: if you're going to take a long lunch and get out on a ride in the middle of the day, it's easier to change out of casual clothes than a nice business suit. Also, you don't feel so bad climbing back into those clothes afterward, all unshowered and gross.

This "keep it ridiculously simple" philosophy extends out to my hair, as well. Oh sure, part of the reason I shave my head is because I'm going bald anyway, but another part simply has to do with helmets: if you don't have hair, you never get helmet hair.

Most pro cyclists seem to have very short hair, and I'm guessing it's for that exact reason. And so, when I saw Jan Ullrich's photo in the 2006 T-Mobile team presentation, it kind of jumped out.

"Hey," I thought. "There must be a reason behind that hairstyle."

And of course, just wanting to look nice couldn't be it. That would be too simple. Right?

MALLORCA, JANUARY 22 (FAT CYCLIST FAKE NEWS SERVICE) — Cycling enthusiasts around the globe reacted extremely positively to the January 22 T-Mobile team presentation, wherein the 29 members of the men's team and ten members of the women's team were announced.

More importantly, however, T-Mobile also took this opportunity to reveal Jan Ullrich's new hairdo.

"This hairdo represents the significant investment we have made in Ullrich," said team manager Mario Kummer. "These curls have been scientifically designed to be loose enough to blow elegantly in the wind as he attacks on mountain climbs, but not so loose that they unravel under the intense pressure of a grueling time trial. They are long enough to look cool, but not so long that they will poke out of his helmet and look clownish. They have been demonstrated in wind-tunnel tests to be the most aerodynamic curls known to man."[31]

Continued Kummer, with evident pride: "His curly, highly-moussed locks clearly state, 'I am the team captain. You must ride in support of me and in support of my hair.' I only wish that we had thought of this hair before last year's Tour de France; perhaps we could have kept Vinokourov in check."

"You will note," the manager pointedly concluded, "that this year Andreas Klöden does not have such a hairdo."[32]

TEAM DISCOVERY CHANNEL REACTS

Johan Bruyneel, directeur sportif of Team Discovery Channel, lost no time in preparing his team's response to the new threat Ullrich poses. "Acknowledging the brilliance of Ullrich's new haircut," said Bruyneel from the Team Discovery Solvang camp, "I have tasked one of my most seasoned riders, Viatcheslav Ekimov, to counterattack with a new hair-style which I myself have designed.

"As you can see," said Bruyneel at a hastily-arranged press conference this past week, "Eki's hairstyle is still short up top and on the sides, so as to not interfere with his riding. In the back, however, his hair is considerably longer, and now nearly touches his shoulders. I firmly believe this haircut will effectively neutralize Ullrich."

Others however, are not so optimistic.

"It's a mullet," said Lance Armstrong, who remains actively involved with Team Discovery Channel operations. "Bruyneel has

---

31 I do not know if Kummer is a Swiss scientist, but I was imagining a very precise, formal Swiss scientist in a lab coat when I wrote Kummer's lines. If you would be so kind as to read his words aloud in a Swiss accent, I would appreciate it. And if you can't do a Swiss accent, just go with Austrian or German or something.

32 I believe this is the first time the word "hairdo" ever appeared in any article in any cycling publication.

sent Eki to chase down Jan with a freakin' *mullet*. No way is that going to be enough."

"I'm just glad that I'm retired," said a concerned-looking Armstrong, pensively running a hand through his (rather pedestrian) close-cropped hair. "I mean, I've always said that Ullrich was my greatest opponent. With that new hairstyle, well, I don't know." Armstrong paused for a moment, weighing his words. "To tell the truth, I don't think I could compete with that."

TOUR TEAMS SCRAMBLE

Reacting to the Ullrich hairdo bombshell, pro teams are now quickly putting their own 2006 hair strategies into action.

Team csc has announced its intention that all team members will grow the same haircut: a short, spiky style, with frosted tips. "We train as a team, we race as a team, and we will now style our hair as a team," said team manager Bjarne Riis.

Euskaltel-Euskadi is staying tight-lipped about its own Tour de France hair strategy, although rumours[33] gravitate around a new hair follicle specially-designed for the team. If these rumours[34] are to be believed, the Euskaltel-Euskadi team will be sporting hairdos up to 15% lighter and 10% more fashionable than comparable hairstyles.

Lampre-Caffita and Bianchi-Liquigas have each extended lavish offers to Mario Cipollini to come out of retirement. Regarding these offers, a spokesman for Cipollini said, "While Super Mario has not ridden his bike in several months, I can assure you that his hair is every bit as glorious as it has ever been. If he so chooses to come out of retirement, I can assure you that he will not disappoint."[35]

Phonak, in an act of desperation, has hogtied Floyd Landis and shaved off his goatee.[36] "Look, nobody has ever liked Floyd's goatee," said a source close to Phonak, on the condition of anonymity. "And now with that new look Ullrich's got, we were put in full-on damage-control

---

33   I used this spelling as a personal little joke to myself because the editor of Cyclingnews, John Stevenson, is British. I doubt he noticed my hilarious use of this quaint spelling.

34   Here's that spelling again. Ha ha!

35   When Cipollini briefly did come out of retirement to ride for Rock Racing, consensus is that his hair was the highlight of the team's existence.

36   Sadly, it has returned.

mode, man. That scruffy thing had to go."

Team Gerolsteiner is perhaps in the most desperate straits of all, as evidenced by this photograph:[37]

ULLRICH: READY TO RIDE

Ullrich himself has approached the subject of his new haircut with his usual modesty. "It is an honor for me to wear this very fashionable hairdo for T-Mobile, and I hope to do it justice with my riding. I believe that with training, focus, and the support of my team, my hair and I will emerge victorious in this year's Tour de France."

> COMMENT FROM AL MAVIVA
>
> I understand that Chris Carmichael has personally looked at Ekimov's hairstyle, and found that it is conducive to effectively managing one's efforts in the earlier stages of a race, whilst simultaneously preparing to rock out and then celebrate at the tail end of races. Carmichael and his crack team of 91 million elite CTS certified cycling coaches have boiled down this scientific study into a short maxim that everyday athletes can use and understand, which he restated on his pay-per-view website as "business in the front, party in the rear."

> COMMENT FROM ZED
>
> And here I thought Ullrich did it out of his intention to join N-Sync after retiring from cycling.

> COMMENT FROM SUSAN
>
> I think all you boys missed one important point. Ullrich's not only the most talented cyclist around, but he looks damn fine! Anyone man enough to admit you secretly covet those curls?

> COMMENT FROM UNKNOWN
>
> Leipheimer looks like he's hooking up with a Devo reunion.

37   I am happy to say that I have personally shown this photo to Levi Leipheimer. He reacted as well as could be expected.

NEWS FLASH! LEVI LEIPHEIMER "TOTALLY OK" WITH IVAN BASSO JOINING TEAM DISCOVERY

Lance had retired. I was just getting comfortable with the idea of Leipheimer being the guy for whom I cheered. And then: wham. Ivan Basso gets brought onto the team.

I thought about how Levi must have felt about this turn of events. How it must have felt like he had been bypassed for a pay bump and a nicer office. Suddenly I had a new piece of fake news to write.

AUSTIN, TEXAS (FAT CYCLIST FAKE NEWS SERVICE) — Top-tier professional road cyclist Levi Leipheimer is "totally OK" with Ivan Basso signing with Team Discovery, according to a company spokesperson.

"Levi is very excited about this development," said Johan Bruyneel, team director. "This is, after all, the team where Levi really launched his professional career as a domestique for Lance Armstrong. So of course, it's a very exciting prospect for him to return, years later, now as one of the top cyclists in the world and as a bona fide Grand Tour contender and team leader...and do exactly the same thing he did last time he was on this team."

"Oh, except now he'll be working for a different guy," clarified the directeur sportif. "So that's new, anyway. And, um, very exciting for Levi."

Asked to comment, Levi Leipheimer verified that he was, in fact, eager to move from de facto team leader to super domestique before he ever raced for Team Discovery. "Ivan Basso's a huge talent, you know, and I'm very happy to have him on the team," said Leipheimer. "I can hardly wait to fetch water bottles for him as he tries to get a double grand tour win."

"After all," continued the 34-year-old Leipheimer, "I'm still really in the early part of my career. I've got another three, maybe four years left in me.[38] Why *wouldn't* I be excited to put my own goals on hold in order to facilitate securing Basso a couple big wins? I mean, Basso really inspires me to work hard; I'm extra enthused to race for someone who may or may not have been doping, but refuses to take the steps that

---

38 It turns out he had more than a few years left in him.

would clear his name, if he's innocent."

Leipheimer paused for a moment, then continued, "Which, I'm sure, he is."[39]

NOT CONSIDERING A DIFFERENT TEAM

Asked whether he is considering leaving Team Discovery in order to go to a team that will make him the team leader he perhaps deserves to be, Leipheimer was quick to respond. "Yeah, you know what would happen if I did that? I'll tell you what would happen. Say I went to team CSC. I'll bet you anything that fifteen minutes later they'd hire Ullrich. And then they'd hire Landis, who I'm sure would magically be cleared all of a sudden."

"And Hamilton," finished Leipheimer. "They'd probably hire him, too."

NEW PERKS

Team Discovery, aware of the possibility that Leipheimer might experience some frustration at being replaced as the team's main GC racer before doing a single grand tour, has prepared a special set of incentives for the racer.

"We haven't forgotten Levi," said the Discovery spokesperson. "In exchange for the hard work he'll be doing on behalf of Ivan Basso, we're going to give him a number of very nice prizes. For example, we are giving him a signed 8x10 photograph of Lance Armstrong, which would sell for $80 or more on eBay.[40] We're letting him pick out any bike from the Trek catalog he'd like for his own use and we're giving it to him *at cost*. That represents significant savings!"

"I should clarify, perhaps," continued the spokesperson, "that this offer does not extend to the Lemond bike line."[41]

"Perhaps the most exciting perk, however," said the spokesperson, "is that Levi will get to *share a hotel room with Ivan Basso* when they're racing! Just think what valuable advice Levi will be able to collect from Ivan during their 'together time.'"

---

39   Wow, fake Levi seems really bitter here.
40   I believe I actually checked at the time to see how much signed photos of Lance were going for at the time. At the moment I'm writing this, an autographed 8x10 of Lance goes for $231. Inflation, I guess.
41   I'm really not sure where I was headed with this line.

Concluded the spokesperson, "Levi must consider himself very fortunate indeed."

NEWS FLASH! FLOYD LANDIS
DOPING CHARGES DISMISSED!

I was so certain that Floyd wasn't doping, I contributed to the Floyd Fairness Fund. And I bought his book, Positively False, *which, as it turns out, was more aptly named than any of us guessed.*

Still, at the time, I really thought he'd be vindicated. And so I tracked the total lack of progress on his case. Tirelessly. Endlessly.

And I asked myself, "What if this case is never resolved?"

Of course, now I kinda wish it hadn't been.

PARIS, SEPTEMBER 7, 2035 (FAT CYCLIST FUTURE NEWS SERVICE) — Floyd Landis, winner of the 2006 Tour de France, is free to race his bike again, with the advent of all charges being dismissed today.

Strangely, however, the charges were not dropped due to a unanimous — or even majority — vote by the selected CAS-AAA arbitration panel, but simply because all three of the arbitrators have now reached retirement age.

USADA would normally have the right to select new panelists in this event, allowing the arbitration to continue into its 29th year. However, two circumstances have prevented this from happening:

- USADA **has not existed for more than twenty years**, since the momentous day in 2014 when they, along with WADA and UCI, admitted they had no idea what they were doing and were going to close up shop, leaving Dr. Dan Richardson[42] to handle all legal cycling matters from that point forward.
- **Nobody else now wants to take up the arbitration.** In fact, very few people even remember what the case was about.[43]

Said Dr. Richardson, "I'm happy to welcome Mr. Landis back into the professional cycling peloton. Also, I should probably apologize to

---

42   Dan Richardson is the name of one of the people who actively commented on my blog as "BotchedExperiment." Botched had some very well-formed opinions on the subject of doping, so I figured that in my hypothetical future, he would be in charge of this matter.

43   I'm pretty sure it was because Floyd spalmed with testosterone. Right?

Floyd for not having dismissed his case sooner. The thing is, though, I've been really busy...um...for the last thirty years."[44]

HISTORY

Shortly after winning the Tour de France, Floyd Landis fell under suspicion for testosterone doping. He immediately challenged this accusation and the arbitration panel, having heard the evidence, retired (i.e., they went into a sequestered room, as opposed to *actually* retiring, which is what they have done today) in early 2007 to consider the evidence at hand.

They have been, evidently, considering it ever since.

Most people thought that a month or so would be enough time to sift through the testimonies and render a verdict. Practically everyone thought a quarter of a year would be plenty. Virtually nobody thought that the arbitration panel would make it their life's work and then retire without having yet come to a conclusion.

In 2009, suspecting the worst, Floyd Landis had himself cryogenically frozen, with the instructions that he was to be thawed "when and if those guys ever make up their minds."

Wakened today, Mr. Landis was heard to remark, "Holy crap, my hip is *cold*!" Then, hearing the news, Landis wryly responded, "Well, that figures," and then got on his bike, evidently preparing for what would certainly be a remarkable comeback.

NEW CHALLENGES AWAIT

Landis has his work cut out for him if he hopes to win the 2036 Tour de France. He will, of course, have to race against the 21 clones of President Lance Armstrong (teams are limited to one clone per team), not to mention the Trek Synthuman/Madone hybrids, the integrated bicycle/purpose-specific lifeforms engineered to spin a cadence of 480RPM at a wattage of 912. For three months straight. Without need for sleep or food.

"Whatever," commented Landis.[45]

44　This was a friendly little jab at Dan, because in real life he tends to procrastinate a bit.

45　You've got to admit: that is probably what he would actually say.

THE CYCLING WORLD REACTS

Noted cycling authority Al Trautwig remarked on this occasion, "Lance Armstrong! Lance! Seventeen time Tour de France champion! President of the United States and King of Texas!" This was not remarkable, because this is all Al Trautwig has said for eight years. In Trautwig's defense, he does say it with enthusiasm and a deep, resonant voice.[46]

Phil Liggett and Paul Sherwen, each looking great considering how old they are, took the occasion to note that they knew Mr. Landis was innocent right from the beginning. Nobody dares contradict them, for fear of being called "youngster," then being forced to listen to more than a combined 120-years worth of cycling stories and history.

Dave Zabriskie said something, but it was practically impossible to understand. One is tempted to put this down to old age, but the truth is, Zabriskie's *always* been practically impossible to understand.

Elden "Fatty" Nelson, most beloved cycling blogger in the world and four-time Grammy winner,[47] commented, "This is extremely strange, because 28 years ago, I predicted this *exact thing* would happen."

COMMENT FROM CLYDESTEVE

All fairly believable, except that the Kingdom of Texas has never admitted that they have a king.

COMMENT FROM BYRDBTH

Have you ever noticed how Dave Z. does not move his mouth when he talks, I would love to figure out how to do that.

COMMENT FROM AL MAVIVA

Hey, you left out the part where Tyler Hamilton protested Floyd's results.

---

46   By 2036, I expect I shall be done with busting Al Trautwig's chops, by the way.

47   In twenty years, it will be possible to have a beautiful singing voice surgically implanted. When this happens, I will be a lock for a singing career. In spite of the fact that I will be 65 years old.

ULLRICH BIKES "DISAPPOINTED, BAFFLED" BY LACKLUSTER FIRST-YEAR SALES

If there's ever been a more unfortunate time to launch a bicycle line, it would be a couple months before you are fired from your cycling team, a few months after which you "retire."

Someday, Jan Ullrich will catch a break. Someday.

Meanwhile, consider how difficult it would be to avoid talking about the elephant in the room at the shareholders' meeting on the first anniversary of the launch of the Jan Ullrich bike line.

But I guess it would be easier if, somehow, magically, your shareholders were totally unaware of what had happened during the past year.

KARLSRUHE, GERMANY (FAT CYCLIST FAKE NEWS SERVICE) — Reporting to anxious investors at the first annual shareholders' meeting for Jan Ullrich Bicycles, LLC, Tobias Steinhauser, co-developer of the Jan Ullrich signature bike line, looked worried.

"I do not want to beat around the bush," said Steinhauser. "I am sad to say that the first-year earnings of our bicycle company have not been as brisk as we would have liked. We have picked up very little market share and, as of this moment, our sales are actually declining precipitously."

Almost as if choreographed, several hands simultaneously shot into the air.

"Why is this so?" asked one dignified-looking gentleman. "Didn't you get press in *Cyclingnews* for the launch of this bike line?"

"Yes, yes we did. And the bikes were received extremely positively," said Steinhauser, staring hard at the podium.

"Did you not tell us last year," piped in a woman in a sensible business suit, "that you would be launching the Jan Ullrich bicycle line just before the Tour de France, when interest in Ullrich would be very high?"

"Yes, we did that too, just as we promised," said Steinhauser, squirming slightly.

"Well, isn't Jan a winner of the Tour de France?" asked a lad of no more than eleven, wearing cycling knickers[48] and a junior-league cycling jersey.

"Of course he is, and he has taken second many times as well. There is no more famous cyclist in all of Germany," replied Steinhauser, reddening a little.

"Well," said several shareholders, in unison,[49] "Why is the Jan Ullrich bicycle line doing so poorly?"

"I don't know," said Steinhauser, dejectedly. "I just don't get it."

NO EASY ANSWERS

Interviewed after the devastating investor meeting, Steinhauser tried to make his case for the Jan Ullrich bicycle line.

"These are handmade Italian bicycles. They are beautiful to look at, lighter than air, and designed with the input of one of the winningest, most experienced pro cyclists in the history of the sport. I honestly cannot understand why anyone would *not* want to ride a Jan Ullrich bike."

Asked for an explanation of why, from his perspective, so few bikes have been sold since they have been made available to the public, Steinhauser seemed puzzled. "That's exactly the question I have been asking myself, endlessly. You have no idea how much sleep I have lost over that precise question.

"Did we overprice the frames? Our focus groups say that for a bike of this quality, we did not.

"Do we not have enough name recognition? That is ridiculous; everyone knows who Jan is — that's one of the reasons we went with his name on the bikes.

"Maybe we should have offered complete bicycles instead of just the frame/fork combination," mused Steinhauser. "That's really the only thing I can think of."

Trying to stay upbeat, Steinhauser went on, "Well, that's all water under the bridge. We'll learn from our mistakes, and redouble our marketing and PR efforts."

---

48   Knickers is a funny word. Only slightly-less funny than "potato." If you can somehow find a way to get the word "knickers" and "potato" into the same sentence, that sentence is guaranteed to be very funny.

49   Has a large group of people ever spontaneously said *anything* in unison? Because that would be *weird*.

Concluded Steinhauser, "Hopefully this next year will be a better one for Jan Ullrich Bicycles."[50]

COMMENT FROM AL MAVIVA

Yeah, they're fine freakin' bicycles.

The only problem is, to ride the dang thing, you have to take all the old air out of the tires, capture it in plastic bags, store it in a refrigerator in Spain overseen by a high priced Spanish physician with a Bermuda Med T-shirt, who will then purify the air and fortify it with O3 molecules, leave the tires flat and flabby all winter, then pump up the tires with somebody else's pump, then re-insert the air you took out of the tires six months earlier a couple days before your first race. Then she's ready to ride.

You can see why the bike is having sales problems. People would buy it if they didn't know about the elaborate draining/bagging/storage/replacement procedure, even if they suspected there might be more to the bike than meets the eye.

But once they actually *know* how the bike operates, it just seems sort of... well... dopey.

(ANOTHER) COMMENT FROM AL MAVIVA

Personally, I'm riding a brand new Basso. It has no wheels, no handlebars, no brakes, a straight pipe for a saddle, and in the end it is likely to leave me badly hurt. But it is good riding in the meantime, especially through the rough patches, since it relies on a new form of passive shock absorption similar to Zertz inserts, called Suspended Disbelief. As long as the Suspended Disbelief holds up, the Basso is sittin' pretty. And yes, the Basso rides pretty darned well. We're just not sure how durable it's going to be, is all.

Yep, the Basso may be sketchy, but it sure beats the Hamiltonian. *That* thing just lies there.

COMMENT FROM EUFEMIANO FUENTES

Al, I am really not that high-priced. Ask around and compare prices.

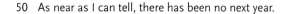

50   As near as I can tell, there has been no next year.

8.

Practical Guidance from an Expert

HERE ARE A COUPLE OF INTERESTING AND IMPRESSIVE FACTS FOR YOU:

1. I have been a cyclist for about eighteen years. By that, I mean that riding a bike is pretty much my one and only hobby.
2. During this eighteen years, I have totally failed to learn all of the following:
   - Fix a chain when it breaks in the middle of a ride
   - Repair a derailleur
   - True a wheel
   - Adjust brakes properly
   - Keep my drivetrain reasonably clean
   - Ride a wheelie
   - Drop a ledge

In short, the only thing I know about riding is how to turn the cranks over. You may want to bear that in mind as you read this section.

A PASSING SCORE

(This piece was originally published in BikeRadar.com and is reprinted without permission. Except the "without" part, though.)

The idea for this story came to me in two parts.

One day, I was riding up toward Suncrest, Utah from my house in nearby Alpine. Far ahead, I saw another rider. I killed myself trying to pass that rider for the next two miles, in spite of the fact that the other rider almost certainly did not know we were racing.

Finally, as I triumphantly passed, I saw that my "rabbit" was a teenage kid, riding a road bike with flat pedals.

Pffff.

Another time, on the same road, I was riding my bike to work. I saw another rider riding behind me. I tried to hold him off, but eventually he caught and passed me. At which point I engaged him in conversation, ensuring that he knew my messenger bag had a full change of clothes and a very, very heavy computer in it, denying him the thrill of victory, if I could help it.

At this point, a brilliant thing occurred to me: there needs to be a standardized rating system to measure exactly how much chest thumping a given pass entitles you to.

It doesn't matter whether it's during a race or a recovery ride.[1] As cyclists, we simply can't help ourselves. Every time we get near another rider, we must chase them down. And any time we pass another rider, it's a victory.

Just how *much* of a victory, however, depends on a number of factors. Fortunately for you, I have created an objective and thoroughly scientific method for determining the value of each cyclist you pass.

The objective of assessing your passing score for each ride is simple: get as many points as you can on any given ride. Equally simple are the basics: each time you pass a rider, you get to add one point to your score.

Of course, it would be ridiculous for you to get the same credit for passing a four-year-old on training wheels as a semi-pro in a time trial tuck. That's why you must apply the following score adjustments.

---

1   I'm speaking about recovery rides in a purely hypothetical sense. I don't believe I have ever successfully gotten on my bike and then ridden in recovery mode. I tend, instead, to recover by not riding. Oh, and also by eating nachos.

And, of course, you must apply these same adjustments *in reverse* whenever you are passed, subtracting points based on these same factors. Hey, that's only fair.

Let's begin, shall we?

BIKE FACTORS

Every cyclist I've ever met is confused by the title of Lance Armstrong's first book, *It's Not About the Bike.* "Well, what else could it possibly be about?" we ask. We're not being argumentative; we simply just never think about anything else. Naturally, then, the bike your opponent — that is, the person you're passing — rides is a crucial factor in your score.

Expensive Bike: If the person you're passing has a bike that costs more than 50% more than your bike, give yourself an extra point. If the bike costs more than double your bike's cost, give yourself two points.[2] Regardless, be certain to comment on what a nice bike the person you're passing has. There's nothing quite so satisfying as a backhanded compliment.

Misidentified Bike: If you've pushed yourself as never before to catch a cyclist on the road, thinking how awesomely fast you're going to appear as you blow by, only to discover that the person you're passing is on a mountain bike or a hybrid with frame material that can best be described as "rebar," subtract a point from your score.[3]

Silly Bike: If you pass a recumbent, add ten points to your score, as long as you are going at least six miles per hour faster than he. Be sure to snort in derision[4] as you go by.

LEGS

It's very nearly creepy how carefully cyclists study one another's legs. I of course exclude myself from this assessment of creepiness, because I never evaluate other cyclists' legs, knowing that mine are bound to be far more awesome. That said, your passing score relies heavily on the attributes of your opponents' legs.

---

2   And if the bike is so nice that there's no possible way that the person riding it actually bought it, but is instead a sponsored rider, give yourself three points.

3   And if the bike is a brand that can be procured at a big-box store, subtract two additional points.

4   Or say, "Nice beard."

Hair: If the person you pass has shaved legs, give yourself two extra points. If he has shaved legs and you do *not,* give yourself *four* extra points, because he's going to eat his heart out when he sees that he just got passed by what appears to be a Fred.

Rookie Mark: If your victim has a chainring mark on his right calf, subtract a point from your score. If he has a chainring mark on his *left* calf, add two points to your score, but only if you can find out how he managed that trick.

Tattoos: If the person you pass has a bike-related tattoo on one or more of his calves, add ten points to your score.[5] You have just defeated someone who identifies so closely with cycling that he is advertising it permanently. Say "Nice tattoo," as you go by. You may also want to add, "What is it, exactly?"

CLOTHING

This one's tricky. The truth is, many riders will wear a jersey in support of their favorite rider or team and that doesn't mean anything. Thus, to assess how many points to give yourself for what the cyclist you're passing is wearing, you must look at the full package.

Full Kit: By this, I mean *everything* matches: helmet, shorts, jersey, socks, gloves. If he's outfitted like a full-on pro, give yourself seven points. If it turns out that he *is* a full-on pro, give yourself ten points, unless you stop him and ask for his autograph. In which case you must reset your score back to zero and give up biking forever, because you are shameless.

Club Kit: If he's wearing just the jersey or just the shorts, no point adjustment is made. If wearing both, you should give yourself two points. If the club kit is ridiculously ugly, give yourself three points. This is a judgment call, but I think I can trust you on this. Unless you're one of those people who design really ugly club kits. If you've designed a jersey that is regarded as ugly even by *your club,* you must start every ride for the rest of your life with a score of –10. You brought it on yourself man.[6]

---

5   If the person you pass has an Ironman tattoo, give yourself an extra six points, but also be sure to pass wide, because the person you're passing is likely to swerve wildly, due to the fact that triathletes...swerve wildly.

6   Here I'm not referring to a specific person, so if you think I'm referring to you, Mr. I-Designed-An-Ugly-Jersey, you just need to calm down.

WHAT THEY SAY

There's a fair chance that the guy you pass will say something as you go by. This tells you something about how deep the wound has gone or, in other words, how complete your victory is.

Greeting: A simple "hello" or "how's it going?" means nothing. Your score does not change.

Congratulations: A "Hey, nice climbing" or "Keep it up" means that they unfortunately bear you no ill will.[7] Subtract a point from your score.

Excuses: This is the holy grail of passing someone. They are so deeply humiliated by your passing them that they want a chance to explain themselves, usually by saying something about being at the tail end of an all-day ride or being told by their coach they must keep their heart rate under 80. When this happens, smile knowingly as you go by, then double your score because I guarantee the person you just passed will be able to think of nothing else for the next 72 hours.

OTHER FACTORS

There are a few other miscellaneous factors that affect your passing score. Be certain to make a careful note of each of them.

Gender Misidentification: If you think you're passing a man and it turns out to be a woman, subtract two points. If you think you're passing a woman and it turns out to be a man, add three points. Why the inequality? It is not for you to question.[8]

Knee In Gut: If the other guy's knees squash into his gut on the upstroke of his pedaling, you get no points for passing him. Unless your knees squash into your gut, too, in which case you get an extra three points.

Re-Pass: If, after passing the other guy, he makes a superhuman effort and passes you again, give yourself an extra two points. This may seem counter intuitive, but this kind of re-passing is your victim's way of admitting that you have cut him and cut him deep.[9]

No-Pass: If it turns out that the other guy really *was* just spinning

---

7   Or, worse, weren't aware that you existed until this moment and therefore weren't trying to fend you off.

8   And also, I'm afraid of women punching me.

9   If, however, you totally let off the gas after passing that person so that he just cruises right by you, subtract five points.

along and is now happy to ride at your pace and chat, and seems capable of riding at your pace and chatting even though you are at your absolute upper limit, and continues doing so until you explode and collapse in a quivering mass on the road, set your score back to –25, for you have just been totally creamed.[10]

FINAL RESULTS

After each ride, be certain to tally your score and then evaluate yourself on the following scale:

50+ points: You are the stage winner. Puff out your chest. Add this score to your race resume, for it is a magnificent accomplishment.

20–49 points: Not a bad ride, but you may want to exaggerate your score when comparing with your friends. Since there's no way for them to disprove your score, you should feel confident in your "exaggeration." Hey, you think your friends aren't "augmenting" their scores, too?

Fewer than 20 points: You may want to consider changing your training route, so as to encounter different riders. After all, it isn't how you play the game, it's whether you win or lose.

---

10   Originally, I used the word "pwned." I believe this was due to a misguided attempt to appear current with the (teh?) lingo kids use now.

STRANGER IN A STRANGE BIKE SHOP

The thing I like about going to Racer's Cycle Service — my long-time favorite local bike shop — is that I don't have to explain anything at all to Racer. He knows that I love bikes, but tend to keep technical details, like how anything works, at all, at arm's length. Racer knows I like to ride the good stuff and he doesn't tease me about the fact that I don't know anything at all about how bikes work.

But when I go into other bike shops, I have a problem. Specifically, I have to either pretend to be a novice who knows nothing about bikes or pretend to be an expert who knows everything about bikes.

When, in fact, I'm a little bit of both.

So this piece is really just a plea for the rest of the bike shops in the world to treat me like Racer does.

As you are no doubt aware, I am a famous and beloved figure in the cycling community. I am regarded as both insightful and witty. Knowledgeable and self-deprecating. Gruff yet tender. Well-known yet easily accessible. And very, very prolific.

In short, I am the cyclist everyone remembers Bob Roll as being, back before he was primarily known for babysitting Al Trautwig through the Tour de France and (hilariously!) mispronouncing the name of this race, in the name of never ever ever burying a very old hatchet.[11]

As such, I am comfortable in practically any bike-related situation. I am happy to join a group ride even if I don't know anyone; I know I will either hang and find someone with something interesting to say or I will get dropped and turn on my iPod. Both outcomes are very nice.

I am comfortable meeting strangers on the road and trail. After all, we're doing the exact same thing at the same place at the same time, so we must have other stuff in common.

I am comfortable giving directions to cyclists, both on the road and off, though I am generally quite certain that my directions are wrong.[12]

---

11   The big difference between Bob Roll and me is that he knows what he's talking about. And he's on TV. And he used to be a professional cyclist.

12   Unfortunately, this part is not a joke. I have given what I know are faulty directions dozens of times in my life.

I figure that, even though I am probably giving people directions to a place other than where they want to go, once they arrive at the place to which I have directed them, they will be glad of the journey. Plus, there's relatively little chance I'll ever run into them.[13]

I am *not*, however, comfortable going into a bike shop where nobody knows who I am. I *hate* going into foreign shops. And by "foreign shops," I don't mean "shops in a foreign land." I mean "any shop besides the one where I don't have to tell them how to set up my brakes or what height to set my saddle, because they already know."

I have my reasons.

ESTABLISHING CREDIBILITY WITHOUT COMING OFF AS A VAIN, BORING TURD

When I walk into a bike shop, I don't really need much. I just want to be revered as the famous and beloved cycling personality that I am.[14] Would it be too much, for example, for the senior staff to drop whatever they're doing, including helping other customers, and come attend to my needs? That question was rhetorical. You shouldn't feel compelled to answer it.

Also, a comfy chair and a back rub while I wait for my bike would be nice. And I wouldn't mind it if someone would come up and honor me a little bit. You know, ask for an autograph, beg me to tell some of my favorite biking stories, that kind of thing.

Instead, for some reason, I think I give off a strange "I don't know anything at all about bikes" vibe to bike shop employees. Maybe it's my gut. Maybe it's the Dockers.[15] Maybe it's the male pattern baldness (yes, I shave my head, but you can still tell I have male pattern baldness). But they always act like I don't know *anything* about bikes.

When I moved to Washington a few years back, for example, there was a bike shop about a mile away from my home. I came in, figuring

---

13   So far, I have never re-encountered and been confronted by someone I have given bad directions to. Which means, perhaps, that my bad directions are really, *really* bad.

14   I have never actually gone into a bike shop and been recognized. Someday, perhaps I will be. When that happens, I hope some friends are with me, so I have proof that it really happened.

15   I wrote this back when I had to go to an office most days for my job. Now I tend to work in the nude. No, not really.

this was destined to be my home away from home.

Instead, when I said I wanted some advice on a good lube for riding in Washington, they gave me a look that was specially designed to make me feel like I was retarded.

Of course, I *wanted* to explain that I actually know quite a bit about bikes. That I've been riding for years and years and years. I am not just a guy who casually and occasionally rides, either. I ride all the time. I talk about bikes all the time. I'm the guy in the neighborhood to whom everyone asks their bike questions. I'm the bike shop's favorite kind of customer.

And I would have liked to explain this to them. But I just couldn't find an opening. For some reason, it's not easy to go into a bike shop and announce, "Hi, I'm a really experienced cyclist, so please accept me into the pack. You may, in fact, want to treat me as the alpha male."[16]

So I'm working on a couple introductions to make it clear that the next time I go into a strange bike shop, I'm really into cycling. Tell me what you think:

- **The Casually Hardcore Opening:** "Hi, how's it going?" (Wait for response.) "Oh, good. Hey, I was thinking of doing an easy century today and wanted to know if you had any route suggestions." (Wait for response.) "Oh, I'm sorry, I wasn't clear. I meant an easy *mountain bike century.* You know, something with no more than 14,000 feet of climbing."
- **The Know-it-All Opening:** "Hey, how's it going?" (Wait for response, but don't appear to pay attention.) "I see that, without needing to walk around or glance at any of the price tags, most of your bikes here are in the $400 to $1,200 range. Is that what your customers tend to want? (Don't wait for a response.) Where do they go to get their *second* bike, when they fall in love with riding and want something nicer than what you've got here?
- **The Put-Them-on-the-Defensive Opening:** "Hey, this is a cute shop. You got anyone here who isn't just doing this as his summer job?"

Some of these ideas are still works in progress and may have unintended consequences.

---

16   Or the pack equivalent of the court jester.

FREQUENT BUYER DISCOUNT, OR LACK THEREOF

When I go into my LBS,[17] I know that I'm going to get the best deal possible. Better than the best deal possible, even. If that's possible. Which, now that I think about it, it's not.

Anyway.

Here, nearly word-for-word, is the conversation I had with Racer when it was time to settle up and pay for my new Fillmore.[18] I'm not saying what the actual numbers were, because I have a feeling Racer's wife[19] would not approve.

Racer: "That will be $xxx."

Me: "What?"

Racer: "OK, I'll drop it by $50."

Me: "That's not what I meant. I don't mind if you make a little bit of profit when you sell me a bike, Racer."

Racer: "Whatever."

Me: "Charge me $100 above that price. That's the lowest I'd feel good about paying."

Racer: "I'll add $25."

Me: "$75."

Racer: "I'll add $50, but that's my final offer."

Me: "This has been a very weird transaction."

I don't expect this kind of discount from anywhere but my local bike shop, but I'm pretty sure that non-local bike shops (NLBS) make up for the discounts they give to their friends by overcharging interloper customers.

Last week, I'm pretty sure I paid $8 for a tube, for example.[20]

I FEEL OLD

I realize that bike shops tend to hire younger people. Kids work for cheap and they generally don't have to feed a family. But I swear that when I go into most bike shops, they are staffed by teenagers *exclusively*. Looking for a light setup for the Kokopelli Trail Race last year, I went into a shop

---

17 Local Bike Shop. Mine's Racer's Cycle Service. Tell them Fatty sent you.

18 The Lemond Filmore was an inexpensive, heavy singlespeed road bike. Eventually I gave mine away as part of a contest. I really miss that bike.

19 Hi, Maren!

20 I am not kidding.

near where I work and — I swear I am not making this up — the kid in the shop tried to get me to buy a couple of commuter lights.

He simply didn't have a point of reference for any kind of riding that didn't involve mad skillz on the halfpipe while wearing Vans and a BMX helmet.

I realize that I am 41. But please, bike shop owners who have never met me, have the courtesy to do the following:

- Have someone at the shop who is older than 20. Otherwise, I feel like I've somehow managed to stumble upon a boy scout troop.
- Forbid all your employees from ever calling anyone "sir." I don't know anyone who likes to be called "sir." I understand the military is considering no longer using the word "sir."
- Tell your employees that not everyone over 40 will necessarily want a hybrid, cruiser, or recumbent.[21]

THE SOLUTION

Of course, I wouldn't gripe and gripe and gripe if I didn't have a solution. What I'd like to propose is a universal LBS members card. This is not something for which you could apply, but when an LBS owner/manager feels you have become a truly loyal customer, she or he could issue you this card in a super-secret ceremony involving things like taking oaths, reciting slogans, and swearing to obey the law of the pack.[22]

Then, whenever you're at an NLBS, you could just show your card, therefore avoiding the posturing and hint-dropping. The card, in effect, would say, "This guy rides. Treat him/her like one of your own." And then the NLBS employees could relax, joke around with you, call you by your first name, and give you the good buddy discount.

Oh, also, there would be a super-secret-bonus version of the card that tells the NLBS that the carrier is a much-beloved cycling celebrity, and that, as such, a comfy chair and back rub may be in order.

---

21 Though I'd be interested in checking out what they have in hybrid recumbent cruisers.

22 My second boy scout reference in this piece. I don't know why.

COMMENT FROM AXEL

My technique is to start the shopping by asking for spokes. Spokes are perfect in that they are not expensive, they indicate that you take your bike seriously, and they are not available on a rack in the middle of the store, but back in the shop. Anyone who confidently orders three 235mm spokes will immediately be recognized as a serious rider and treated with the proper respect for the price of less than $2. If you are not in the mood to get more spokes, turn down the ones they have as 'low quality' and proceed with the rest of your shopping.

COMMENT FROM HELLKITTY

Try going into the LBS being a female. They NEVER take you seriously, no matter what.

COMMENT FROM DUG

I think I see your problem. You should never under any circumstances go into anything other than your LBS. It's very much like infidelity.

COMMENT FROM UTRACERDAD

The funny thing is that I was standing in the shop watching Racer build a particular Filmore when this particular situation took place and I do have to say that I have had the exact conversation as well.

TEST YOUR BIKE REPAIR IQ

This is one of those "based on a true story" kind of pieces, except it's not based on just one true story. It's based on about eighteen years' worth of true stories. Or possibly one story that's eighteen years long.

The truth is, me writing a quiz about bike repair is as ironic as...as....

Nope, I've got nothing. I'm trying to think of something as ironic as me writing something about repairing a bike, but I just can't.

This piece was originally (but not ironically) published in BikeRadar.com.

An important part of being a cyclist is knowing how to identify common mechanical troubles and knowing how they can be repaired, as well as how to give accurate information to bike mechanics, on the rare occasion you find one necessary. Take this handy quiz to help you identify how much you know about diagnosing and repairing common bike problems.

1. You hear a creak coming from somewhere in your bike. What should you do?

a. Immediately stop and call your bike mechanic. The bike is seriously damaged; any further riding will make the problem worse and almost certainly will cost thousands of dollars to repair.

b. Lubricate all moving parts with whatever lube is handy.[23] You are bound to get the correct one eventually, right?

c. Ignore it. The squeaking is caused by friction, so it stands to reason that eventually that the two things that are rubbing against each other and making that infernal racket will wear each other down, and the sound will go away, or at least subside.[24]

d. Turn up your iPod. Hey, the sound went away!

2. Whichever thing you did in question 1 didn't work. What do you do next?

a. Fix the bike yourself. You have tools and a bikestand, so you must be a mechanic.

b. Quickly admit defeat and meekly take your bike into the shop.[25]

---

23   Chain lube, motor oil, Vaseline, Pam, etc.
24   In my head, this logic is totally sound.
25   Yep, those are your only two options.

3. After you unwisely chose answer 'a' in question 2, your bike now squeaks louder, and the gears skip all the time.[26] What do you do?
　　a. Take the bike to the shop, but don't admit to having monkeyed with the bike yourself. Stare blankly at the mechanic when he asks you how the cassette got reversed.
　　b. Take the bike to the shop, and confess everything, sobbing pitifully; beg for mercy.
　　c. Take the bike to a different shop than you usually go to, and say, disgustedly, that the mechanic at the *other* bike shop totally screwed it up and you're hoping you can get better service here.

4. The bike mechanic asks you what the problem is. What do you say?
　　a. "It makes a 'skhreekh-skhrokh' sound when I pedal."
　　b. "Well, if I knew what the problem was, I'd be halfway done fixing it, wouldn't I?"
　　c. "Nothing. What's *your* problem, buddy?"

5. After somehow ascertaining that your bike makes a creaking noise, the bike mechanic asks *when* it makes the noise. How do you answer?
　　a. "When I ride it, stupid."
　　b. "When I'm pedaling. Or maybe it's just when I'm coasting. Or it might be when I'm pedaling, but only when I'm out of the saddle. One of those, for sure."[27]
　　c. "And sometimes it makes the sound when I hit a big bump or do a wheelie drop. But not always."
　　d. "When the moon is waxing gibbous."

6. Now the mechanic wants to know *where* the sound comes from. What is the proper thing to say?
　　a. "Either from the headset or from the bottom bracket."
　　b. "Either from the front or rear shock."
　　c. "Either from the pedals, chain, or wheels."
　　d. "You know, come to think of it, I think that sound may be coming from my right knee."

26　Even if you ride a singlespeed.
27　"I'm pretty sure it doesn't make the sound when I'm coasting and riding hands-free."

7. When you shift from the third to the fourth cog, the chain often grinds for a moment before making the switch. You do not have this problem shifting between other gears, and don't even have the problem shifting from the fourth to the third cog. What should you do?

a. Be grateful the drive train is working as well as it is. Bike drive trains are dark magic with which you should not tamper.

b. Turn the barrel adjuster on the left clockwise one half turn. No, wait, that just adjusted the front brake. OK, try turning the barrel adjuster on the right — yeah, that's the one — clockwise. Hmm. That didn't work. Maybe try a full turn. Nope, that made it worse. OK, let's try three full turns in the opposite direction. Hey, now it's shifting great! Except I no longer have access to my lowest gear and the chain skips the fourth cog altogether.[28]

c. This is an indicator that the rear derailleur is misaligned. Lay the bike on its side, find a good sized rock, and drop it on the derailleur from a height of four feet (2.1 kilometers).[29]

8. You're on a group ride, when *someone else's* chain breaks. What do you do?

a. Get out your chain tool and fix it, because you're the annoying guy in the group who has a tool for everything. As you fix the chain, make sure you deliver a nice, self-righteous lecture on why it's important to be prepared for every situation.

b. Keep riding. Chains don't just break. They break because you didn't replace them when you should have, or didn't lube them properly, or put too much stress on them. The other rider's neglect is not your problem.

c. Stand around and watch the annoying guy who has the chain tool, trying to learn how to use that chain tool you've carried around for two years, but have no idea how to use.[30]

9. After completely screwing up your drivetrain with your attempts to repair it, you take the bike into the bike shop mechanic. How do you

---

28   I have epoxied my barrel adjusters into one position, just to prevent me from being tempted to turn them.

29   I know. Four feet isn't really 2.1 Kilometers. It's actually 2.1 parsecs.

30   I have done this approximately plenty-six times.

explain the problem?

a. "I think the cables are stretched or something; it's not shifting right. Could you give it a once-over?"

b. "You know that really annoying know-it-all guy who brings that massive toolkit on every ride? He messed up my bike. Could you try to undo the damage?"

c. "Hey, I was just riding along and the shifting started going totally wonky. Did you let one of the junior mechanics touch my bike or something?"

10. **Your bike is fixed, but the mechanic took the liberty of using some new parts as part of the repair, then having the audacity to charge you for them. As a result, the bike repair cost $30 more than you expected. How should you react?**

a. Tip big, be glad you've got your bike back, and ride away.

b. Ask the mechanic to take care of a couple of other "little" things that just occurred to you on the spot, figuring you can slip them under the radar.

c. Complain. A lot. Try to wheedle the mechanic down. After all, those bike shops are just rolling in the dough. Tell yourself you would have tipped, if they hadn't charged you an arm and a leg.

d. Act surprised. "What? I didn't ask to have the bottom bracket replaced. I just wanted you to clean the drivetrain. Hey, I sure hope we're not going to have to get our legal teams involved in this."

ANSWER KEY

Use the following handy guide to determine whether you answered correctly:

If you think you got an answer right, you probably did.[31]

---

31 I originally planned on having a detailed answer key. Then I got lazy.

WHY I HATE THE SONG, "BIRDHOUSE IN YOUR SOUL"

Really, it should have been a dream race. A fun road rip with good friends. An awesome course. Hanging out afterward. The stuff of which great memories are made.

But for this particular event — The Laramie Range Enduro — my overarching memory is of one part of one song, playing endlessly in my head.

I still shudder in horror.

Some people listen to music while they ride. I never do.[32] When I'm on the bike, I like to hear what's going on around me, and I like to let my thoughts wander.

Mostly, this is fine. My mind bounces from one topic to the next, sometimes landing on a funny or interesting thought, or occasionally suddenly solving what I had previously thought was an unsolvable dilemma.[33]

Once in a while, though, my mind gets stuck on something. On the way in to work Friday, for example, I found myself — for no reason I can think of — mentally chanting the list of common linking verbs a teacher had taught my class back in fifth grade.[34]

I didn't want it in my head. I tried to get it out of my head. But it wouldn't leave. To make things worse, I couldn't remember the whole chant. Just that one part. So while part of me was trying to get the stupid thing out of my head, another part of me was trying to puzzle out how the rest of the chant went.[35]

Luckily, my ride to work isn't that long, and the chant is now out of my head. Or at least it was, until I started writing about it.

---

32   This is no longer true. Sometimes I do ride with an iPod now. And you know what? Nothing kills an earworm (see below) faster and deader than listening to an actual song.

33   For example, I've solved the "irresistible force vs. immovable object" paradox. And the "next statement is true: previous statement is false" problem. I'd explain them here, but I don't want this footnote to just go on and on endlessly.

34   Amisarewaswerebebeingbeen.

35   As explained to me in the comments section, these are called — at least by some people — "earworms." Which sounds gross, but appropriate.

SCAR TISSUE

Everyone gets songs (or, more rarely, chants about grammar) stuck in their head from time to time, but cyclists are especially prone to them. The rhythm of the cycling cadence, along with steady, fast breathing, lends itself to looping a song through your head, over and over.

It's not always bad. I remember that for one of the laps of 24 Hours of Moab one year, Red Hot Chili Pepper's "Scar Tissue" ran through my head continuously. Since *Californication* is in fact one of my favorite albums of all time, I was OK with this particular song auto-repeating in my brain. I even sang snippets of it out loud, causing concern among riders as they passed me or, much less often, were passed by me. I hit the words at the end of lines with an extra-hard exhale:

Soft spoken with a broken jaw
Step outside but not to brawl
Autumn's sweet we call it fall
I'll make it to the moon if I have to crawl

To tell the truth, I would have preferred "Parallel Universe," my favorite song from the album; it's got a bass line that forces a fast cadence.[36] But one of the rules of endless loop music seems to be that you don't get to pick the song.

Alas.

BIRDHOUSE IN YOUR SOUL

This repetitive song phenomenon is no big deal, usually. Sometime soon after the ride ends, the song fades and you get on with your life.

If you're on an endurance ride, though, an endless-loop song can become downright evil.

Several years ago, Dug, Racer, and I drove to Laramie, Wyoming for what would turn out to be the final Laramie Range Enduro (that was a good course, rest its soul).[37] As we parked the car and unloaded our bikes, They Might Be Giants' "Birdhouse in Your Soul" came on the radio. Not paying much attention to it, I finished unloading my bike and lined up at the start.

---

36 Flea, if by some chance you ever see this: Thank you for being a genius.

37 Much like a zombie, a race with the same name has risen from the grave, though — also much like a zombie, it no longer resembles what it once was. Which is to say, it's a different course. Although, from what I hear, it's still very cool (unlike zombies).

About twenty minutes into the first climb of the race, the song came back to me. The problem was, I didn't know the lyrics to anything but part of one verse and the chorus, and was even sort of sketchy on that. So I'm singing:

There's a something something of me
Of my primitive ancestry
Who stood on something and kept the something shipwreck free
Though I respect that a lot
I'd be fired if that were my job
After killing Jason off and countless screaming argonauts
Something something something
Something it's always near
Look at a canary over by the light switch
Who's watching over you
Build a little birdhouse in your soul
Not to put too fine a point on it
Say I'm the only bee in your bonnet
Build a little birdhouse in your soul
And while you're at it
Keep the nightlight on inside the
Birdhouse in your soul

Even taking the "something somethings" into account, I could tell I was getting it wrong; I couldn't get the words to fit the meter. And the more I sang it, the worse it got, until I could no longer be sure I was getting the lines even remotely close to the right order.

And still it played on in my head. For *five hours.*

After a while, I started looking for a suitable cliff off of which I could ride, so I could end that infernal song. I imagined the conversation other racers would have as they saw me go over:

Racer 1: That guy just rode straight off a cliff! On purpose!

Racer 2: Did you notice the insane grin on his face?

Racer 3: More importantly, why was he singing that "Birdhouse in Your Soul" song as he went over?

Racer 1: I don't know, but he was getting the lyrics all wrong.

I had a really fast time at that race, but took no pleasure in it. My dominant memory of that day is of that song, playing over and over and over.

And over.

I will hate that song forever.

IT GETS WORSE

As long as you don't have children, you can at least take comfort in the fact that it's your music that's getting stuck in your head. Once you have kids, though, it's a whole new ballgame. For example, my wife, in a fit of temporary insanity, purchased the animated video, "The Princess and the Pauper." That would be awful enough, but the DVD comes with a bonus soundtrack CD. Which, of course, the girls want to be played in the car CD player.

Always.

And since there are only seven songs on that CD, you get to hear each of them quite frequently.

So: if I ride my bike head-on into traffic someday in the near future, you know why: I was doing whatever it took to get "You're Just Like Me" out of my head.[38]

COMMENT FROM ALLAN

I did the entire Off-Road Assault on Mt. Mitchell with The Killers' *Somebody Told Me* going through my head. Unfortunately, I only knew the chorus. I had that 30–45 second loop of music going over and over for 8 hours. I almost threw that CD away after I finished.

COMMENT FROM BIG MIKE IN OZ

I often get *Another One Bites The Dust* by Queen going around in my head. Not comforting while riding on a busy road, not comforting riding anywhere, really. But not surprising since the permanent announcer at the biggest velodrome venue in our state thought he was a DJ. For about two years, whenever there was a fall he would crank out the chorus over the PA. I heard it a lot, and it often referred to me.

---

38 Shortly after I wrote this post, the "Princess and the Pauper" CD mysteriously disappeared. What a shame.

UNIVERSAL SIGNS

I am not a good driver. I admit this openly, to the amazement of people around me and to the terror of people who are just climbing into my car for the first time. I tend to get distracted. I have poor reaction time. My blind spot seems to include a much larger area of my vision than other people's blind spots.

So when I nearly cause traffic accidents, I wave and mouth "sorry" to whomever I almost crashed into. It's a weak gesture.

Unfortunately, I tend to have similar issues when biking. And since I'm a civic-minded individual, I want to apologize when I'm at fault. This all-too-frequent desire is what inspired this piece, which was originally published in Cyclingnews. And is used with their permission, though I'm pretty sure they wouldn't have noticed if I had published it even without their permission.

To the best of my knowledge (and I am a very, very knowledgeable person), there are only two universally recognized hand gestures. The first — the wave — is for "Hi." The second — the flipoff — is considerably more intimate, as well as considerably less friendly.

As cyclists, we have a few more gestures, most of which are used when riding in a paceline. We can point out obstacles. We can tell a rider to take a turn pulling. We can say we're turning or stopping.

And that's about it.

Frankly, we need more. Much more. Hence, to facilitate communication, avoid accidents, and generally increase the opacity[39] of cycling to outside observers, I hereby propose the following as Universal Cycling Hand Gestures.

THE ANTI-FLIPOFF

I sometimes make mistakes while biking in traffic.[40] And I regret them. In fact, I sometimes feel downright stupid. I want to acknowledge my mistake and apologize for it. Currently, I do this weird pantomime where I shrug my shoulders and mouth the word, "Sorry!"

The problem with this technique is it takes too long and requires

---

39 Opacity is the opposite of transparency. That helps, doesn't it?
40 But only very rarely. Ha.

that the person you're apologizing to is no further away than six feet, preferably sitting absolutely still, so as to catch the nuance of the shrug and mouthed apology.

What I need instead is an Anti-Flipoff: something that quickly says, "Oops, my bad. I'm an idiot. Sorry."

To perform the Anti-Flipoff, rap yourself on the helmet three times, as if checking to see if your head is hollow. It's quick and it's self-deprecating. I worry, however, that this one won't catch on, because while people are generally happy to point out other folks' errors, they're only rarely aware of their own.[41]

THE MAGNANIMOUS FLIPOFF

You know, not every grievance is equally bad. Sometimes, motorists do something that's just annoying enough that you want to call their attention to it, but not really bad enough to warrant a flipoff. This gesture says, in effect: "You may well deserve to be flipped off, and in fact most people would flip you off. But I am your moral superior, so I instead choose to forgive you."

To perform the Magnanimous Flipoff, extend one arm so it's easily visible, hand splayed, then wobble that hand up and down as if to say, "Your mental faculties are only so-so."

My guess is that the condescending nature of this gesture will mean it is perceived as more infuriating than the original flipoff.[42]

WHITE FLAG

You're on a group ride. You're not at your best today though, and have been repeatedly spat out the back. Considerately, the group has slowed down each time, letting you rejoin the paceline, when all you really want to do is lick your wounds in privacy.[43] You need a gesture to let the group know that this time, you'd really prefer they don't hold back and let you catch up.

The White Flag gesture needs to be visible from a good distance away, for obvious reasons, so it needs to be large. Execute this gesture by repeatedly weaving left to right as you pedal. Let your head loll.

---

41 Myself excepted. I'm acutely aware of every single thing that happens around me.
42 I have since confirmed that this suspicion was correct.
43 This is an especially good idea if your wounds are in a private spot.

On second thought, scratch that. That gesture may be indistinguishable from how you were riding in the first place.

Instead, hold your right hand high in the air, with a big "thumbs down" sign to indicate: "I'm cooked. Don't wait for me. Let me die in peace. Seriously. I mean it."

HELP? HELP!

One of the things I really like about cyclists is that pretty much every time I've ever been on the side of the road and another cyclist goes by, they ask, "You OK? Got what you need?" Usually I don't need the help. Sometimes I do.

But the exchange is horribly inefficient. You've got to slow down enough to shout a question and hear the answer if you're the would-be-helper. You've got to make yourself understood if you're the one on the side of the road.

The following gestures allow you to continue to be a courteous cyclist and to respond to other courteous cyclists, without shedding the precious momentum you've built up:

- **Do you need help?** Stick your thumb out, as if you were hitchhiking.
- **Yes, I need help:** Stick your thumb out the same way in response.
- **No, I don't need help:** Stick your thumb out, but pointing down.
- **I'm just resting here by the side of the road. I don't need help. Please don't ask why.** Windmill your arm once or twice, finishing by pointing in the direction the rider is going, as if you were a member of ZZ Top.[44] (Note: This gesture must be given *before* the approaching rider offers the "Do you need help?" gesture or it will be construed as horribly rude.)
- **Hey, I can see you've got a mechanical there and could use some help, but I don't have any tools at all, and besides, I'm a terrible mechanic, so I'm just going to keep going:** Stick your thumb out as if you were hitchhiking, but then let your thumb and hand droop down into a thumbs-down position, as if your thumb is very disappointed in itself.

---

44   This joke will be understandable only to those of us who are young enough to remember who ZZ Top is, and can furthermore remember their videos, which were very awesome indeed.

I ONLY *SEEM* SLOW

Yesterday, you did intervals. Today, you're supposed to spin along nice and slow, keeping your heart rate below 60. So you're noodling along when some guy pulls even, gives you "The Look,"[45] and shoots off the front. Of course, you're tempted to counterattack; show this jerk who's boss. But you don't want to spoil your carefully designed regimen just for this guy's benefit.

To indicate that the cyclist is passing you only because you are letting him, put your hand — the one the other guy can best see — in the air and do a slow "walking" motion with your index and middle finger. This gesture conveys the message, "I'm letting you go right now because it's my rest day. Believe me, if I wanted to, I could attack and drop you in a hot second. Now be off with you, before I change my mind and teach you a lesson you won't soon forget."

NEW PACELINE GESTURES

Riding with a group in tight formation requires a high degree of trust. By working together, you're all faster than you would be individually. And while there are already some perfectly good gestures for indicating debris and speed changes, those hardly cover the array of information you might want to convey.

- **Whoa, sorry I didn't call out that pothole/rock/broken glass we just hit:** Sure, you try to call out every little obstacle on the road, but sometimes you just don't see them 'til too late. When this happens, give yourself a quick, visible kidney punch, to show that you're aware you deserve to be smacked. If you just dragged the paceline through a really nasty patch of glass, you may also want to follow up with a quick rap on your helmet three times to underscore the point.
- **I'm about to fart. It's going to be bad. You may want to drop back:** Generally, it's a good idea to keep the group together, but if you've got really vile gas, most riders are more than willing to make an exception. Wave your hand behind your butt three

---

45 How many millions of cyclists have given millions of *other* cyclists "The Look" since Lance did his famous "The Look?" The answer is of course, "Way too many." Thanks a *lot*, Lance.

times to indicate the oncoming moment of flatulence.[46]

- **Hey, you're surging every time it's your turn to pull. Cut it out:** I'm not sure why some people feel it's their duty to try to up the pace for the first thirty seconds of each of their pulls, but I do know there's one in every group. To let this guy know you've had enough of this nonsense, when he drifts by you on the way to the back of the line, punch your fist forward quickly, then pull it back slowly. Repeat a couple times. If this person continues to surge at the beginning of each of his pulls, stop punching the air, and instead actually punch the person the next time he drifts back.[47]

- **Your complete and utter refusal to take a turn pulling has gone beyond annoying. It's crossed the threshold of outrageous selfishness and will have permanent implications on your group ride invitation status unless you get your butt to the front *now*.** Make eye contact with the offender and simply point your finger to the front of the line. Don't do it unless you mean it.

JUST THE BEGINNING

As cyclists become more and more confident with their gestures, more are sure to surface, ranging from "Hey, nice jersey" to "I'm totally out of food and water. I will name my firstborn after you if you'll just give me something to eat so I don't fall over on my side."

So please, let me know how these gestures work out for you. I'll be interested to know your experiences.

As for myself, I intend to just keep flipping people off.

COMMENT FROM UNKNOWN

An alternative to the magnanimous flipoff: the head shake. Similar to the MFO, simply and slowly shake your head back and forth to indicate what a lowly specimen the offending person is. This way you get to keep both hands on the bars in case you need to suddenly begin interval training. The HS is especially aggravating to the male of the species.

---

46   Out of all the gestures in this piece, this is the one I most often wish people understood. TMI, I know.
47   I'm really surprised this one hasn't been adopted.

THREE TRIES

I'm really lucky. When I first started riding, my friends had already been riding for a couple years. They had already set their own set of rules; all I needed to do was follow them.

The "Three Try" rule is perhaps the most useful rule ever invented. It allows you to practice, to become a better cyclist, and to try, try again, without worrying whether everyone else is looking at their watches.

It also keeps you from pounding your head against the wall so often that you make a hole in it (here, "it" could be either your head or the wall).

The Three Try Rule may be the most or, in fact, only, useful piece of information in this whole book. Read it carefully, understand it, and institute it in your own cycling group.

If I have a gift in cycling, it's in the ability to keep turning the cranks. Which is to say, I certainly don't have any special talent in the technical mountain biking arena.

And yet, if you were to compare my technical biking skill, it would be very nearly above average. I can ride up and down minor ledges. I can go over moderate-size logs.[48] I can navigate hairpin turns, as long as they are not terribly tight. I can, if the situation requires, ride up short stretches of loose shale.

How is it I can perform all these magnificent feats of derring-do? I think I can narrow it down to one particular thing.

The Three Try Rule.

HOW THE THREE TRY RULE WORKS

I started riding with The Core Team (Bob, Dug, Rick, Brad, Kenny) after the Rule had been established, so I'm afraid I can't offer any insight into its history. However, the premise of the Rule is elegant both in its simplicity and usefulness.

Any rider can try any move three times.

This means that if, as you're riding on a trail, you dab (put a foot down), crab (hit a rock with your pedal, throwing you off your line or off your bike), or just plain fall over, you get to go back and try it another two times.

---

48   And very small rocks.

By itself, that doesn't seem like much of a Rule.[49] The Three Try Rule, however, has an extensive set of supporting corollaries that give it its true power.

- **A Move is What You Think it Is:** If, either on-trail or off-trail, you find a series of logs, rocks, ledges, roots, or any other interesting challenge, you can call it a move and commence to try to clean (that is, successfully ride over) it three times.
- **Exception 1:** If you've been declaring move after move after move, to the point that the group hasn't moved 50 yards in the past four hours, people will start to find you annoying.[50]
- **Exception 2:** If everyone's tired from a whole day of riding and just wanting to get back to the trailhead (except you), there are no moves.[51] Just shut up, will you?

STICK TOGETHER
Once a move has been declared, all shall gather around the move to analyze, admire, pick lines, and give advice.

PEER PRESSURE
When at the move, nobody is required to do the move. However, you are a chicken if you don't. You're not a chicken, are you? C'mon. Just try it once. Everyone's doing it.

TURNS
After trying the move, you shall return to the back of the line to wait your turn for the next try.

- **Exception 1:** If you actually cleaned the move, you get to remain at the top.
- **Exception 2:** If you missed the move but had an epiphany that will almost certainly get you a "clean," you can ask for, and usually receive, cuts in line and an immediate extra turn. If, during your extra turn, you fail, you are a dork.[52]

---

49   Here, "Rule" is capitalized for additional importance.
50   Actually, I've been on rides with The Core Team where we haven't gone more than 50 feet in four hours, and *I'm* the only one who finds it annoying.
51   This is probably just wishful thinking on my part.
52   It is up to the other riders to decide whether they wish to *call* you a dork or just give you a meaningful look.

ADVICE FROM THE SUCCESSFUL

If you clean the move, you may remain at the top of the move and offer advice, encouragement, and commentary, though not to the point of being distracting while the next person is attempting the move.

- **Addendum 1**: Encouragement, advice, and commentary may be useful or useless in nature, but must be at least moderately entertaining. If you aren't funny, shut up.[53]
- **Addendum 2**: If you clean the move on your first try, but nobody else does, you are The Champ.[54]
- **Addendum 3**: If you are The Champ, your advice must be taken seriously. The move is your throne.
- **Addendum 4**: The Champ gets to make a short speech, usually thanking all the little people, and concluding that this is something they can't take away from you.

ADDITIONAL TRIES AVAILABLE BY REQUEST

If you were *soooooo close* on your third try, you may make an emotional appeal for another try, and another. And another.

- **Ennui Override:** At some point, you need to let it go. You'll get it next time. Let's move on. Seriously. It's getting dark.
- **Mulligan:** If you make a boneheaded mistake in the approach to the move — can't get clipped in, slide out in gravel, feel a certain bad juju in the air — you may call "mulligan," and try again. One mulligan per person per move, please.

ACCEPTABLE USE

The Three Try Rule may be used alone or in groups, but is much more fun in groups.

> COMMENT FROM UNKNOWN
> I'm trying to get my boss to implement a three tries rule at work. Him: "You screwed up that project, dummy." Me: "Yup. I call a mulligan."

---

53   The problem is, sometimes it's really hard to tell whether a joke you've got in your head is funny. It seems funny when you say it in your head, but magically transforms into something un-funny on the way out of your mouth.

54   Capitalized, again, for emphasis and to lend an air of importance.

9.
Food

WHAT, YOU THINK THERE'D BE A FAT CYCLIST BOOK WITHOUT A SECTION ABOUT FOOD? PFFF.

The truth is, I don't really obsess all that much about food. I don't even think about food very often, in the same way I don't think about breathing very often. And maybe that's the problem. In the same way I'm almost always breathing without even thinking about it, I'll frequently discover that I am in the kitchen, two-thirds of the way through making a sandwich.

Strangely, this section is quite possibly the most useful one in the book. It contains actual working recipes, including the one for The Best Cake in the World, which was originally posted the day after my post on "The Best Place in the World," proving that I was in a superlative mood at the time.

Be warned, though. This is also the section that ends with a story about barfing.

WHY I AM FAT

I wrote this post when I was pretty much at my fattest — close to 190 pounds. While I was trying to be funny, the frustration I felt was real.

And while I haven't gotten to quite the same weight again, I've been close, like, in the mid 180s. This is fat enough to start feeling like the fat pants are getting kind of tight. When that happens, I make a steely resolution: I will lose weight!

Then, three out of five times, I do it; I lose weight! And then I put it back on again.

As I write this, in fact, I am coming off the fastest, fittest summer I have ever had.

And now it's autumn; I'm back up to 165 pounds. The reason why hasn't changed:

I'm fat because of weekends.

I have a serious "grazing" instinct. If I'm in the house, I often find myself near the fridge or pantry without ever consciously intending to go there. I'll fix myself a snack, even though I'm not hungry. And if there's nothing I want to eat immediately obvious, I treat it as a Grazer's Challenge. This has resulted, in recent memory, in the following:

- Peanut butter and mozzarella cheese on a tortilla, heated in microwave for 25 seconds. Actually, it's very tasty.[1]
- Cool whip and powdered chocolate milk mix, blended together and used as a dip with graham crackers.[2] Again, very tasty.
- Saltine crackers with chipotle-flavored Tabasco sauce (my new favorite hot sauce, by the way).[3] Once again, very tasty, but probably would have been better if I had mixed the Tabasco with sour cream.
- A milkshake created using vanilla ice cream, milk, a handful

---

1   I don't understand why so few people never try combining the taste of mild cheeses like mozzarella or provolone with peanut butter. They work *great* together. Seriously, next time you make a peanut butter sandwich, go with a slice of provolone instead of honey or jam. You'll thank me for it. And then later, you'll hate me for it because you'll have a new bad-for-you craving.

2   It's like an instant mousse. Kind of.

3   That was just a passing phase. I'm back to Cholula.

of M&MS, and a large piece of chocolate cake. **This was possibly the best thing I have ever tasted and could be the basis of a successful milkshake chain: "Cake Shakes!"[4]**

This ability to always find something to eat — and then eat it, naturally — is pretty easy to suppress for short periods of time. When I'm at home for 60 hours at a stretch, though, eventually my willpower breaks down.

Which explains why my weight has gone from 181.4 pounds to 184.4 in less than a day. In one case, around 7:00PM on a Sunday night, I just started eating and eating and eating. Handfuls of Cap'n Crunch. Improvisational burritos (everything's better with a tortilla around it). A bowl of Frosted Mini-Wheats (I could happily eat nothing but cold cereal and Mexican food for the rest of my days). The leftover part of an ice cream cone one of my twins didn't finish.[5]

This conduct, in short, makes me a train wreck.

Originally, I intended to spend some time detailing the weirdness I've been through in the years surrounding this behavior, and try to link it to my current weight problem. I think this is the more honest answer, though:

I'm fat because I run out of willpower before I run out of weekend.

Mark my words, you'll see a variation of that on a fridge magnet someday.[6]

COMMENT FROM MIKEONHISBIKE

This holds true at my house too. I do some heavy duty grazing without even being hungry at all when I'm at home. I do a heck of a lot better when I'm chained to my desk at work all day.

COMMENT FROM JEFF

You're completely onto something with the cake shake. That sounds like the most fantastic human invention of the past century. I applaud you until my hands become raw.

---

4   Someday, try it. But use a smallish piece of cake. You'll thank me for it. And then later (again), you'll hate me for it.
5   Who doesn't finish an ice cream cone? That's just strange.
6   Or, quite possibly, on a Fat Cyclist T-Shirt.

THE BEST CAKE IN THE WORLD

I have my sister Kellene to thank for this recipe. It's genuinely my very favorite cake. Try it; you'll love it too.

While I'm on the subject of my sister Kellene, though, I'd like to lodge a complaint. Kellene is about my age and loves food about as much as I do. She is an excellent cook. And she is totally skinny.

This is just not fair. I mean, we both bike. We're about the same age. We like the same stuff. We have the same parents. But she's always thin, and I'm known to thousands of people as "Fatty."

Where's the justice in that?

It occurs to me that I have been spending far, far too much time in this blog on the "Cyclist" part of "Fat Cyclist." So, today, I'd like to present what has been determined by Renowned Scientists and Certified Dessert Experts around the globe as the Best Cake in the World.

It is a Chocolate-Chip-Oatmeal cake. It is not a fluffy, airy cake that collapses away to oxygen and a whiff of chocolate when you put it in your mouth. No. It is a substantial cake, something of which you could make a meal.[7] The oatmeal keeps it dense and moist and the chocolate keeps it chocolaty.

Do not put frosting on this cake. Frosting is what most cakes need to hide the fact that they are dry, overly airy, and flavorless.

I promise you, if you make this cake, you eat will three pieces before nightfall. You will gain three pounds before dawn.[8] And you will look for reasons to make this cake again soon. You will make this cake whenever you are asked to bring a dessert over to a picnic and you will be invited to an increasing number of picnics when people learn that you will bring this cake.

Your enemies will approach you to resolve your differences, just so they can have some of this cake.

I will, by coincidence, be making this cake later this afternoon for my wife, for it is her birthday. I will also give her an iPod, onto which I will copy our entire library of music — importing this library into

---

7   And believe me, I have.
8   And you'll eat it again for breakfast.

iTunes has been a tedious labor, and ordinarily my wife would appreciate the work that has gone into it. But when she sees that I have made this cake, I expect she will toss the now-forgotten iPod into a box and will throw her arms around me, grateful that I have gone to the effort of making her The Best Cake in the World.

I only hope that I have not undersold this cake.

RECIPE FOR THE BEST CAKE IN THE WORLD

1 ¾ cup boiling water — *Do not put your fingers in this water, for it is hot!* [9]
1 cup oatmeal — *Use regular oatmeal, not instant, you cretin.*
1 cup brown sugar — *How come it tastes so good?*
1 cup white sugar — *I have no clever comment to add to this ingredient, unless you consider this comment clever.* [10]
1 stick butter — *No, don't use margarine. Use butter. Margarine is gross.*
1 tsp baking soda — *I tried brushing my teeth with baking soda. Once.*
½ tsp salt — *Or go crazy and put in a whole teaspoonful.* [11]
1 ¾ cup flour — *Warning: flour may contain wheat products.*
2 eggs — *From a chicken; ostrich eggs are too big and taste nasty.* [12]
1 pkg milk chocolate chips — *Or semi-sweet if you think you are too good for regular milk chocolate chips.* [13]

Pour the boiling water over the oatmeal and stir. It's best if the aforementioned pouring of boiling water over said oatmeal occurs in a bowl. Stir and let set for ten minutes. About five minutes into this ten-minute period, put the butter in so it can melt.

Meanwhile...

Stir flour, baking soda, and salt together in a different bowl.

Once the ten minutes has elapsed...

Stir the brown sugar and white sugar into the oatmeal mixture.

---

9   I've sometimes thought it would be fun to do a whole cookbook with lots of asides and silly comments. You know, to make the recipes fun to read. And then I realized that a full book of this kind of nonsense would be the *most aggravating cookbook ever.*

10   This is sorta-kinda a *Raising Arizona* reference.

11   I just sort of shake some in.

12   OK, I've never actually eaten an ostrich egg.

13   I've done it both ways and like each equally well.

Beat the eggs in a separate bowl, then stir the eggs into the oatmeal mixture.[14]

Mix the flour mixture into the oatmeal mixture. You should now have one mixture. If you have more than one mixture, you need to reevaluate some life choices you made in your childhood.

Stir half the chocolate chips into this mixture. Do not snitch more than 5% of the chocolate chips as you do this.[15]

Grease and flour (or, in my house, just spray with Pam) a 9 x 13 pan. Pour the cake batter in, then sprinkle the other half of chocolate chips on top.

Bake at 350 degrees for 30 to 40 minutes, or until the center of the cake is not a gooey mess.[16] Let cool at least a little bit or the molten chocolate will burn the living daylights out of the roof of your mouth.

Serve warm, or at room temperature if you must, with vanilla ice cream if at all possible.[17]

Eat.

Rejoice.

COMMENT FROM UNKNOWN

I didn't think anybody else knew about this cake. My mom has been making this cake for me on my birthday for as long as I can remember because I hate frosting.

COMMENT FROM DAWN

This is the best cake ever. Because it has oatmeal in it, you can eat it for breakfast and feel good about it.

COMMENT FROM WILD DINGO

FINALLY! For 39 years I've been wondering why my two favorite snacks haven't been combined. I mean, why in the world would anyone put RAISINS with oatmeal? I just don't get that. I searched high and low for oatmeal chocolate chip cookies and never found one. This is even better.

---

14 I know, this recipe is starting to seem kind of complex, and it uses a lot of bowls and stuff. Trust me, it's worth it.

15 5% is actually quite a bit. Like a good-sized handful, I think.

16 I always have to let it go an extra ten minutes, it seems.

17 But not when you're eating it for breakfast.

VERY RATIONAL THINGS I BELIEVE

This post came about because of grapefruit.

See, I really do love grapefruit, at least when I can find nice, juicy good ones that aren't pulpy and dry. And I have noticed that if I regularly eat grapefruit, my dieting efforts tend to go better. Sure, this may be because I'm not eating something else much, much worse for me, when I'm eating grapefruit, but I choose to dismiss that possibility as irrelevant.

It occurred to me that my "grapefruit = dieting success" belief may have crossed the threshold that separates "encouraging theory" from "wacky nonsense." And it furthermore occurred to me that my grapefruit theory was not the only superstition I have about food.

I am a very clear thinker. I behave rationally and entertain no superstitions. For example, while it is true that I will never cross the path of a black cat, I do this because I simply do not like the path the black cat has taken, not because I see the path as ominous.

Similarly, I do not believe that walking under a ladder causes harm at a psychic level. Rather, I choose to never walk under ladders out of safety concerns.

If I knock on wood, it is because I like the texture of wood grain against my knuckles, not out of some silly notion that this action can ward off bad luck.

If I wish on a star, it is merely because I have empirical evidence that stars have magical wish-granting powers.

As I said, I am purely rational.

As a clear-headed, logical person, I can also assert with perfect confidence that the following items, each of which I unreservedly believe, are not dieting superstitions, but are in fact, self-evident, reproducible scientific phenomena, each impacting how and to what degree my diet works.

GRAPEFRUIT IS MAGICAL

Of all the diet-related things I believe, this is the absolutely most important one: *grapefruit is magical*. I have found, time and time again, that grapefruit has the ability to make me lose weight. I eat a grapefruit before going to bed and my weight is down in the morning.

I'd say it's "just like magic," except for one thing: it's not *like* magic. It *is* magic.

Of course, there are rational explanations for this, in addition to the fact that grapefruit is magic. Here are the reasons:

- **Grapefruit is acidic.** You eat this fruit with lots of citric acid in it and the acid starts dissolving your fat, like battery acid on butter.[18]
- **Eating grapefruit is hard work.** To eat a grapefruit, one must expend considerable energy. One must cut the grapefruit in half. One must cut around the circumference of the grapefruit for *each* of those halves. One must then attend to the labor of spooning out each of the sections. I've broken into a mild sweat at the mere *prospect* of this task. By the time one has completed this effort, I estimate that one has burned more than 2750 calories.[19]

Some people (by which I mean "stupid people who look for arbitrary reasons to disagree with me") make the foolish counterclaim that eating grapefruit before bed actually only helps me lose weight because instead of eating a bowl of cereal and bag of chips, I'm eating a grapefruit.

Those people are fools.

Grapefruit, I praise you, and thank you for your magical ability to help me lose weight.

DIETING GODS ARE VENGEFUL

Another absolute truth in dieting is this: as you diet and train, you begin to attract the attention of the Dieting Gods. As you fastidiously follow the religion of self-deprivation, they reward you with your heart's desire: weight loss.

If you cross the Dieting Gods, they will make you pay.

As an example, suppose you have been strictly adhering to your diet for three weeks, as I have at the time of this writing. The Dieting Gods would reward you with some significant progress. When I wrote this, I was down 11 pounds.

I know, however, that — having shown faith and devotion — if I were to slip up (eat half a candy bar, say) I would reap the dieting whirlwind, in the form of these three punishments:

---

18   See? This all totally makes sense. Right?
19   Give or take.

- **My appetite would increase threefold.** Once I have shown dietary fecklessness, the Dieting Gods would curse me with a wild abandon. The Hunger would come upon me and I would eat anything that came within my easy reach (everything in both the fridge and the pantry are to be considered "in easy reach").
- **My despair would take the form of "despondent consumption."** Any of you who have ever said to yourself, "Well, my diet's screwed today; no point in dieting the rest of the day."[20] And then, the following day, you find yourself thinking that you'll restart your diet the next day. And so on, until you are ten pounds heavier than when you started the diet in the first place.
- **I would gain weight.** This is a direct curse from the Dieting Gods and is not a result of having eaten myself into a coma.

THE MANTRA IS MEANINGFUL

As I diet, I find myself saying, over and over, "One Hundred and Forty Eight:" my goal weight. This is because if you consciously utter your objective often enough, that objective seeps into your subconscious, which is where the action really is.[21]

Some would say that the fact that I have never reached my goal weight nor lost any weight at all while using this method is a clear indication that this mantra is useless. To them I say, "Shut up, stupid."

THE SCALE IS JUST PLAIN MEAN

It is widely known that bathroom scales are inhabited by pixies that have been banished from their magical fairyland after being convicted of accounting fraud.

These pixies — unrepentant criminals from a folk that are mischievous and unreliable to begin with — then tell us how much we weigh. Rest assured that any time you show a weight loss the morning after a night of heavy drinking and eating, this is just a Pixie giving you a jolt of irrational pleasure so that the following day, when you show a nine pound gain, your disappointment and horror will be that much more exquisite.

---

20   I don't know how many times I have said this, but I would estimate it at just over one thousand. Or maybe a million.

21   I know it seems like I'm just being ridiculous and I probably am, but I really do this.

WHEN YOU EAT MATTERS — A LOT

Did you know that a recent scientific study conducted at Yale University proves that after 7:00PM, food actually *triples* in its caloric content? Don't believe me? Look up the study yourself.

Totally factual.

COMMENT FROM DUG

Here's the thing — you used the word "fecklessness." I LOVE that word. The Dieting Gods will reward you accordingly.

Kim bought us a new digital scale and threw out the old analog scale. The new digital scale told me I had gained 5 pounds overnight. I gave the new digital scale a severe beat down and I threw this feckless item out. I then rescued the old analog scale from the curbside trashcan.

I love my old analog scale. It is full of robust feck.

COMMENT FROM EUFEMIANO FUENTES

Jan also believed the dieting gods were vengeful. And that they were racist against Germans. He would purge for days and still not lose weight

He also liked the grapefruit juice in his Sea Breezes; for some reason he likes traditionally feminine drinks. It always struck me as odd, but who was I to say, right?

MASHED POTATOES

*I would rather eat mashed potatoes — the way I prepare them, I mean —
than anything else. Anything. They're my favorite thing in the world to eat.*

*Unfortunately, I'm pretty sure they're also the worst thing in the world for
me. I go a little bit crazy with the cheese. And the sour cream. And the salt.
Really, the chances of you getting any actual potato in my mashed potatoes
is about one in two.*

*So, to prevent me from killing myself with an acute case of clogged
arteries, I restrict myself to making these mashed potatoes no more often
than twice per year: once for Thanksgiving and once for Christmas.*

*Naturally, however, it's OK to make a nice big batch. Which means
there will be leftovers. In fact, there will often be enough leftovers from the
Thanksgiving batch to take me pretty close to a week before I make the
Christmas batch.*

And then the Christmas batch will generally last 'til February.

Still, I think it's good I restrict myself to making them only twice per year.

Something's changed. It's the same something that changes every year
around this time. And that something is my motivation level. Sometime
in late September, I stop thinking about how strong or fast or light or
heavy or slow I am, and start thinking about mashed potatoes.

Oh, how I love mashed potatoes.

I should be more specific: I love *my* mashed potatoes. *Everybody*
loves my mashed potatoes. If there were a mashed potato contest, I'd
enter it with confidence. And if I didn't win, I'd feel robbed.[22]

My kids love my mashed potatoes more than any other food in the
world. They'd rather eat my mashed potatoes than dessert. And so
would I, for that matter.

Friends and relations call early in the year to invite me to Thanksgiving
dinner, even though they don't care for me personally, because my
mashed potatoes are so good.

Nobody puts gravy on my mashed potatoes. This is because people

---

22   I have never entered a food contest, because I know they put a lot of emphasis
on presentation and my presentation is perhaps too simple: a giant bowl, full of
mashed potatoes. The end.

intuit that while other mashed potatoes need gravy, my mashed potatoes do not need such a crutch.

HOW TO MAKE GREAT MASHED POTATOES

People always ask me, "Fatty, how do you make such incredible mashed potatoes?"

I do not tell them.

It's not that there's a secret. There's not. And it's not that these are difficult to make. They're not.

It's that if I tell people how bad these mashed potatoes are for them, they'll never eat them again, and that would be a shame.

The thing is, though, most of you won't ever be eating Thanksgiving with me anyway. So I don't mind telling you about my mashed potatoes. And then you can make them, call them your own, and be famous within your own circle of friends for the best mashed potatoes in the world.

Start by peeling a ten-pound bag of potatoes. Cut each potato into six or eight pieces. Put the potatoes into heavily salted water[23] and boil until the potatoes reach "ready to mash" consistency.

No, I don't know how long that is and I can't explain what that consistency is. If you can't tell, perhaps you don't have any business making my mashed potatoes.

Drain the water out. If someone else is making gravy, you can offer your water to them, because salty boiled potato water makes great gravy. Not, mind you, that you'll need gravy.

It's important you do this next part while the potatoes are very hot.

Toss in two sticks of butter. Do not use margarine, no matter what.[24] Toss in a fistful of grated mozzarella cheese and a much smaller fistful of grated Jack.

Now start mashing. Use a masher, not a mixmaster or other appliance. You don't want these to be smooth and fluffy. That's what mashed potatoes from flakes are. You want these to be recognizable as potatoes.[25]

Continue until the potatoes are mashed and the butter and cheese are melted.

---

23   Sea salt. It makes a difference. Really.

24   In fact, don't use margarine, no matter what, *ever*.

25   I know opinions differ on mashed potato texture. I like mine a little chunky. I'm not going to fight you on this, though.

Now, put in a big double wooden-spoonful of sour cream. Mash some more.

Taste.

If you don't weep with joy, you did it wrong.

I wonder why I always gain weight during the autumn?

COMMENT FROM BOTCHEDEXPERIMENT

You know, I think my wife makes better mashed potatos than these. Her mashed potatoes have sour cream AND cream cheese in them. But, being the scientific type, I'll propose a head-to-head: a Mrs. Botched vs. Fatty mashed potato cook-off. I'll get her to make both kinds, then I will eat both of them and declare a winner.

COMMENT FROM KATIE

That feeds how many people? 50?? I can feel my arteries clogging from here.

COMMENT FROM ROCKY

It's the hibernating instinct. I can't eat enough during the early autumn months and I need frequent naps during the day. One day, I am afraid that I will doze off and wake up to freshly blossomed daisies and spring weather. I guess that would be a good thing.

EPIC DESSERT MAKING:
BANANA CREAM PARFAIT

I am not an angry person. If, for example, you were to tell me I am a fool, that would not make me angry. If, for another example, you were to borrow my bike and then crash it, scratching the paint badly, that would also not make me angry.

But when I hear about people make banana cream parfaits (or pies) using instant pie filling, that makes me angry. Because it doesn't taste right, nor does it taste good, no matter what Bill Cosby says.

Some things just take a lot of time and attention. And those things, generally, are worth the time they take.

And also, once your family and friends try this dessert, they will love you more than they already did. So it's a good investment of time, I'd say.

I don't know how to cook many things. If, for example, you were to ask me to make Chicken Cordon Bleu, I wouldn't know what ingredients to buy. I wouldn't even know which part of the chicken to use.[26]

That said, I am famous for making the few things I know how to make extremely well. Better than anyone else in the whole world, in fact.

Here are the things I am the very best in the world at making:

- **Mashed potatoes (see previous).** Yes, I know a lot of you also think you make the best mashed potatoes in the world, which might be true if I didn't have an actual certificate stating that I make the best mashed potatoes in the world.[27]
- **The Best Cake In The World.** Actually, I'm no better at making this than anyone else. This cake is superlative in its own right.
- **Chili.** I have an honest-to-goodness, bona-fide secret ingredient I use in my chili.[28] Nobody has ever identified it, but

---

26   The bleu part?

27   If you and I are ever in a mashed potato-making contest and it comes down to a draw, with the judges stymied over the exquisite perfection of our respective mashed potatoes, you can bet that I'll present that certificate in the hopes of swaying the judge.

28   OK, it's just a handful of semi-sweet chocolate chips, and apparently everyone else does it too. Imagine my disappointment.

everyone agrees that my chili is better than everyone else's. Oh, also I sometimes make fry bread to go with the chili. I have received several marriage proposals based solely on my fry bread and chili.[29]

- **Hamburgers**: There is nothing secret or fancy about the way I make hamburgers. I just use top-quality beef, add more Worcestershire sauce than most people think you should (you've used enough when it actually changes the color of the burger), sprinkle some sea salt in, knead and shape the patties by hand, and grill the burgers over charcoal. The reason my burgers are the best in the world is because I am apparently the last person in the universe to grill with charcoal. I'll tell you what, though: when gas-grillers eat my burgers, they see, however briefly, the error of their ways.[30]

- **Kitchen Sink Quiche**: I call it "Kitchen Sink Quiche" because I put so much stuff into it, there's hardly any room for the eggs: cheese, peppers, bacon, grilled chicken, onions, mushrooms, tomatoes, avocado, and anything else that strikes my fancy. And yes, I've heard the "real men don't eat quiche" line. To which I respond, "By all means, feel free to not to have any." But everyone tries a bite, and then they apologize. Kitchen Sink Quiche is best with Cholula hot sauce.

- **Banana Cream Parfait**: This is the most difficult thing I make and it's the subject of my post: endurance dessert-making.

ENDURANCE DESSERT-MAKING

I make the Banana Cream Parfait exactly twice per year, just like my mashed potatoes: for Thanksgiving and for Christmas. And while a *good* reason to make it so rarely would be because it's fattening beyond belief, the *real* reason is because it's an incredibly laborious process. More to the point, it's a pain in the butt.

But it's *so* worth it.

---

29   I only make fry bread very occasionally, though, because my chili with fry bread is such an incredibly heavy, dense meal you will fall asleep almost instantly after finishing your second helping (oh yes, you will want a second helping), and will not wake up for a couple days.

30   I'm not saying there's anything wrong with grilling with gas. It's just that there's nothing especially right with it, either.

I'm now going to share with you my recipe for making the Banana Cream Parfait, but I think it's worth making a few observations first:

- You will have to stand at the stove, stirring continuously, for a full hour.[31]
- Even after spending all this time stirring, you are not done. In fact, you need to count on spending about two hours to make this dessert. And I don't mean that, of the two hours, you're letting something bake in the oven for ninety minutes. I mean two hours of constant work.
- Because this is so much work to make, the recipe is *big*. Big enough to make some for yourself, your family, and your neighbors.[32]
- Once you have made this dessert for your friends and family, be prepared for them to demand you make it again. You will then need to, as I have, declare that it is an annual tradition and that you will make it for them again next year.
- I expect that I have now frightened most of you away from making this dessert. That's OK.
- Don't you *dare* make substitutions to this recipe. When I say "whole milk," I mean it. When I say "butter," I mean it. And if you think you can just substitute pudding from a mix for the cream filling, you and I no longer have anything to talk about and I never want to see your face again.[33]

I feel quite strongly about my Banana Cream Parfait.

Let's begin.

INGREDIENTS

2½ cup sugar
1 cup cornstarch
2 teaspoons salt
3 quarts whole milk
16 egg yolks, beaten

---

31   No, don't you dare bring a stool over to the stove and sit while you stir. People will be able to tell you didn't suffer as much as you should have.

32   I warn you, therefore, not to double this recipe. There's such a thing as too much pudding, after all. Theoretically.

33   Tough love, baby. Tough love.

8 tablespoons butter
⅓ cup vanilla
12 bananas
1 quart whipping cream
2 boxes Nilla Wafers

THE LONG, ARDUOUS PROCESS

First of all, you need to plan on spending an hour up front making the filling and then another hour, two or three hours later, actually *assembling* the parfait. And then the parfait is not going to be ready to eat for another three hours. And it's going to be at its best about 24 hours after you make it. So plan ahead.[34]

Let's start with the filling.

In a big ol' saucepan — I use my pressure cooker pan — mix your sugar, cornstarch, and salt together. *Slowly* stir in the first few cups of milk, until you're certain there are no lumps of cornstarch. You can then pour in the rest of the milk, stirring as you go.

Now, get ready to stand for a while, because you need to stir this mixture *continuously* over medium heat until it comes to a boil. And that's going to take about 15–20 minutes. Or more. During this time, here's what you should **not** do:

- **Stop stirring for a minute, because what could go wrong?** Here's what could go wrong: the bottom of the pan will get scalded milk all over it, and you'll wind up with gross, chewy, burned flecks of milk in your parfait.
- **Turn up the heat to speed up the process.** If you go above medium heat, your mixture will indeed boil sooner. And the result will be a nice sweet, grainy, thin gruel that never sets up, instead of the smoothest, most perfect cream filling that has ever been created. This is an endurance race, bub. If you try to treat it like a sprint, you'll be sorry.[35]

Once the mixture has thickened and come to a boil, keep stirring for another minute, then remove from the heat and keep stirring another minute longer. Even though it's off the heat, the milk can still stick to

---

34   Wow, I've about talked *myself* out of ever making this again.

35   I'm speaking from experience. It's a massive disappointment to go to all this effort and then wind up with something that is completely useless.

the bottom of the pan.

OK, time to add the egg yolks. If at all possible, have a second person available to help you with this part, because this is tricky.

Your egg yolks should be in a mixing bowl big enough to hold at least half the milk mixture. S-l-o-w-l-y pour a little of the milk mixture into the beaten egg yolks, while briskly whipping those egg yolks. The idea here is to do this slowly and a little bit at a time, so you don't wind up cooking those egg yolks all at once. Really, who wants scrambled eggs in their cream filling?[36]

Once you've slowly stirred in a couple cups of the milk mixture, you can speed up just a bit. Keep pouring the milk mixture into the egg mixture (stirring the whole time) until you've mixed half of it in.

And now, you've got to reverse the flow. Slowly pour the egg mixture back into the milk mixture in the saucepan. It should now be a lovely yellow color.

And hey, guess what! You're finished!

Just kidding. You're not even close.[37]

Put the saucepan back on medium heat and keep stirring until it comes to a boil again. And yes, it's going to be another 15 minutes or so. Once you've got a boil, stir for another minute, and then take the saucepan off the heat.

Now you're ready to add the butter and vanilla.[38] Toss them in, but not from a great height. You might discover that boiling hot pudding splashed on your face, well, *stings*. Not that I'd *personally* know anything about that.

Stir the butter and vanilla in until the butter is melted and both are well blended.

Dip a spoon in so you can taste what you've made. Blow on the filling until you feel a little bit ridiculous, then blow on it some more, because you would be *amazed* at how hot this stuff is and how much heat it retains.[39]

When you do finally taste it, your eyes should roll back into your

---

36 I tried to come up with someone who might want this and I couldn't. So I think it's entirely possible *nobody in the world* wants scrambled eggs in their cream filling. Wow: something on which the entire world probably agrees.

37 That was a mean trick. I'm sorry.

38 Real vanilla. Duh.

39 When you bring it off the burner, it's the same temperature as molten aluminum.

head and you should involuntarily let out a low moan. If you don't, you didn't make it right.

Now let this filling cool down for a couple hours.

LAYER UPON LAYER

Once the cream filling has cooled down enough that you can sneak a spoonful without burning your mouth at all, you're ready to start assembling the parfait.

There'll be a skin on the filling by now. Peel it off and eat it. It's delicious.

Whip the whipping cream to nice soft peaks. I find that adding a little sugar makes the whipped cream hold its shape a little better.[40]

Now, in as many large, deep bowls as it takes, do the following:

1. Spread a layer of filling.
2. Put down a layer of Nilla Wafers.
3. Spread a layer of whipped cream.
4. Put down a layer of banana slices.
5. Repeat steps one through four until the bowl is full. The last layer should always be whipped cream. And be *sure* the last layer is not bananas, because they'll look all brown and gross if they're exposed to the air for long.

You may wonder if the order of the layers is important. It is. I've thought it through. Don't mess with it.

BEFORE SERVING

You should refrigerate this dessert for at least a couple hours before serving it; it's definitely best cold.

And, if you can manage to wait, this is one dessert that actually gets better as it sits in the fridge with the flavors blending. It's at its very best 24 hours after you finish making it.

And, finally, prepare yourself for some rather embarrassing displays of affection. The Banana Cream Parfait tends to bring out that sort of behavior.

---

40 And go ahead and put in a little vanilla, too, if you're so inclined. Which I am.

BARF

I know, it's a little bit cruel for me to finish off the section on food with an anecdote about barfing. But to be honest, I couldn't find another place where it should go and it's definitely a story I wanted to include in this book.

Though I kinda suspect that my eldest son would prefer I didn't.

About 5:00PM yesterday, one of my twin five-year-olds started barfing. She barfed about every twenty minutes or so until 8:00PM, at which point she was so exhausted she went to sleep, waking up every couple hours to barf and dry heave again.

The other twin, on the other hand, was happy and not at all sick as she went to bed.

That changed around 11:30PM, when she woke up barfing.

The cleanup was not easy.

She did not go back to sleep until 3:00AM.

So I'm not functioning at peak capacity today.

THAT'S NOT EVEN REMOTELY MY BEST BARF STORY

The thing is, the twins don't throw up often. My oldest boy,[41] on the other hand, used to have a barf trigger that was known far and wide for how little it took to make him throw up.

Back when he was a little kid, my wife and I cleaned up barf so often, our efficiency and capability at this task actually became a source of pride. We could strip the sheets, clean the carpet, swap out new pillows and blankets and get everything hosed down and cleaned up in five minutes or less.

Except once.

I was feeling particularly pleased with myself because I had heard the noise coming from his bedroom: the gagging noise that meant I had two seconds to get into his bedroom and try to catch the barf in a bowl. I had sprinted across the hall, grabbed the bowl we always kept by his bed, and managed to catch the entire stinky mess. No cleanup tonight!

And then, as I carried the bowl o' barf out of his room to the bathroom, I tripped.

---

41 Now in college. *College*, for crying out loud! So now he has to clean up his own mess. Ha!

The bowl fell, staying magically[42] upright, landing flat on the floor.

Those of you who have studied physics and know things about equal and opposite reactions and the way a parabola-shaped object can distribute matter know what this means.

For the rest of you, let me simply say this: the room was painted in barf.[43]

And so was I.

I do not believe I have ever been so angry, embarrassed, and grossed out before. Or since, for that matter.

It would be months before we stopped finding dried-out barf chunklets in the room and I don't think the smell ever went away entirely.

COMMENT FROM RICK S

Goat cheese ravioli, one hour before climbing Tibble Fork — enough said.

COMMENT FROM BOB

Back when I was a Mormon missionary, I barfed all over a woman during a prayer. And then I barfed all over her couch and living room floor and front door (I couldn't get it open fast enough) and gate (I couldn't open that either). When I finally wrapped up my dry heaves, the whole family was throwing sand on the vomit as efficiently as a CTS Decon *(Fatty note: Crime and Trauma Scene Decontamination)*. They stayed with Catholicism.

COMMENT FROM BARRY1021

So hey, what's for lunch??

---

42   And, as it turned out, tragically.
43   Floor to ceiling, including both the floor and ceiling. And the walls in between.

10.
Tour de Lance

I BOUGHT MY FIRST ROAD BIKE IN 1998 FOR ABOUT $500. IT WAS A NEW BIANCHI, ALTHOUGH DEFINITELY THE LEAST EXPENSIVE ONE THEY SOLD. I didn't want to spend a lot of money on it; I didn't know if I was going to like it.

To tell the truth, buying a road bike was a defensive move; everyone else in The Core Team had bought road bikes and had fallen in love with them. I was tired of getting left out of more than half the rides.

The next year, 1999, I watched the Tour de France for the first time. Back then, that meant watching the daily hour-long recap late at night on ESPN. I was watching so I'd know what The Core Team was talking about during all those road rides.

That was the year Lance Armstrong — about whom I knew nothing — won the Tour de France for the first of what would be seven consecutive years, each of which I watched.

Coincidence? I don't think so, although I'm still waiting for that "Thanks for helping me win all those races!" card from Lance. Should arrive any day now.

I started blogging the last year Lance raced the Tour de France before retiring (the first time). Oddly enough, quite a few posts about Lance, the Tour de France, or both wound up in my blog.

2005 TOUR DE FRANCE PERSONALITY TEST

As Susan and I watched the Tour de France together, it quickly became clear that we were rooting for different people. At first, she was rooting for Ullrich; I was rooting for Vinokourov.

Then, as they started up the final climb and Vinokourov was shot out the back as effectively as if he had turned around and started riding in the opposite direction, my wife continued to root for Ullrich. I began rooting for Basso.

As Basso and Ullrich were shed, leaving only an elite four, Susan continued to root for Ullrich. I, on the other hand, easily switched loyalties to Armstrong.

Surely this said something about our different personalities. Specifically, it says that Susan liked to pick a horse and stick with it. It also said that my loyalties are more complex: I want the underdog to win, but am not willing to stick with him once it's clear that King Kong has crushed the life out of him. In the end, my loyalties are with those who most earn my admiration.

Which made me think (seriously, it did): The Tour is big and sophisticated enough that one could use it to make an assessment of the fan's personality: for whom you root, to which kinds of stages you most look forward, etc., tell a lot about who you are. And who better to parse meaning out of your preferences than the Fat Cyclist?

Well, who indeed?

Take this fast and easy quiz to reveal your personality to yourself. Or to at least reveal what my personality's take on your personality is, as filtered through the narrow prism of what you like in a single sports event.

Hey, it's cheaper than therapy and nearly 20% as effective!

QUESTION 1.
WHO DO YOU *WANT* TO WIN THE TOUR DE FRANCE?

   a. **Jan Ullrich:** You love a comeback kid, a perpetual underdog, a likeable loser. If American, you voted Democrat.[1] If you

---

1   This is an interesting thing to read for me, because it actually makes me cringe reading it...and I'm the guy who wrote it. If I were to write something — even something like this — about politics in my blog now, the comments section would be overwhelmed with a political flame war. Luckily for me, in real life I'm just about as apolitical as I am in my blog.

are a cyclist, you are more likely to be overweight than not and use Jan as a shining beacon of what it's possible for a fat cyclist to achieve.

b. **Ivan Basso or Alexandre Vinokourov:** You fancy yourself a thinker, an analyst, but you're actually just a flibbertigibbet. You've looked at Basso's results from the past and think he's a good bet for the future.[2] When Basso doesn't wind up in the top ten after this year's tour, you will hardly notice, however, because you'll already have moved on to the next big thing.

c. **Lance Armstrong:** You are a pragmatist, and like to surround yourself with winners. If American, there is a strong chance you voted Republican.[3]

d. **Levi Leipheimer or Floyd Landis:** You are a dreamer and hold to those dreams even in the face of harsh reality. If American, you vote Libertarian.

e. **Iban Mayo or Roberto Heras:** You are an idealist, and tend to remember the old days as better than they actually were.

f. **Someone else:** You are simply obstinate.

QUESTION 2:
WHO DO YOU *THINK* WILL WIN THE TOUR DE FRANCE?

a. **Lance Armstrong**: You are a realist.

b. **Someone else:** You live in a parallel universe, a beautiful place filled with magic, light, and wish-granting fairy godmothers.

QUESTION 3. WHAT IS YOUR FAVORITE KIND OF STAGE?

a. **Individual Time Trial:** You are a fatalist and obsessed with the idea of fairness. Everyone should pull his or her own weight in this world. You do not often get invited to parties and nobody has ever referred to you as a team player.

b. **Team Time Trial:** You enjoy the beauty of fine machinery.

c. **Flat stage:** You are one of the organizers of the Tour or a sprinter on a pro cycling team. You love to tell shaggy dog jokes.

d. **Mountain Stage:** You love the excitement of the unknown

---

2   So, how'd that bet turn out?
3   I think it probably seems like, from this remark, I am a Republican. In reality, I do not affiliate with any party. I'm no good at parties, anyway.

and are willing to suffer to achieve joy, which is a nice way of saying you are a masochist. There is a 40% chance that you are one of those people who insist that problems are challenges and that obstacles are opportunities.

e. **That last stage of the tour where everyone rides around and around and around in a circle all day:** You are a nincompoop.[4]

QUESTION 4.
IF YOU COULD CHOOSE, WHICH KIND OF RIDER WOULD YOU BE?

a. **Sprinter**: You were a bully at school and have stopped being a bully as an adult only because you have been threatened with legal consequences.

b. **Climber:** You are a good person.[5]

c. **Time Trialist**: You like to tell people that you enjoy exploring your limits and pushing the envelope. In reality, you know exactly where the edge of the envelope is and discovered long ago that you do not have the capacity to push through it.[6]

d. **GC**: You have a difficult time making up your mind. You are completely helpless when eating at a buffet-style restaurant.

e. **GC lieutenant**: You evidently take great pride in having a part in the accomplishments of others. At night, when nobody is watching, you cry into your pillow, agonizing over your own mediocrity.[7]

QUESTION 5. WHAT PERCENTAGE OF RIDERS IN THE TOUR DE FRANCE DO YOU THINK, IN YOUR HEART OF HEARTS, ARE CHEATING, EITHER BY DOPING, BLOOD TRANSFUSIONS, OR HIDDEN TRIPWIRES TO MAKE THE COMPETITION SUDDENLY AND WITHOUT WARNING, FALL FROM THEIR BIKES?

a. **0% — they're all clean:** I just put this here in order to be comprehensive. I don't think *anybody* believes they're *all* clean, so am not going to make up something about what this says about you.

b. **1–20%:** You believe, in general, that people are good and want

---

4   I don't even record that stage. I just don't care.

5   Can you tell what kind of rider I want to be?

6   Wow, that was just mean of me, wasn't it?

7   I felt it was OK to write this because I can't imagine a single person would pick this option, given a choice.

to do the right things for the right reasons. You believed in Santa Claus a full two years after the rest of your classmates.[8]

c. **21–40%:** You consider yourself tough but fair. Others consider you a fence-sitting nancy-boy.

d. **50–100%:** You suspect everyone of everything. You assume the worst of everyone and think that this protects you from being taken advantage of. In reality though, you're just being paranoid and tend to make yourself a target of practical jokes. You were the kid in school who told everyone there is no Santa Claus. Jerk.

e. **"Hey, you skipped 41–49%!":** You are anal retentive and are furthermore taking this way too seriously.

QUESTION 6.
WHO IS YOUR FAVORITE TOUR DE FRANCE ANNOUNCER?

a. **Phil Liggett, Paul Sherwen (Originally I gave these two individual bullets, but the fact is they're inseparable):** In general, you're a well-balanced person, though you do have a penchant for wacky idioms and pretending you know what other people are thinking.

b. **Bob Roll:** You are boisterous and wear a lamp shade on your head, even when you are not drunk.

c. **Al Trautwig:** You accept everything anyone says about anything. You laugh at knock-knock jokes. You are not aware you have a comfort zone because you have never left it. You are a chimpanzee.

QUESTION 7. HOW IMPORTANT IS IT TO YOU TO AVOID STAGE "SPOILERS," I.E., FINDING OUT WHAT HAPPENED IN THE MOST RECENT STAGE BEFORE WATCHING IT UNFOLD YOURSELF?

a. **Crucial — I avoid all cycling websites until I get home from work and can watch the stage myself:** You are self-disciplined. I wish I had the self-control to do that.

b. **Not important — the race is the thing; how it ends is just an interesting data point:** Yeah, that's what I tell myself every day after I break down at work and check Cyclingnews.com.

c. **Not relevant — I get to watch it live.** Shut up. I hate you.

---

8   Like I did.

AN OPEN LETTER TO THE NEWLY-UNEMPLOYED LANCE ARMSTRONG

I had just gotten some well-intentioned, but totally useless, advice from a relative on what my next career steps should be, specifically, that I should go back to school and not leave until I had an MBA. My feelings weren't at all hurt; this person had such a weak understanding of who I am and what I care about that his perspective was good, solid entertainment.

From there, it was an easy leap to think about what kind of advice this person might give someone like Lance, having no clue about pro racing, nor the fact that Lance had retired, i.e., not been fired.

Dear Mr. Armstrong,

I'm very sorry to hear that you have lost your job as a bicycle rider. Being unemployed is a difficult, demoralizing experience, and to tell the truth, I'm not absolutely sure that anything I have to say will help.

However, like you, I have found myself "between jobs" before and I'm happy to say that, if you treat this as a learning experience, you can gain some important life lessons from these admittedly difficult circumstances.

Here's how you can take those lemons and make lemonade![9]

DON'T BE PROUD

From what I understand, Lance (I hope you don't mind if I call you Lance), this is not the first time you have lost your job. In fact, I hear that last year the United States Postal Service fired you.

Maybe now is the time for you to go back to them, apologize for your shortcomings, and ask for a job. It seems like common sense to say that there will always be work for mail carriers. If you can start being more consistent in your work, perhaps you'll find you have a reliable career that can last a lifetime![10]

---

9   People are always advising those in possession of lemons to make lemonade, as if that was the only good you can do with a lemon. How about lemon meringue pie? Lemon sherbet? Lemon tarts? How about just slicing that lemon up and dropping a wedge of it into a nice, cold Diet Coke?

10   Even in 2005, the USPS was in trouble.

DON'T BE AFRAID TO ASK FOR HELP

No doubt you're wondering how you're going to make ends meet now that you have no job. Well, I understand you have a girlfriend who is a singer. In fact, if I don't miss my guess, I believe she once had a hit song, "All Girls Wanna Do is Just Have Some Fun!"

And while I think it's safe to say that one-hit wonders are a dime a dozen, she can probably still find work. In fact, I have several friends with younger children. I may be able to help her make some bookings for their upcoming birthday parties. In any case, if you need money, you should ask her for some. But keep a strict accounting of every penny you borrow, and an even more strict accounting of every penny you spend, to show that you're not just throwing her hard-earned and somewhat unsteady money around foolishly. Pay her back as soon as you can.

DO SOMETHING FOR OTHERS

I hope you don't mind me being a teensy bit direct with you now, Mr. Armstrong. I can tell, just by looking at you, that you have always had it easy. You've probably never been sick a day in your life.

Well, now may be the time for you to think about some of the less fortunate people in the world. Help the sick; give back a little. You're a strapping young man. I'll bet any hospital in the world would be happy to take you on as a candy striper.

THINK ABOUT A CAREER CHANGE

You've given bicycle riding a shot. That's great that you've chased a dream. Now it's time to come down to the ground and realize that it's simply not a practical job. Try to find something at which you can be more successful.

Perhaps you could get a job with Amway or Nu Skin.

Or maybe you could get a job making/selling those rubber bracelets that are so popular with kids these days. Or maybe you could take your former "career" experience and turn it into something practical: you could be a mechanic or salesman in a bike shop!

If you want to be a salesman in a bike shop, however, I recommend you stop acting like such a know-it-all about bike riding. Remember, the *customer* is always right![11]

---

11   I'm pretty sure this letter was the inspiration for the Mellow Johnny's bike shop.

You can't help that you've lost your job, Mr. Armstrong. But you *can* help what you're going to do now. Please accept this advice in the spirit in which it is given.

Kind Regards,

LANCE ARMSTRONG COMES OUT OF RETIREMENT

This piece was not my idea. I'd love to claim credit for it, but I can't. The fact is, James Scott, a reader, emailed me a thought along the lines of, "What if Lance had too much time on his hands now that he's retired? What if he became the neighbor who drives everyone crazy?"

I'm pretty sure James also suggested that somewhere in the fake news piece, Lance wash a car with one of his yellow jerseys.

Thanks, James!

AUSTIN, TEXAS (FAT CYCLIST FAKE NEWS SERVICE) — Less than six weeks after winning what was presumably the final race of his career,[12] Lance Armstrong today announced in a hastily-called media conference that, as widely rumored, he is coming out of retirement.

Said the rumpled, unshaven seven-time Tour de France champion, "Uh, I guess I'll be racing the Tour de France next year."[13] Then, after pausing for a few seconds while exchanging glances with Sheryl Crow, Armstrong continued, "I'll also be racing the Giro d'Italia." Another five silent seconds elapsed, after which Armstrong finished, "And the Vuelta a España."

Armstrong concluded the media conference abruptly by saying, "No questions. I have to go ride my bike now."

CROW GIVES THE GO-AHEAD

Rock star Sheryl Crow, fiancée to Armstrong, explained his decision. "He's racing again because I was going to completely lose my mind if he didn't get out of the house and do something."

"I swear," continued Crow, "If he isn't at Home Depot buying new power tools or downstairs playing Halo[14] (I haven't yet told him Halo 2 has come out), he's catching up on seven years' worth of television.

---

12 Ha.

13 I toyed with the idea of him having the beginnings of a gut, but decided against it. Too bad.

14 If I were writing this post nowadays, I'd have included something about sitting at the computer, spending hour after hour following 1,200 Twitter accounts. And maybe Skyping with Bike Snob NYC.

Yesterday, he watched the *entire second season* of 24. You know how long that took? All day and all night."[15]

Crow took a deep breath and continued, "Back when he was preparing for the Tour, Lance and I used to talk about how great it would be when he was retired and he'd have time to do nothing but relax." She then gritted her teeth and said, "I had no idea he meant that *so literally*."

At this moment, Crow stopped and took three deep breaths before continuing, "So, yeah, he's going to start racing again."

NEIGHBORS ENTHUSED FOR ARMSTRONG COMEBACK

Armstrong's next-door neighbor, James Scott, reports being pleased with Armstrong's decision to re-enter the peloton. "A few weeks ago, I was washing my car and Lance comes over, wearing pajama bottoms and 'I won the Tour de France 7 times and all I got was this lousy t-shirt' shirt."

"As *usual*, we start talking about the Tour," said Scott, "and he's helping me wash my car. Nice guy, really. And then I realize he's rubbing down my car with one of his yellow jerseys. I told him he should be protecting them for posterity and he says, 'Oh, I've got a million of 'em. You want it?' And of course I said 'yes.' I mean, who wouldn't want one of Armstrong's jerseys?"

"That was nine jerseys ago," continued Scott. "Now *anytime* I go outside to water the lawn, trim the hedge, whatever, he's out there with an excuse to talk about glory days and try to unload one of those jerseys. I've started avoiding him, if you want to know the truth."

ARMSTRONG REACTS

"I'm ready to get back into the routine," said the record-holding Tour winner when reached for comment. "At first, it's fun to be a full-time dad, but after a couple days you find yourself trying to remember which of the twins always wants to wear purple and which wants to wear pink,[16] and how you're going to get Luke back home from soccer practice when it's the girls' nap time and there are still dishes in the sink from two days ago."

---

15   Which makes sense, when you think about it.

16   At the time, one of my twin girls (who are pretty much the same age as Armstrong's twins) always wanted to wear purple. The other always wanted to wear pink.

"And have you ever been forced to watch 'Dora the Explorer?'" asked Armstrong, his face growing animated. "Now, *there's* a time trial for you. And they want to watch the same episode like, three times per day. I swear, if I hear that 'I'm the Map' song one more time...

"There've been times when I'm making three different kinds of soup for lunch," continued Armstrong. "Grace likes chicken and stars with the chicken bits taken out, Isabelle wants cream of chicken, and Luke wants cream of tomato, unless he changes his mind after I've made it and decides he wants SpaghettiOs. That's when I think, 'OK, who's the domestique now?' So no, I'm not too upset about having to get back on the bike."

Asked about his plan to race all three grand tours in 2006, Armstrong said, "Can I win all three? I have no idea. That's not even the point. I'm just doing what I'm told."

And when will Armstrong retire permanently? "I dunno," says Armstrong. "When will the twins be in school full-time?"

2006 TOUR DE FRANCE DECLARED "YEAR OF THE ASTERISK"

The 2006 Tour de France was the strangest, saddest Tour ever. First, impor-
tant contenders (Lance Armstrong, Jan Ullrich, Alexandre Vinokourov,
Alberto Contador, Ivan Basso) weren't there. Second, the initial days of the
race were incredibly dull.

Then it got better. In fact, it became incredibly inspirational, with Floyd
Landis turning in the most heroic-looking comeback since...ever. So much of a
comeback, in fact, that he won the Tour with that one gigantic, heroic move.

And then he got nabbed for doping, which kind of let the air out of the
whole thing.

My point being, 2006 was even more the year of the asterisk than I
thought at the time I wrote this piece.

PARIS, FRANCE (FAT CYCLIST FAKE NEWS SERVICE) — In a press conference following the ejection of Tour favorites Jan Ullrich, Francisco
Mancebo, and Ivan Basso from the Tour de France (TdF), race director
Christian Prudhomme announced that the 2006 TdF had been officially declared "The Year of the Asterisk."

"I am pleased to announce that the asterisk (*) will play an exception-
ally prominent role in this year's tour," said Prudhomme. "Of course,
it already had a starring role, due to Mr. Armstrong's absence and the
universal certainty that the only reason he wasn't going to win this year
is because he isn't racing.

"Now, however, with Basso and Ullrich gone, combined with efforts
to remove other racers like Vinokourov, we feel certain that any victories won in this year's tour will be very nearly meaningless.

"We are taking measures to really make the asterisk play a special
role this year," continued Prudhomme. "Instead of a stuffed lion, stage
winners will be handed a stuffed asterisk. Instead of excited discussion
about who raced how in a given stage, Phil Liggett and Paul Sherwen
have been instructed to talk about who would have raced better had
they been present.

"Most importantly," concluded the race director, "the leaders' jerseys have been specially modified. The yellow jersey will be a much paler, washed-out yellow; in fact, it will be hard to tell it's yellow at all. The white jersey will be more off-white than white, and may prominently feature a coffee stain if we don't get around to washing it soon. The polka dot jersey will have red asterisks instead of dots, and the green jersey will have a camouflage pattern.

"And of course," concluded Prudhomme, "all jerseys will have a big asterisk over the right breast."[17]

RACERS REACT

"I'm so glad all of these dirty racers have been caught," said one professional cyclist, who, on the advice of his lawyer, asked to remain anonymous. "You see, all the rest of us are absolutely clean."

"Yes," agreed another cyclist, who also asked not to have his name printed, "With all[18] of the leading names in cycling gone from this race, viewers — if there are any — can have high confidence that the person who wins has never taken drugs. You have my word on it."

"Isn't it amazing," asked a third unidentified racer, "that there are so many of us who are dirty, but none of us were able to beat Lance? It just goes to show: clean living pays in the end."

FANS REACT

Elden Nelson,[19] an avid cycling fan who was so excited about the Tour de France he recently purchased a Slingbox so he could watch it wherever and whenever he wanted,[20] looked despondent upon hearing the news. "This thing cost me close to $200," said Nelson, close to tears. "And now I don't know if I'll even bother watching at all."

"That's not all I'm upset about," said Nelson, who appears to be approximately twenty pounds overweight.[21] "I was more excited for this

---

17   OK, that would just look weird. Like you were wearing a single pasty or something.

18   Well, maybe not *quite* all. But you get my point.

19   This is the only time I have ever included myself in a fake news piece. I just wanted to put my actual feelings into it. Sort of a bubble of sincerity bobbing along in a vat of snark.

20   Wow. I had totally forgotten about the Slingbox. We had to do such crazy things to remote-view stuff back then.

21   A little self-deprecation, apropos of nothing.

TdF than I have been for three years. I mean, finally: a tour where there could be honest debate about who would win."

"Now," said Nelson, glumly, while idly scratching his paunch, "I guess people could still debate who's going to win, but it's not easy to get worked up about it. I guess I'll cheer for Floyd, but that's just kind of a fallback position."

Nelson then wandered away, evidently looking for something to eat.

RACE PREDICTIONS

With Ullrich, Basso, and Mancebo out of the tour, other racers suddenly have newfound opportunities to shine. Expert cyclist analysts say that faces to watch include:

- **David Millar:** Oh, the irony. It is rich, is it not?
- **Floyd Landis:** Dollars to doughnuts, Floyd will win the whole thing. And he might have won the whole thing even if Basso and Ullrich were racing. But now we'll never know, and it's suddenly tough to care.
- **David Zabriskie:** OK, I'll admit: if Zabriskie shines, there's reason to get excited. Really excited.
- **Others:** There are likely other candidates for a strong showing in this year's tour, but unfortunately, the expert analysts got bored of listing them, mumbled something about "doesn't matter anyway," and walked off.[22]

OLN FAILS TO REACT

OLN, the network broadcasting the Tour de France, was unavailable for comment on this development, because everyone involved in the broadcast (with the sole exception of Al Trautwig, who had no idea what had just happened) were too busy weeping.

---

22   Wow. Those expert analysts need some Prozac or something.

2006 TOUR DE FRANCE SHOCKER!
STAGE 9 CANCELLED DUE TO
LACK OF INTERESTINGNESS

The first week of the saddest Tour de France ever (see previous story) had come to a close. In it, there had been nothing but flat stages and one time trial, which I'm afraid I just don't remember at all. Which may speak more to my advanced stage of middle-agedness than the blandness of the stage, but you get my point.

What would the second week of the Tour bring? Another interminably-long flat stage, right off the bat!

Yaaaaaaaay.

PARIS, FRANCE (FAT CYCLIST FAKE NEWS SERVICE) — Tour de France (TdF) head honcho Christian Prudhomme took advantage of the relative calm of the rest day to announce that tomorrow's stage (Stage 9: Bordeaux – Dax) will be cancelled, due to the fact that it looks like it will be the least interesting stage in the history of the Tour de France.

"I really don't know how that stage snuck in there, but I don't see any way out of it: that stage is a yawner," said Prudhomme. "169.5 kilometers of very-nearly-straight road, completely flat."

"Seriously," concluded Prudhomme, "What were we thinking?"[23]

A PERFECT STORM OF MALAISE-INDUCING EVENTS
Prudhomme's decision would not likely have been made if not for several precipitating events earlier in the tour. Consider:
- **One Successful Breakaway per Customer, Please**: Each flat stage, a group of cyclists shoot off the front in order to give commentators something to talk about. Once per tour, someone from the breakaway is allowed to win the stage. That was yesterday. Sorry, no more successful breakaways.

---

23   I really do think the planners of the Tour were either angry at the world or just not paying attention. Or maybe there was some subtle-yet-compelling reason why it was important to have a long, flat stage hot on the heels of several other long, flat stages. If so, I didn't get it. Still don't.

- **Stage Winner a Foregone Conclusion**: Robbie McEwen would win the sprint. Again. It's not even entertaining to watch anymore. Commentators have been reduced to discussing what kind of victory salute Robbie will do as he crosses the line. For example, consider the exchange between Phil Liggett and Paul Sherwen at the end of Stage 6:

   Liggett: "Paul, if I were a betting man, I'd wager that today when Robbie wins the stage he'll do his 'I've been vindicated for some perceived slight' salute. He's a very angry man, you know."

   Sherwen: "I'm afraid I'm going to have to part with you on that assessment, Phil. Robbie looked to be in a pretty happy mood this morning. I'll wager he'll do his 'Jolly Jogger' salute as he crosses the line."

   Liggett: "Of course, there's always the possibility he'll do his 'I'm a very important person' salute. That's one of my favorites, you know."

   Note: Sherwen made the correct guess for stage six with his "Jolly Jogger" prediction.

   Note #2: Surprisingly, Robbie McEwen actually supports the cancellation of Stage 9. "I need time to regroup and think of a new clever salute," McEwen stated in a recent press conference.

- **The Only Interesting Contest in the TdF Currently Has Nothing to do With Flat, Sprint-Ending Stages**: Most major GC contenders took a major blow to their position in Saturday's individual time trial, and everybody's very interested to see whether this damage will get worse or better in the mountains. "I'm very excited to get into the mountains," said a very un-excited-sounding George Hincapie. "As everyone will remember, I showed last year that I can win stages in the mountains. No, seriously, I can. I can see in your eyes you think it was just a fluke, but it wasn't! I'll show you. I'll show you *all*!"[24]

---

24   He did not show us all.

COMMENTATORS EXPRESS RELIEF, DISAPPOINTMENT

Reached for comment on the cancellation of this exquisitely meaningless stage, Paul Sherwen responded, "To tell the truth, I'm quite pleased at the prospect of not having to commentate this stage. Do you think it's easy to talk about a peloton that isn't trying, while pursuing a breakaway that won't succeed? I have run out of clichés and colorful metaphors, and have told every anecdote from my professional cycling days more than a thousand times."

"Plus, Phil keeps falling asleep during the flat stages and then it's up to me to wake him up while I try to keep talking."

Phil Liggett, however, expressed mild disappointment at the cancellation of Stage 9. "I saw this stage as the Pro Cycling Commentators' Mt. Everest, really," said Liggett. "I mean, if I can talk in a friendly, informative, engaged manner about the most dreadfully dull stage imaginable, that says something about me, doesn't it?"

"Plus," finished Liggett, "I just finished uploading the audiobook version of *The Da Vinci Code* onto my iPod and planned to listen to a few chapters during the stage."

RACERS REACT

"You mean I don't have to — I mean, won't be allowed to — race 170 kilometers in close proximity to more than a hundred other stinky men, while risking some bozo crashing me out because he touched the wheel of the guy in front of him?" said Floyd Landis, presumably rhetorically. "You mean I won't have to ride all day with no chance of changing my overall standing on a stage where nobody else's standing will change either?"

"Wow," said Landis. "That's just tragic."

No other racers were asked to comment, because it's looking like in the absence of Ullrich, Basso, and Vinokourov, Landis is the only relevant rider left in the field.

> COMMENT FROM CARA
> You know the flat stages are getting boring when this comparison was made: "It was like Robbie pulled off an invisibility cloak from Harry Potter."

COMMENT FROM UNKNOWN

Today's rest day promises to be more exciting than tomorrow's stage.

COMMENT FROM BOB

The flat stages have always been boring, yet mesmerizing to me, kind of like watching golf on a Saturday afternoon. It'll get better in the mountains. Or not.

COMMENT FROM TYLER

You beat me to a post I was going to write tomorrow called "Tour de Boring." Seriously, guys. Five flat stages. A time trial. A flat stage. A rest day. A flat stage. And they're not even the "breakaway-style" flat stages ("a bit lumpy" — Paul) where a Jens Voigt would have a good time stomping everyone around for a while. Just flat. Come on, get 'em over with.

COMMENT FROM JIM

I Tivo every race, but have been so bored that I skip to the end and watch the last ten minutes instead of the painful two to three hours. If things get any "more interesting," I might have to check out re-runs of *Monk*.

LEVI LEIPHEIMER CALLS 'MULLIGAN' ON 2006 TOUR DE FRANCE

This post originally appeared in Cyclingnews, though they were a little bit apprehensive about it, to the point of including around three disclaimers before the story itself, and bolding the "Fake" in "Fake News Service."

PARIS, FRANCE (FAT CYCLIST FAKE NEWS SERVICE) — Following a closed-door meeting with Tour de France (TdF) Officials, Team Gerolsteiner held a press conference today, wherein team leader and former GC contender Levi Leipheimer made the following announcement:

"Based on the fact that until yesterday everyone, especially me, has been having a totally sucky tour, I have requested that we call 'mulligan' on this year's Tour de France to this point, start over with the prologue tomorrow, and try to get it right this time.

"I hold in my hand an Official Do-Over Petition, which has been signed by a clear and wide majority of riders, race directors, journalists, and cycling fans.

"Let's just say that everything up until Stage 11, where I took second after a long, brutal day in the mountain, was kind of like a dress rehearsal. I mean, you can see that our hearts just weren't in it for the first week."

Concluded Leipheimer, "Let's take it from the top and do it for *real* this time."

CHRISTIAN PRUDHOMME REACTS
Tour de France director Prudhomme, also on hand for the press conference, noted that there is indeed a mulligan clause in the Tour de France rules. Said Prudhomme, "It's an obscure rule, but Article 7.9.867-5309[25] does clearly indicate:

"In the event that a majority of race contenders are ejected from the Tour before the beginning of the race, and in the further event that the people left in the race tend to lurch around haphazardly from stage to stage as if they were drug addicts who had suddenly gone cold turkey, and in the final event that by the time the second half of the race begins only a single serious contender remains in actual race contention, the metaphorical reset button shall be pushed and the Tour shall commence again."

"Well," concluded Prudhomme, "I think this year's Tour pretty much satisfies those conditions."

RACERS REACT

George Hincapie, mistakenly treated as Discovery team leader for the first 11 stages of this year's Tour, had this to say: "Can we all *please* just accept that the climbing stage I won last year was just a fluke and that the yellow jersey I wore last week just goes to show what a freaky Tour this has been? If we could start over and all get behind Popovych or Salvodelli, maybe we could get someone on the podium.

"So yeah, I guess I'd be OK with starting the Tour over."

Hincapie then hesitated for a moment and said, "But can I still keep that yellow jersey?"[26]

Iban Mayo, who completely self-destructed without warning or reason as soon as the roads turned uphill this year, concurred, "Yes, a do-over would be an excellent idea," the Euskaltel-Euskadi rider said. "If given another chance, I will ride with honor and will win stage after stage.

"Or, I suppose," finished Mayo, "it's possible I may just blow up again. That's kind of my signature move."

Bobby Julich concurred that it would be an outstanding idea to restart the tour, providing he gets six weeks for his wrist to heal (and, presumably, to reconnoiter the course).

LIGGETT, SHERWEN REACT

Well-known commentators Phil Liggett and Paul Sherwen were enthusiastic about the idea of restarting the Tour. "You know, I am sick to death of talking about nothing but what an unusual Tour this has been," remarked Liggett. "Because everyone knows that when I say 'unusual,' what I really mean is 'ridiculous.'[27] We commentators don't look too good when we talk about what a strong time trial Leipheimer is going to put in and then he gets passed by a recreational cyclist, you know."

---

26 I think he should get to.

27 "Or sometimes I mean 'horrible.' And occasionally, I mean 'ridiculously horrible.'"

"Absolutely," agreed Sherwen. "Let's erase the tape of the Tour thus far, reach into our suitcase of courage, and start from scratch. From the way these guys have been riding, they can't be too tired yet."

FLOYD LANDIS REACTS

"You know, most people would probably expect that I wouldn't want to restart the Tour, since I'm winning it and everything," said race leader Floyd Landis. "But that's not the case. I'd love to start over.[28] This time, though, I'll hire a better mechanic and maybe someone to watch the clock for me, so I ought to be in yellow by the end of Stage 1. That should be cool."

OLN SCRAMBLES

The American broadcaster has had to react quickly, adjusting its schedule and making name changes to the program names.

"Considering that this race has been anything but 'Cyclismic,' we are going to go with something a little more subdued for the series title. We're thinking 'Cyclezzzzz' has a nice ring to it."

---

28 Yeah, I'll bet he would.

AN OPEN LETTER TO LANCE ARMSTRONG: SUGGESTED CHANGES TO YOUR SCREENPLAY

In 2006, there were a lot of rumors in the cycling world about a Lance Armstrong big screen biography. I still think there should and could be such a film, although it gets harder and harder to figure out where that movie would end. As he wins his first Tour de France? Or maybe seventh?

When he retires the second time, maybe? No, definitely not then.

Oh, how about after he retires the fifth time, at age 52? C'mon, you know it's going to happen. He can't help himself.

For the record, no, I have not actually seen an actual screenplay, and to my knowledge, there isn't one. However, in the off chance that Mr. Armstrong ever reads this, may I suggest: make it a musical.

FROM: The Fat Cyclist
TO: Mr. Lance Armstrong
SUBJECT: Minor Changes to Your Screenplay

Dear Lance,

First off, thanks for letting me be one of the first people to see the screenplay you've just completed for your autobiographical movie. I loved it and am absolutely positive that every cyclist in America would love it too.

Cyclists will flock to this film, just as it's written; they'll love this window into your world, as well as the drama and pageantry that swirl around the Tour de France. In short, I feel confident, Lance, in guaranteeing that every single cycling enthusiast in America will go see this movie when it comes out.

Which is my gentle way of saying, Lance, that as written, your movie would be a complete and total disaster.

There are only about 6,000 cyclists in America, Lance. And this statistic is no less alarming even when you take into consideration that I just made it up. My point is: if you want this movie to succeed, you need to punch it up. Make it Hollywood-friendly. Give it some heat.

Here, then, are my suggestions for a rewrite of your screenplay, if you'd rather it be a summer blockbuster than an anonymous direct-to-DVD bust.

CHANGE THE NAME

Yes, Lance, I know that your book, *It's Not About the Bike*, was a huge success. But that book was for a different audience. Specifically, it was for an audience of people who know how to read.

For a movie, you can't go telling people what it's *not* about. That would be like serving your head on a platter to the critics. I mean, can't you just hear Roger Ebert opening his review of your movie saying something like, "Lance Armstrong's movie tells us it's not about his bike. That's all well and good, but I wish he would have taken the time to decide what it *is* about."[29]

So, then, what should you call the movie? I have a few suggestions:

- *Ride*: People love one-word titles. They're easy to remember. Also, it's both an imperative verb and a noun, so it both describes what you do and what the film is. It sounds strong, confident. Manly. This is my number-one recommendation.[30]
- *The Cyclist*: This title makes it sound like you are really the only cyclist in the world. Everyone else is just a pretender. There's also a decent chance that many people will mistake "Cyclist" for "Cyclone" and we'll get a fair number of tickets purchased by the disaster-film crowd. Hey, let's not be picky; let's get butts in seats any way we can.
- *Lance Loves Sheryl*: This one's risky. If you call it this, we'll need to make sure that the movie trailers emphasize the love story aspect of your movie. The only way we'll get a greater than .000001% of the female audience for this film is if we make them think it's a romantic comedy.[31]

PUMP UP THE PLOT

Your life makes an inspiring story, Lance. Born into a humble, one-parent home, you showed great initial promise as a professional cyclist. Then you got cancer, but suffered through the treatment to emerge a stronger, more disciplined rider.

Once you started riding in the Tour de France, you caught fire and

---

29   Note to Roger Ebert: I have copyrighted this sentence. Hands off.

30   And I just checked IMDb; it doesn't look like any major feature films with that name have been made within the last five years. It's wide open. *Take* it.

31   I hereby retract my suggestion for this, both as the title of the film and the subject matter. I think people — Sheryl Crow, for example — would find it awkward.

won seven times in a row, showing a drive and consistency that is perhaps unmatched in the history of sport.

This kind of storyline is what we in the biz call a "non-starter."

You know what they're going to do when we pitch this movie with this storyline, Lance? They are going to tear us to *shreds*. Here are the easy questions they'll ask, and how I propose we revise your screenplay so we can be ready for them:

- **Where's the villain?** Of course, cancer is the real villain in your life, but that doesn't exactly work on film, does it? We need someone who is doing his level best to thwart you, not just in racing, but in your personal life. I suggest Jan Ullrich is the right character for this role. We'll have to tweak his personality a little bit since Ullrich is in fact, one of the nicest guys in the whole world, but the motivation part's easy: with each loss to you, Ullrich becomes more and more bitter, until (let's say in 2002) he snaps and vows he will stop at nothing — nothing!!! — to defeat you. He commences a campaign of underhanded tactics all geared toward securing the top spot on the Tour de France podium.[32]

- **You mean once he starts winning, he just *keeps* winning? There's never a serious doubt that he'll keep winning?** I'm sorry, Lance, but the first act (early promise) of your screenplay is incredibly ordinary, and the second act (enduring cancer treatment) makes you seem more like of a movie prop than an exciting film protagonist. We can tell those parts of the story in about twenty minutes anyways. Then there's the third act: Tour de France champion. It goes like this: You win the Tour de France. Then you win again. Then you win again. Then you win again. Then you win again. Then you win again. Then you win again.[33] It gets a little predictable, Lance. Think about this for a second: Rocky lost in the first movie, and *that's the only one that was any good.*[34]

- **At the end of the movie he just *RETIRES*?!** I'm sorry to use bold, all-caps, and excessive punctuation, Lance, but that's

---

32   I am not ashamed to admit that I think this would actually be a really interesting plot. Although, if I wrote the screenplay, I'd change the names and stuff.

33   Yep, I used copy and paste there.

34   I'm just being a snob here. I actually liked the second one too. After that, they all start blending together.

the way they're going to say it. I can't think of a more anti-climactic end to a movie than retirement. I suggest that in the movie, after your final tour, you vow to fight crime or you discover a cure to cancer while celebrating in a hotel or something. Remember this Hollywood axiom, Lance: any scene featuring a retirement must be followed with a scene wherein the newly-retired person[35] is gunned down by his enemy. See any cop movie that has ever been made for an example of this.

CHARACTER CONSOLIDATION

I'm sure you don't have trouble telling Floyd Landis from Roberto Heras from Tyler Hamilton from Jan Ullrich from Ivan Basso, even when they've got their helmets on. You probably can also identify every team immediately with just a quick glance at what they're doing.

I promise you, though, Lance: the movie-going audience will be completely baffled by all these different people and uniforms. They will wonder, "How come there are so many people in this race? Didn't some get eliminated in semi-finals?" And you know what? They'll never figure out that there are several teams, with domestiques (Mr. Midwest: "Domestique? What's a 'domestique?'") riding in support of captains.

So here's what we do. First, we get rid of all but about seven racers, and five of them will be anonymous. Their job will be to wipe out, drop off the back, acknowledge your superiority, and whatnot. We'll consolidate Floyd, Roberto, Tyler, and Ivan into one all-purpose competitor, who we will call "Henry." Henry will not have a last name, and will communicate mostly through the medium of sweat.

TACTICS MADE EASY

As part of the general simplification of cycling for the moviegoing masses, we'll also simplify tactics. We won't show you drafting along behind your team for 99.8% of a given stage, for example, because John. Q. Moviegoer would say, "How come Lance can't beat that guy?" Instead, we'll show you just shooting off the front at the beginning of the stage and then staying off the front.

People will get that.

When you think about it, Lance, the whole idea of "stages" is fairly

---

35 Or more often, the guy *about* to retire.

problematic. Put yourself in the place of someone who has never watched pro cycling before. You come to this movie. It shows a guy coming in 20th or so, day after day. Maybe he wins one or two stages. Then, at the end, they say he won the whole thing.

"No he didn't," Mr. NASCAR Dad will reply. "I saw him lose *over and over.*"[36] So we're going to tweak the results a bit. We won't go and actually say you won *every* stage in the movie, but we'll only show the stages that you *do* win. That ought to do the trick.

MISCELLANEOUS CHANGES

There are a few other little things we'll need to change, Lance. Nothing big:

- **Costumes:** I think you'll agree that cycling uniforms look, well, silly. I'm in consultation with one of the hottest costume designers in Hollywood — she did both *Daredevil* and *Pirates of the Caribbean.* She's going to start from the ground up. I promise, you are going to be blown away by her designs. Think high-gloss leather with a chamois.
- **Location:** Americans are very patriotic right now, Lance. Being a Texan yourself, you know that. What if the "Tour de France" became the "Tour de Freedom" and went from Alaska to Hawaii? That would rock.
- **Podium Ceremony:** Girls in knee-length dresses, giving you a peck on the cheek and a stuffed lion? I don't think so, Lance. I'm thinking full on rock-concert-level celebration with Vegas showgirls doing the honors.

I've sent a copy of your script, along with these suggestions, to a top-notch team of Hollywood script-doctors. They asked me to give them some latitude as they wrote and I figured you'd have no problem with that. I'm excited to see what they cook up.

Like I said, Lance, with a few tweaks here and there, we're going to have a great film that stays true to your story and the sport.

Kind Regards,

---

36 | I'm betting this is sounding terribly familiar to those of you who have tried to explain the Tour to friends and family.

11.
Who We Are

HERE WE ARE. THE LAST SECTION IN THIS BOOK. IF EVERYTHING HAS GONE AS I'VE INTENDED, YOU STARTED WITH THE FIRST STORY AND HAVE READ continuously through each and every essay, in the order presented.

In this section, everything all comes together. The stories you have been reading will suddenly take on new and highly significant meaning as you read these last few stories. Waves of epiphany will crash over you and you will become truly enlightened.

What?

You've just been dipping into this book, reading stories randomly, and rarely, if ever reading these section introductions?

Well, I guess you can forget about all that enlightenment. Without everything else, these last few stories are simply pieces about how cycling affects us; how it makes us who we are.

And how we smell.

I AM A CHANGED MAN, PART I: MY BODY

Do you ever play the "What if" game? What if you hadn't introduced your-self to that person with whom you're now spending your life? What if you had chosen a different major in college?

What if you had said "no thanks" to the friend who invited you out on that first ride, the one that got you hooked?

Well, in addition to all the fun I'd have missed, I'd look different. And my body would work different. Probably, that's not so unusual.

But where did this story came from? Easy. I was sitting in a meeting at work, staring at my ring finger, thinking about how odd it looks, the way it bends up at the tip. I started making a mental list of other ways that cycling has affected me.

After that, all I needed to do was add some verbs and punctuation.

Biking has changed me during the ten-plus years[1] I've been riding. Both physically and mentally. Here I'm going to talk about the physical part. In my next story, I'll talk about how biking has changed me mentally.

Unless I forget or change my mind.

RING FINGER

Back when I was first mountain biking, maybe just a year or so into it, one of my riding group's favorite yardsticks was known as "The Frank Time Trial." The first time I tried doing this course for time, I was as nervous as I ever have been for any race. After all, since Frank has a lot of climbing and a technical descent, your time said a *lot* about what kind of mountain biker you were.

I took the downhill in a manner I'd like to call "aggressive." My friends called it "spastic and out of control."

In a banked chute toward the end of the ride, I picked a bad line and supermanned off my bike, landing with all my weight on my hands.

---

1   And it's continued to change me ever since. I've now got so many scars I can't remember which scar goes with which story. I should have gotten identifying tattoos to caption the scars I wanted to remember, as insurance against the mind-wipe middle age is turning out to be.

That hurt.

I was so intent on finishing with a good time, though, that I didn't even worry about my left hand. That's significant, because normally I probably would have screamed bloody murder.

I got back on my bike and finished the loop. I remember getting a 1:06, which was respectable for a new rider. I think the fast guys were doing it eight minutes faster.

When I got back to work, I thought about calling a doctor, because the tip of my ring finger seemed to be pointing in an odd direction; it went up at a 30-degree angle. Then I decided not to bother.

My finger continues to point at that weird angle even today. I think my typing has improved because of it.

MY RIGHT SHOULDER

Whenever my friends and I go to Moab, you can bet that one of the rides we'll do is Reverse Porcupine. This simply means that we ride part of the famous Porcupine Rim trail, but we ride up the part most people come down. This section of trail ridden in this way is full of difficult moves, and provides an excellent opportunity for technically skilled riders to show off their talents.

And for technically unskilled riders to fall a lot.[2]

Guess in which category I belong?

Maybe seven years ago, I was trying one of what I thought was the safest of these moves: do a slow-mo 120-degree left turn around a scrub oak, thread the needle between two tight rocks, and then wheelie up a ledge. I didn't expect to make it, but I wasn't scared of trying.

Then, at almost exactly zero miles per hour, as I pivoted around the scrub oak, I lost it. The sand kept me from getting out of my pedals in time and I fell over heavily on my right side, sending the combined force of my weight and falling momentum through my outstretched right hand and up my arm.

The screams were incredible.

---

2   As I write this footnote, a Moab trip with The Core Team is less than two weeks away. Thinking about what's in store for me — the unknown new injuries I am about to incur — I find my stomach is suddenly knotting up.

I had dislocated my shoulder[3] for the first time, and I can promise you the first time is the worst. That is where what is now known as the "Elden Scream" was first heard.

After I was able to stop screaming — yes, screaming — I walked my bike back to my car. I couldn't ride with a dislocated shoulder[4] and I didn't know how to set it back then. I drove the three hours home to go to the hospital, where the emergency room doctor put my shoulder back where it belongs.

My shoulder now pops out quite easily, thank you, and while it still hurts each time, I now know what to do. But I can't sleep on my right side, I can't throw, I can't rotate my right arm in certain ways or lift it very high, and I always know when it's going to rain.[5]

And as an aside, I think it's a testament of my friends' dedication to their craft, as well as their quality as human beings, that nobody volunteered to go back with me (and I was driving a stick shift, by the way).

Hey, at least I know where I stand.

MY LIP

It's hard for me to talk about this injury. No, not because the pain is too vivid of a memory, but because I just don't really understand what happened.

The short (and long) version[6] is, I wiped out on one of my favorite trails (Dry Canyon, coming down off Frank) one day for no apparent reason. I tore my lip all the way to just below my nose. I guess it says something about me that when the doctor gave me suggestions on steps I could follow to minimize the visibility of the scar, as well as a recommendation for a plastic surgeon who could essentially make it disappear. I brushed him off.

So now I have a nice, white scar that is always visible, increasingly so with every day I skip shaving. I sometimes wish my wreck would have a more interesting story behind it, but at least I got it while doing what I love best. And by "what I love best," I am referring to biking, not wrecking and sliding on my face.[7]

---

3   Actually, recent MRIs and whatnot reveal that what I've been doing all this time is dislocating my shoulder and tearing my labrum. Regardless, the pain was exquisite.

4   Torn labrum, whatever. Google "SLAP tear" for more info.

5   So it's not all bad.

6   See *How to Fall Down*, p. 52.

7   I just want to be clear on that point.

The only really unfortunate thing about this scar is that it totally screws up my goatee. I used to be able to grow one of the nicest goatees you had ever seen; when combined with my sinister-looking eyebrows, this beard made me look intense, as well as evil. Complete strangers would stop and comment on how evil I looked. "Hey, fat dude on a bike, you look full-on wicked evil!" they would say.

Now, however, the scar breaks up the beard and makes it look asymmetrical. Which is more disconcerting than evil.

MY LEGS

I sometimes like to imagine the present-day me challenging past me to a bike race. Even though I weigh about ten pounds more than I did when I first started riding, I am absolutely confident I could kick my own past self's butt. "Who is that fast, fat guy with the scar on his lip?" the me from the past would ask.

The thing is, riding a bike for ten years or so changes your legs. Even at my fattest and most out of shape, I could, with total confidence, challenge some generally ultra-fit non-cyclist to a bike race and utterly humiliate him.[8]

Anyway, this foundation of leg fitness stays with you. Once or twice, I've stopped biking during the winter and picked it up again in the spring. Sure, you hurt at first, but it's nothing like starting over.

I don't know: maybe if I stopped riding for a full year, that magical leg strength would vanish, but I prefer to think instead that by biking all these years, my legs are now fundamentally and permanently different from what they were before.

And that change, to me, easily makes all the other changes worth it. Because those physical changes are the entry fee for the mental changes which I will talk about next.[9]

---

8   Or her, I guess, except I'm married and even before I was married was not the kind of person who would casually challenge women to sports contests.

9   And which are not, in spite of everything you know about me, absentmindedness and a tendency to ramble.

COMMENT FROM UNKNOWN

That does it. I really must start cycling. It sounds fun. It might be quicker and cheaper and perhaps more of a rush to step in front of an express train, though. I'm conflicted. Please advise.

COMMENT FROM ANDREW

A *real* mountain biker, or perhaps just a really bad mountain biker, ends up with a distinctive line of teeth marks on the back of the right calf, a result of the big ring digging into you during a gravity check. Whenever I'm in a spinning class, I consider any guy who doesn't have that permanent tattoo on his calf to be a contemptible sissy.

COMMENT FROM UNKNOWN

Now y'all have done it. I had a nice mountain bike ride planned for today. I was even going to do Buck Hill, but after reading all the comments, I'm afraid to ride. Guess I'll take the day off and polish my trophies. That'll probably take all day.

I AM A CHANGED MAN, PART II: IT'S ALL IN MY HEAD

I do not have a favorite shirt. I do not love my car. My house is important to me only because that's where my family is.

I don't love stuff.

But I love bikes. Love them something awful.

The reason why is easy: they make me happy. Not just in a momentary way, either (although definitely in the momentary way, too). Bikes have made me a happy person in general. Riding has gotten me through difficult times. Riding has inspired me. I've solved difficult work and personal problems while riding. I've seen more beauty while riding a bike than I have in any other way.

My life is good. And a huge part of that wellness is due to the bike.

In the previous story, I talked about the obvious physical changes ten years of biking has made in me. Most of the changes I talked about — and most of the comments that came after — were about scars and other injuries.

Which brings up the question: So *why* do we bike?

Well, I bike because what's happened in my head more than offsets anything that's happened to my body.

I'VE LEARNED I'M AN ATHLETE

In high school, I actually did "letter" — in debate[10] and humor interpretation (yes, reading funny stories to audiences is actually a competitive event in the U.S. and I took it *very* seriously). But not in sports. Oh no, not in sports. In fact, I took some kind of cockeyed pride in not being a "jock."

This is a tragedy, because I went to high school in Fruita, Colorado, which any mountain biker worth his salt knows is one of the best

---

10   I was in Lincoln-Douglas debate, because the one-on-one style, combined with the emphasis on persuasion, as opposed to mountains of evidence, is a great way for someone who plans to be a lawyer to get started. Yep, in high school I was absolutely convinced I would be a lawyer. It did not occur to me that I might be an analyst for an IT research company, possibly because at the time there was no such thing.

mountain biking destinations in the world.[11]

As I got older, I rollerbladed[12] (I can admit it without shame) to keep in shape,[13] and played quite a bit of racquetball.

But I was never an athlete until I tried endurance mountain biking at age 30. The discovery that I have a gift for staying on my bike and turning the cranks long after most people would fall over exhausted was incredibly gratifying. It made me wonder: what *else* have I not discovered about myself?

And who *wouldn't* want to find out, three decades into their life, that they're an athlete? That you just needed to find out what kind?

I'VE LEARNED I CAN SUFFER WELL

I have ridden through the night, I have ridden in the cold, I have ridden when I am completely bonked out of my mind. I have ridden uphill for twenty miles with the jagged end of a seatpost where my saddle should be. I have finished a race with a dislocated shoulder. I have ridden six hours after falling six feet right onto my chest, forearms, and face.

And while part of me despairs (or even screams), I have never quit a race.[14] Even while I am suffering, there's a part of me that's grimly amused at what a fool I am. That sarcastic guy has goaded me through a lot, and I now know that I can make it through circumstances that would shut a lot of people down.

That's a pretty cool thing to know about yourself.

I'VE LEARNED HOW TO BE SMART

Kevin Millecam, a manager of mine back in the old days at Novell, used to give me challenging assignments. He'd tell me he wanted a database that could act as a back end to a shopping cart he wanted created using Java. And he would ask for those things knowing full well I was still just learning Java and didn't have database programming experience.

Then he would send me off on a mountain bike ride during work

---

11 In my defense, mountain biking hardly existed at the time.

12 Or is the past tense of "rollerblade" "rollerbled?"

13 For a couple years, I also rollerbladed to commute to work. Eight miles each way, each day. I got in pretty good shape. And I'm still not convinced rollerblading is objectively any dorkier than cycling.

14 When I wrote this originally, it was true. Sadly, it is no longer true. I crashed out of the 2009 Leadville 100.

hours, telling me to come back in three hours or so.

I'd take off, totally freaked out, knowing I was doomed. Within a half hour on the bike, though, I'd have forgotten all about what Kevin had assigned. And then, within an hour, little things would start popping into my head. By the time I got back, I'd have a working plan for how to get started.

Any time I've talked with a cyclist, road or mountain, I've heard similar stories. You get out on the bike and somehow your difficult problems get pushed into the background. Then, when they're ready, they come popping back to the foreground...but they're not as difficult as before.

I'VE LEARNED TO LOSE MYSELF

Every once in a while on a nice long ride, there will come a few miles where I go completely blank. I'm never aware of going into that state, but I'm always aware of coming out of it. And I realize, wow, I haven't thought about *anything* for...well...I don't *know* how long.

Was it a minute? Five? How far did I go? What did I see? What was going on in my head?

I never have answers to any of those questions, but I always feel great afterward.

I don't know anything about Zen, but I'm pretty sure this blankness is a state adherents strive toward. I know Schopenhauer[15] called it "the sublime," but he went after it in all the wrong ways.

Schopenhauer should have bought a bike.

I'VE LEARNED I LOVE THE OUTDOORS

My dad is an avid hunter and fisherman. I, to his dismay, am not. I don't have anything against hunting and fishing, I just couldn't get into them as a kid. Believe me, I tried. Somehow, I got my disinterest in these two activities confused with a dislike of the outdoors.

Wrong.

Once I started mountain biking, I discovered I *love* the outdoors.[16] And I have seen a lot of it. I've seen banana slugs as big as...well, bananas. I've seen stars while out in the desert; there are a lot more of

---

15   From one of the philosophy classes required for pre-law folks. Ha. See *Section 1: How It Began.*

16   I should try to get my dad to try out mountain biking. He owes me.

them than I had realized. I've seen wildflowers high up in the Uintas. I've seen moose and elk and eagles and wild turkey and mountain lions and foxes and raccoons and porcupines and skunks and rabbits and bears and deer, countless deer.

So, yeah. Biking comes with its bumps and bruises and scars and occasional permanent debilitating injuries and death.

But hey. Lots of upside, right?

COMMENT FROM UNKNOWN

I was not an "athlete" when I was a kid. I was always the last one chosen for the team. You know the one. I was 13 when the bike came along. It was a revelation to find a sport at which I excelled. In high school, I had the sublime experience of being a Cat 2 bike racer at the same time that the gym-class physical-fitness test said I was a 20-percentile weakling.

COMMENT FROM ARIANE

Yeah, you know, now that you mention it, cycling is the only thing I've ever done where I can zone out like that. Though I wonder if I've ever almost died, as after I'm back to myself, I haven't the least recollection anything that's taken place, including whether or not I've paid attention to rush hour traffic, road signs, and stop lights.

CYCLING STINKS

I'm always a little bit embarrassed to give co-workers, friends and miscellaneous folk rides in my truck. Not so much because it's a mess (though it is) as because my truck — thanks to years and years of post-ride riders riding in it — always smells quite a bit like a locker.

But somehow worse.

In fact, the only thing that smells worse than the inside of my truck may be my bike stuff bag, which holds my helmet, gloves, shoes, socks, jerseys, and shorts.

You might be surprised to know that this bag is quite pungent.

You might not, however, be surprised to learn that opening my sports bag at the end of one particularly warm day after it sat broiling in my truck was the inspiration of this story.

I love biking. I love mountain biking. I love road biking. I have a sneaking suspicion I'm going to love track racing.[17]

I love getting ready for a big ride. I love the rhythm of riding on the road. I love picking a line on new singletrack. I love riding rocky jeep roads. I love the way I feel after a big workout.[18]

I love the way bikes look. I love the way bikes sound. I love talking about bikes and telling biking stories, and I love hearing other cyclists' stories.[19]

To recap: I love biking. And yet, there is one inescapable truth about cycling that I do *not* love:

Practically everything about cycling stinks.

JERSEYS

It's easy to tell whether a person on a bike is a cyclist, or just a person who happens to own a bike. Just look at what he's wearing. T-shirt? Person. Brightly-colored polyester skintight jersey with a zip-up front and pockets in the back? Cyclist.

---

17   This suspicion is still, unfortunately, sneaking.

18   You could be forgiven, at this point, for saying, out loud, "OK, I get it. You like bike stuff. Move on."

19   If, by now, you have *not* said, "OK, I *get it* already. You *like bikes*. What's your point?" then I have not done my job. Which, apparently, is to drive a point right into the ground.

The benefits of jerseys are many: they help you be seen by traffic. They give you a place to carry food and a phone. They evaporate sweat, so you don't feel like you're riding with a big ol' soaked sponge for a shirt.

But that last bit, that bit about evaporating sweat, is a two-edged sword. Because while your jersey is doing a fantastic job of getting rid of the water part of the sweat, it's doing an equally fantastic job of *holding on* to the stink part of the sweat. The fibers of biking jerseys are, in fact, specially designed to trap every little molecule of stench[20] your upper body excretes, compound it by a factor of seven, and then time-release that smell for the next eon or so.

As a young, naïve cyclist, I used to think washing a jersey would get rid of that smell. It doesn't. Washing it again doesn't help, either. And in fact, if you wash the jersey too many times, you'll just make the washing machine start to stink.

Special Note to everybody who is about to send me mail,[21] describing how they use vinegar, lemon juice, ammonia, or sulfuric acid to good effect in combating the "jersey stink" phenomenon: Feel free to go ahead and address that letter, but please realize that I already know about your so-called remedy and have the following observations to make:

- **Your remedy actually only masks the smell**. An argument can be made that a stinky jersey with a hint of rancid lemon is even worse than plain ol' stinky jersey.
- **Even if your remedy *does* work, I don't care.** I'm barely organized enough to wash my jerseys at all. There's *no way* I'm going to remember to start using time-consuming anti-stink potions every time I do the wash.

HELMET

My head starts sweating well before the rest of my body. And the straps and little pads in my helmet are nowhere near as easy to clean as my jersey. Back in arid Utah, this meant that within a few hours after a

---

20   Yes, there are actual stench molecules. They have scientific names and everything.

21   That's a rhetorical device. I don't actually expect you to mail me a letter. Although you're welcome to send me e-mail. Address: Fatty@fatcyclist.com. Subject: You Stink.

ride, my helmet straps would dry out, becoming stiff, crusty, and above all, stinky.

Here in Washington, though, the humidity keeps the straps from drying out so quickly. In fact, if you ride your bike more than twice a week, your helmet straps will *never* dry out.[22] This means that instead of your straps becoming stiff, crusty, and stinky, they become dank, cold, and above all, stinky.

Interesting[23] **aside:** You'd think that mildew would grow on constantly damp straps like this, but it doesn't. My theory is that this is because the stench frightens the mildew monsters away.

Unlike jerseys, it's possible to clean helmet straps and pads so they don't stink.[24] Unfortunately, to reap this benefit, you must in fact clean your helmet straps and pads. This is such a time-consuming, awkward process — which is immediately negated the next time you go out on a ride — that nobody in the history of cycling has done it more than once.

GLASSES

I just found out about this recently and admit I was astounded. Yes, my beloved Oakley Racing Jackets, the ones with the expensive frames and super-expensive prescription lenses, stink. I discovered this when my wife asked me to keep my glasses in the garage, because they smelled up our bedroom. Challenging her, I put the frames under my nose and inhaled deeply.

Wow.

So I guess thousands of miles-worth of dripping sweat can permeate *anything*.

---

22   This was one of the most surprising things I discovered about moving to Washington: nothing ever dries out. When I moved back to Utah, it took some time to re-train myself to start closing the bread bag again.

23   It's interesting to me, anyway.

24   I've been told that you can wash a helmet just by running it through a dishwasher. I haven't tried this yet, though, because I imagine all the Styrofoam breaking up and dissolving in the wash cycle, and I'd open the dishwasher door to find nothing but a sad little plastic shell.

MORE, MORE, MORE

Really, I could go on.[25] My messenger bag stinks, which is a problem since that's what I use to carry my clean clothes to work. My biking shoes stink, which is probably the least surprising thing I've ever written. My biking shorts stink, which dogs seem to really appreciate. My Camelbak stinks, although, as near as I can tell, that stench hasn't yet penetrated the bladder.[26] This may, however, just be because Camelbak bladders have a stink and taste of their own.

So I have a theory: the main reason people don't get into cycling is because they smell us before they ride with us.

POST-RIDE STENCH

The thing is, this residual stink, the smell that clings to all your cycling stuff, is only a tiny part of the problem. The only thing worse than the smell of a cyclist after a ride is a *group* of cyclists after a ride. Or at least, that's what my wife tells me and my kids won't come near me when I get home from work until after I clean up.

But you know what's even worse than a group of cyclists after a ride? A group of cyclists after an *epic* ride, in a car, for an extended period of time. Why? Well, without getting too explicit, when one is on one's bike for a long time, eating unusual food, one's digestive system, well, *reacts*. And while most people have the most polite intentions in the world, at some point physics takes over.

And, in short, seven stinky guys with gas in a car for an extended period of time can reduce a vehicle's resale value by 18%.[27]

DANGER OF BECOMING DESENSITIZED

If you're an avid cyclist, there's a good chance you haven't recently thought about the stink you make. This is not a good sign, because it means you have contracted Cycling Stench Desensitization Syndrome (CSDS). Here are common symptoms:

- You think your bike clothes don't stink.
- You keep any of your bike stuff in any place other than the garage.
- You wonder why nobody ever wants to be near you.

---

25 I think, over the course of six-plus years, I've proved this sufficiently.
26 And let's hope it never does.
27 Per year.

It's entirely possible that CSDS is incurable. The symptoms, however, are treatable. You must simply realize that just because you don't notice the smell *doesn't mean it's not there*. Every bike-related item you own must be isolated from everything else you own, and treated much the same as if it were radioactive waste.

Or at least, that's what all of *you* have to do. *My* bike stuff smells just fine.

COMMENT FROM TIM

If your jersey stinks after a ride you must not have discovered the benefits of Merino wool.

COMMENT FROM DUG

I knew wool would come up. Whenever talk of stink comes up, wool is always touted as the answer. However, remember this. Wool will eventually make your nipples bleed. And in the end, bleeding nipples suck more than stinky jerseys.

COMMENT FROM UNKNOWN

Ok, so one thing you neglected to clarify in all your glorious details about cycling stink: Girl cyclists do NOT stink nearly as bad as guys! I swear it's true! Our sweat stink is there, but it's only faintly, delicately, barely perceptible.

(ANOTHER) COMMENT FROM UNKNOWN

You guys don't know what stink is! I have played hockey for more years than I care to admit, and when I start comparing the stench of my riding apparel to that of my hockey gear, now that is smelly! Hockey gear is the benchmark by which all athletic odors should be measured. The only time it doesn't smell is when you are in the locker room with your teammates who smell equally as bad.

LIES

I was trying to convince my good friend and manager Matt to get into cycling. "It's not at all an expensive sport," I told him. "All you need, really, is a bike and helmet."

I said it with a straight face, too. Just up and told him that, as if it were true.

Later, when I got home and opened the garage, the full extent of the falsehood hit me in the face: a garage so full of bike stuff that my car would absolutely not ever have a prayer of fitting in there.

So I wrote this story. And hoped that by the time Matt read it, it would be too late.

There are so many ways to lie. Exaggeration. Omission. Misdirection. Statistics. Intentional-but-cleverly-concealed logical fallacy. An anecdote, presented as a pattern. Misleading metaphors.[28] And I'm just getting started (that's a lie; I'm actually running out of steam).

I know all about lies. I have to, because I'm a cyclist. The two go hand in hand. If you're going to be a cyclist, you've got to embrace certain falsehoods.

I have examples.

ALL YOU NEED IS A BIKE AND A HELMET

The Lie: One of the appeals of biking is that it has a very low barrier to entry. I mean, all you really need is a bike which you can get at your local sporting-goods store or big box store. Add a helmet for safety and you're all set.

The Truth: Well, first of all, you're going to at least need a pump and a patch kit,[29] some lube, and some basic tools, or your bike won't last very long, will it? Even beyond that, though: sure, you *can* get yourself a cheap bike, a helmet, and leave it at that. In which case you will never understand why other people love to ride their bikes.

---

28 It's a little bit disconcerting how easily I'm able to come up with different ways of being dishonest, isn't it?

29 The first time I ever got a flat on my first "real" mountain bike, I fixed it using a patch kit. The patch failed within one ride. I have not used a patch kit ever since; the odds against them working just seems too high.

No, if you want to really see what your bike-loving friends are raving about,[30] you're going to need a nice bike, some good biking shorts, biking shoes, gloves, and a jersey. That will be enough for you to started.

After a while, though, you'll need to buy more bikes, for different kinds of riding. And you'll want to upgrade your components. And you'll want more bike clothes, for different kinds of riding weather. There is no end to bike consumerism.

At all.

Ever.

BIKING IS A GOOD HOBBY/WAY TO EXERCISE

The Lie: Riding a bike is a good way for you to get outside and see the world, all while getting fresh air and exercise.

The Truth: When you start biking, you'll notice things like the outdoors, and you'll be glad for the exercise. Soon, though, it won't seem like enough. You'll start taking longer rides, because the short ones just don't seem to work you out the way they used to. And you'll start paying attention to the road or trail instead of the world around you.

Before long, you'll notice that in order to get any kind of workout at all on your bike, you need to go out for a couple hours. And you'll ride the entire time looking at the road or trail, not even thinking about what's off to your side. And you'll want to start riding more and more often, on more and more extreme terrain. At that point, you're no longer a hobbyist.

Congratulations. You're a bike junkie.

YOU CAN SAVE TIME AND MONEY BY BIKING TO WORK

The Lie: You can get to work faster and for cheaper by riding your bike than by taking your car. There's nothing quite so rewarding as passing hundreds of crawling cars as you head to work. Then, once you get to work, you feel energized the whole day. Plus, there's the nice side effect that you've combined your workout with your commute!

The Truth: OK, all of that's actually true. But if you bike commute for long enough, you'll start talking to your coworkers about it, gushing

---

30 Seriously, sometimes we rave. Foaming at the mouth, wild-eyed, twitchy raving. Makes you want to join the club, doesn't it?

about how great it is, and how they ought to try it. You'll go on and on
an on. Coworkers will cringe when you approach.

People will start avoiding you at office parties.

CYCLING IS A GREAT WAY TO LOSE WEIGHT

The Lie: By riding your bike, you can burn 300–1,000 calories per hour
at an aerobic level. This can greatly accelerate any weight loss program.
The Truth: This is an especially insidious aspect of biking, because you
can be snared by either of two opposing, but equally vicious, traps:

- **Cycling begets hunger**: If you ride your bike, you'll get hungry.
  If you ride your bike more, you'll get even hungrier. If you ride
  your bike for several hours, you'll come home and eat everything in the kitchen. I have never done an epic ride in my life
  where I was not heavier the day afterward.[31]

- **Endless loop**: As you ride your bike
  and lose weight, you discover that
  you're faster. So you start trying to lose
  additional weight in order to be still
  faster on your bike. As you become
  very thin,[32] you find that you can climb
  with incredible ease. You are no longer
  riding to lose weight. You are losing
  weight to ride. Why is this dangerous?
  Consider the logical extreme of this
  cycle: Michael Rasmusson, winner of
  the climber's jersey in the 2005 Tour de France.

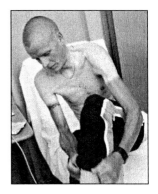

YOU GET USED TO THE SADDLE AFTER A WHILE

The Lie: Sure, your butt hurts when you start riding a bike. After a
while, though, you get used to the saddle and it's no problem. Just use
some of that chamois cream to avoid chafing.
The Truth: Sure, your butt hurts when you start riding a bike. After a
while, though, you get used to the saddle and it's no problem . . . until

---

31 That is the absolute, honest truth. Somehow, I am creating matter by expending
energy. How is it possible that I am defying physics this way?

32 I am no longer speaking from experience, since I have never been "very thin."

you get your first saddle sore, which makes the pain you suffered as a new cyclist seem laughable.

Furthermore, that chamois cream feels *so creepy,* most people would rather have the chafing. At least, that's what they think until the chafing occurs.

COMMENT FROM UNKNOWN
Lie: Seriously, honey, this is the last bike I'm going to buy.

COMMENT FROM ANDREW
Lie: That which does not kill you makes you stronger.
Truth: That which does not kill you only postpones the inevitable.

COMMENT FROM JIM
Lie: The team ride starts at 9am.
Truth: It's 9:10. Joe did say he was showing up, right?

CRASH ETIQUETTE FOR COMPLETE IDIOTS

A while ago, Bob and I rode the Crop Circles/Mr. DNA/Tapeworm trail system. It was raining lightly, even though it was spring in Seattle, so the roots, rocks, and wooden stunts were slippery.

Early in the ride, we came to a seesaw. This one was taller and shorter than the seesaw I had ridden the last time we had been in the area, the board was narrower, and it was made of smooth wood. Also, the approach was downhill and around a bend.

I admit it: I was scared.

I approached the seesaw too slowly. By the time I was about halfway up, my front wheel was wobbling. I nearly stalled out, and my front wheel rolled off the right side of the seesaw.

This, as you may expect, was not a desirable situation.

From a height of probably five feet, I fell over the front of my bike. Ordinarily, I'd put my hands out to catch my fall, but this time I didn't. I pulled my arms in toward my chest, and landed in a nice forward roll, finishing in a sitting position, astounded that I was not hurt even a tiny bit. I sat for a moment, stunned at my good fortune.

Bob shouted, as I sat there, dropped his bike, and ran over. "Are you OK?" he asked.

I admitted that, to my amazement, I was just fine.

Bob then started laughing, recounting how the fall looked from his perspective, describing the contributing factors to my crash, and how surprised he was that I hadn't snapped a wrist on that fall.

It was at this moment that I realized the reason I really like riding with Bob. He knows proper crash etiquette.

Bob's behavior stands in marked contrast to how another friend of mine reacted after I crashed. Let's just call him "Brad." His name is, in fact, Brad.

Brad and I were riding a goat trail coming down from Jacob's Ladder, which is part of the Hog's Hollow[33] network. I had never ridden this descent before and so was surprised when it suddenly terminated with

---

33 I am on a mission to misspell "Hog Hollow" in every way possible, because it really bothers my friend Dug. I think I get extra points for misspelling it in a book.

a three-foot drop onto a dirt road. I flipped over my handlebars and landed on my back. It hurt. A lot.

Brad, naturally, took this opportunity to immediately begin laughing his head off. Without asking if I was OK, without saying, "Sorry I didn't warn you about how this trail ends," without any clue that several years later, I'd be tearing him a new one in the most public way I could imagine.

PROPER CRASH ETIQUETTE

So, let this be a lesson to you. If you don't follow the rules of Crash Etiquette, you may someday reap the consequences. Have I mentioned that this is the same Brad who bailed on his last lap when we were racing the 24 Hours of Moab as a two-person team, and then didn't even stick around to see me finish when I did his lap for him?

Luckily, the rules of Crash Etiquette are quite simple. Most anyone can follow this simple five-step procedure:

1. **At the moment of impact, express astonishment and dismay.** The best possible noise you can make when another person crashes is the noise you imagine yourself making if you were to have that selfsame crash. But an audible gasp or "Whoah!" will do fine.

2. **Immediately check to see if the crasher is OK.** Saying "Are you OK?" is the correct way to do this. If a pool of blood or a compound fracture is evident, you should still ask the question, as a stall tactic, while you get out your phone to call 911.

3. **Recount the incident.** While the crasher is collecting his or her wits, describe the accident, in as dramatic fashion as you possibly can. This will help the crasher feel like the pain is worth it. Anything for a good story.

4. **Once the crasher stands up, you are allowed to laugh.** But not before then. And if the crasher is crying, you are not allowed to laugh. However, you are allowed to pretend the crasher is not crying, awkwardly avoiding looking at the crasher's face as you fuss with his or her bike.

5. **Speculate.** Spend a few minutes describing the root causes for the crash. Slippery rock, mossy root, off-camber trail, and scree are all excellent reasons.

Most of you will learn this procedure quickly and will have no trouble with this important process.

Brad, you may want to print it and tape it to your bike.

COMMENT FROM BOTCHED

"Hey, was your femur bent like that before you wrecked?"

COMMENT FROM ROBERT

There are some situations when it's appropriate to make fun right away: if someone has been boasting too much and needs to be brought down a notch, if someone obviously isn't hurt but did something bizarre, or if someone is named "Brad."

COMMENT FROM DUG

How could you write this, and not mention that after your "best crash ever," that I, the one you call churlish, the one you use as your personal example of mean, *I* was caught on camera sprinting across the desert rock to your aid and rescue, while your "friends" rolled on the ground, laughing, gasping for air, snapping pictures!? You, you, you *churl*.

COMMENT FROM BRAD

I'd do it again in a heartbeat. I only regret that you didn't roll through that cactus in the trail.

COMMENT FROM BRENDAN

In the group with whom I ride, there is etiquette for the crasher too: you must stay exactly where you landed — no matter how uncomfortable — until the others have taken photos of you.

LITTLE THINGS

This story came to me as I was riding my bike to work one day. Traffic was light, I was going downhill, and I had the right of way on a left-hand turn. I carved it just right and it felt beautiful.

"That," I said to myself, "is why I ride."

And here are some other reasons.

As of Saturday, the autumn weather has turned into exactly what it's supposed to be. In the morning, you need to ride in tights and long sleeves, but in the afternoon, it's just warm enough to ride in shorts and short sleeves, provided you keep up the pace. The sun's bright; the sky's clear. There are dozens of hang gliders and paragliders in the air off the point of the mountain. I've got to try that some day.

To cap it all off, on Tuesday a group of us are going to ride Gooseberry Mesa, a serious contender for one of the top 10 trails in Utah, and therefore one of the top 20 in the U.S..

I'm in an incredibly good mood.

Maybe that's why, as I rode to work, I noticed all kinds of things I love about riding my bike. Little stuff. Stuff I normally don't even consider, but which I'm pretty confident anyone who rides knows what I'm talking about.

CATCHING UP WITH A CAR AT SUCCESSIVE LIGHTS

Off the green, you're the first person, until maybe just a few feet past the intersection. Then you get swept up and passed by traffic. But wait a second, there's the next light, and it's red. You ride past everyone who just passed you, back up to the front, getting there just long enough to trackstand for three seconds (which is about as long as I can hold a trackstand) and you are once again the first guy, in front of the same group of cars.

HAVING SOMEONE WAVE FROM A CAR

For every jerk who honks or swerves, trying to unnerve me, I'll bet there are ten people in cars who wave, or, once in a while, yell some encouragement (I can never tell what they're saying). And you know, only about half of those cars have bike racks on them.[34]

CARVING A FAST LEFT TURN

A good supple road tire on a good road bike on a good road can lean at crazy angles at crazy speeds. I get every bit as much of an adrenaline rush from hitting a left turn at speed with no brakes, as I do successfully cleaning a technical move on my mountain bike.

DRIP

Riding in a nice, straight line on a road bike, sometimes it's nice to just put my head down and focus on the effort. As I do this, the sweat runs down from my forehead to the tip of my nose, and then drips, regular as clockwork.

I like watching that drop of water fall to the left of my top tube (I've never thought about it before, but for me it's *always* the left of the top tube), thinking about how cool it is that because the water's going the same speed as me, it looks like it's falling straight down. Then it hits the pavement and — zing! — seems to shoot backward as it stops and I keep going.[35]

FRESH, SMOOTH PAVEMENT

I rarely think about the texture of the pavement I'm riding on unless it's especially bad. When Kenny and I rode the Nebo Loop a few weeks ago, though, we hit a five mile stretch of brand new pavement that was just elegant.

It was so smooth, our riding effort dropped perceptibly while riding it. I notched it up a gear and looked at my speedometer: 27MPH. The speed and silence of a well-tuned road bike on perfect pavement is something to be savored.[36]

---

34 I always check out what kind of bikes are on bike racks. I think they say a good deal about what kind of person is behind the wheel.

35 Simple man, simple pleasure.

36 Related simple pleasure: Where chipseal suddenly ends, yielding to perfect, smooth pavement. The difference is beautiful.

BEING 90% UP A HARD CLIMB

I seek out rides with climbs, whether I'm on a road or mountain bike. I've often wondered, though, why I do this. These climbs hurt, after all. Last Saturday, though, as I came to the final stretch of the north side of the Suncrest climb, it hit me: I love the last 10% of a climb, where I know I'm going to finish, and feel like I can open it up and put my heart into the final push.

It's strange how it both hurts like crazy and feels like victory.

All at the same time.

Acknowledgements

Thanks to Nigel, Brice, Katie, Carrie, Zac, Scott, Kerry, Blake, Melisa, Gene, Janel, Carolynn, Dean, DeVerl, Jackie, Karen, Kellene, Lori, Jodi, Christy, and all your respective spouses and kids. I've got a lot of family and am lucky to have you.

Thanks to Kim Dow for making my book look more impressive than the text warrants. And thanks to Greg Fisher for jumping in and editing this mess.

Thanks to The Core Team, especially Dug, Kenny, Brad, Bob, and Ricky.

Thanks to Racer for taking care of my bikes and keeping to himself how badly I maintain them.

Thanks to Louis Phillips and Lynn Braswell for writing *The Animated Thumbtack Railroad Dollhouse & All-Around Surprise Book (Evening Edition)*. I was ten years old when I first found your book, and I'm pretty sure I read it a hundred times. I don't think anything has ever influenced me quite so much.

Thanks to Matt Carter for telling me I should start a blog.

And especially, thanks to everyone who reads and comments at FatCyclist.com. I really believe that nowhere else in the world is there such a fine neighborhood.